New Frontiers in Regional Science: Asian Perspectives

Volume 54

More information about this series at http://www.springer.com/series/13039

Akihiro Otsuka

A New Driver of Regional Sustainability in Japan

Inter-regional Network Economies

Springer

Akihiro Otsuka
Association of International Arts and Science
Yokohama City University
Yokohama, Japan

ISSN 2199-5974 ISSN 2199-5982 (electronic)
New Frontiers in Regional Science: Asian Perspectives
ISBN 978-981-16-3708-7 ISBN 978-981-16-3709-4 (eBook)
https://doi.org/10.1007/978-981-16-3709-4

This Springer imprint is published by the registered company Springer Nature Singapore Pte Ltd.
The registered company address is: 152 Beach Road, #21-01/04 Gateway East, Singapore 189721, Singapore

Preface

This book highlights the role of inter-regional networks in exploring the drivers of regional sustainability. Many industrialized countries are facing a population decline. As population decreases, concerns grow about a decline in the domestic market size. To counter the decline in certain regions, it is essential to consider connecting regions and improving the performance of economic activities in broad areas. Achieving sustainable economic growth requires that economic performance be increased by improving the quality of inter-regional networks as well as the intensity of regional agglomeration. Moreover, economic growth must be compatible with solutions to global environmental problems. Achieving regional sustainability requires not only increased productivity but also improvements in the efficiency of energy use. Hence, this book provides a new description of critical advances in inter-regional networks, which are vital for enhancing regional sustainability.

This book is a sequel to my previous book, *A New Perspective on Agglomeration Economies,* published in 2017, which focused on Japanese regional economies, primarily during the 2000s. The earlier book focused on agglomeration economies that occurred in spatially limited areas and did not consider geographical externalities from a broader perspective in terms of expanded space through improvements in inter-regional networks. Recent studies have identified that the actual spatial range that would benefit from agglomeration economies is broader than that covered by conventional studies. Based on the current literature, this book defines inter-regional network economies in a regional economy and identifies them in the context of regional sustainability under conditions of population decline and environmental constraints. Some new highlights from the current book are up-to-date discussions of inter-regional network economies and new insights into energy conservation given the increased interest in sustainable development goals (SDGs). The more in-depth consideration of the analytical methods and analytical results will enable readers to propose desirable regional policies aimed at achieving regional sustainability. This book also contributes to evidence-based policymaking (EBPM) in the sense that it deals with the debate about Japan's national land planning. The primary audiences envisioned for this book are scholars, researchers, and policymakers specializing in regional science, urban economics, regional economics, and national land planning.

Much of this book's contents summarize a six-year study conducted from 2016 to 2021 at Yokohama City University, and most of its chapters have been published as journal articles. Each of these articles received constructive and valuable comments from the journal editors and reviewers. I would like to express my gratitude to them. To improve comprehension, each paper has been edited and included in this book as an independent chapter with a wealth of supplementary interpretations and commentary that could not be described in the journal articles due to page constraints. Please read each chapter carefully.

This work was supported by grants from the Japan Society for the Promotion of Science (JSPS: grant numbers 15K17067 and 18K01614). In addition, this work was supported by a grant from the 2021–2023 Strategic Research Promotion (No. SK202106) of Yokohama City University. I would like to thank Emeritus Professor Dr. Michiko Aihara, President of the Yokohama City University. Any opinions, findings, conclusions, or recommendations expressed in this book are those of the author and do not necessarily reflect the views of the JSPS or the author's affiliation.

In writing this book, I had to compile a dataset by drawing from various sources of regional statistics. The book's dataset mainly relies on official statistics but also includes estimates. The estimates of private and social overhead capital were developed by the Central Research Institute of Electric Power Industry, my former affiliation. I would like to thank the institute for allowing me extensive use of its data for academic purposes. Originally, these regional economic data were developed and inherited by the leading predecessors of this institute. I would like to express my appreciation and respect for the great work done by the predecessors of the institute. I hope that the institute will continue to contribute widely to the development of academic science in the future.

Furthermore, while writing this book, I had many opportunities to advise on improving the *National Land Policy Simulation Model* of the Ministry of Land, Infrastructure, Transport and Tourism. I would like to express my gratitude to the planning officers who provided detailed public information on national land policy. They are working hard day and night to develop a sustainable national land structure. I was inspired by their enthusiasm for Japan's land development. I hope that the findings in this book will contribute to their work, even if only a little.

This book is part of the *New Frontiers in Regional Science: The Asian Perspectives* series. This series is a constellation of works by scholars in the field of regional science and receives support from the Japan Section of the Regional Science Association International. I wish to express my gratitude to Emeritus Professor Dr. Yoshiro Higano, the book's editor-in-chief and former president of the Regional Science Association International, for his dedication.

Finally, I received much support from my wife. The cakes and cookies she baked for me kept me motivated and encouraged during my strenuous writing work. I would like to express my gratitude to her. I hope that this monograph will contribute to the study of regional science. Moreover, with this monograph as a milestone, I would like to continue contributing to the development of regional science.

Yokohama, Japan Akihiro Otsuka

Contents

Chapter 1
Executive Summary

Abstract This chapter provides an overview of the contents of this book. This book discusses the impacts of inter-regional networks on the regional economy through economic analyses. This book also has many implications for the national land policy in Japan. Japan's national land plan aims to achieve enormous economic benefits through the upgrading of inter-regional networks. Connecting regions via high-speed transportation networks may help to improve regional productivity and environmental efficiency. However, to the best of our knowledge, few studies have assessed the significance of the national land plan because of the low availability of relevant data and the scarcity of analytical methods for accurately measuring inter-regional network economies. Therefore, this book provides analytical methods that can clarify the role of inter-regional networks in improving productivity and environmental efficiency. Based on plentiful empirical evidence, this book defines the role of inter-regional networks in the regional economy. Notably, the book provides indicators that capture the economic effects of inter-regional networks. Using these indicators reveals that such networks enhance geographical externalities in regions and improve productivity and environmental efficiency. These findings provide readers with guidelines regarding desirable regional economic policies for economies facing population decline.

Keywords Agglomeration economies · Environmental efficiency · Inter-regional network · Productivity · Regional disparity

1.1 Features of the Book

This book highlights the roles of inter-regional networks in regional economies while exploring the drivers of regional sustainability. Many industrialized countries are facing a period of population decline. Furthermore, these countries are aiming to become decarbonized societies to address global warming issues. Thus, it is necessary to not only increase productivity but also improve environmental efficiency to achieve sustainability.

A. Otsuka, *A New Driver of Regional Sustainability in Japan*, New Frontiers in Regional Science: Asian Perspectives 54,
https://doi.org/10.1007/978-981-16-3709-4_1

The spatial concentration of economic agents, such as economies of agglomeration, is crucial for improving productivity and productive efficiency. Many empirical studies have shown that agglomeration economies increase firm productivity and international competitiveness (Rosenthal and Strange 2004; Combes and Gobillon 2015). In agglomeration regions, firms actively exchange diverse ideas, information, and technology, thereby facilitating research and development (R&D) and innovation through knowledge sharing (Capello 2016; McCann 2013). The knowledge created by a firm is then transmitted to other firms through interactions among intellectual workers and exchanges of knowledgeable assets. Through these knowledge spillovers, new technologies and products are created, which increases the productivity of the region as a whole.[1]

Inter-regional networks expand the space in which economic agents can enjoy agglomeration economies because the development of highways, railways, and airports reduces travel time. This makes it easier for remote firms that have difficulty participating in meetings and business conferences to access and benefit from the agglomeration region. Since the resulting increase in knowledge exchange occurs bidirectionally, inter-regional networks increase productivity among firms within and outside the agglomeration region (Burger and Meijers 2016).

High-quality transportation networks also improve environmental efficiency by reducing transportation costs. Spatial economics suggests that reducing transport costs enhances agglomeration and improves productivity (Fujita and Thisse 2002). The economic benefit obtained from productivity growth enables firms operating under environmental regulations to invest in energy conservation, thereby increasing energy efficiency (Porter and Van der Linde 1995). Moreover, efficient inter-regional transportation networks have the potential to reduce gasoline consumption and greenhouse gas emissions by causing a modal shift from passenger vehicles to railways.

This book discusses the impacts of inter-regional networks on the regional economy through economic analyses. The discipline of this book is urban and regional economics. Urban engineering, which analyzes the functions and performance of networks in detail, is outside the scope of this book. This book also has many implications for the national land policy in Japan. Japan's national land plan aims to achieve enormous economic benefits through the upgrading of inter-regional networks. Connecting regions via high-speed transportation networks may help improve regional productivity and environmental efficiency. However, to the best of our knowledge, few studies have assessed the significance of the national land plan because of the low availability of relevant data and the scarcity of analytical methods for accurately measuring inter-regional network economies. This book provides analytical methods that can clarify the role of inter-regional networks in improving productivity and environmental efficiency.

---

[1]In recent years, the role of innovation in economic growth has become even more critical, and empirical studies on knowledge spillovers have been attracting attention in the field of regional science (Carlino and Kerr 2015).

Many studies have examined the role of agglomeration in urban areas and regions to determine their static and dynamic effects (e.g., Rosenthal and Strange 2004; Combes and Gobillon 2015). However, most studies have analyzed the impacts of agglomeration economies only in the area where they are generated; few have assessed the impacts in other areas through high-quality inter-regional networks. The 2016 special issue of *Papers in Regional Science* covers up-to-date discussions on the spatial range of agglomeration economies. Based on this stream of research, this book provides several findings on inter-regional network economies. In mature economies, the strength of the agglomeration economies may weaken as the population declines. The creation of inter-regional networks is, therefore, essential to prevent a decline in agglomeration. Thus, examining inter-regional networks is crucial for correctly identifying the drivers of sustainability in a maturing economy.

The objective of this book is to illustrate the impact of inter-regional networks on regional productivity and environmental efficiency. Based on plentiful empirical evidence, the book defines the role of inter-regional networks in the regional economy, provides indicators that capture the economic effects of inter-regional networks. Using these indicators reveals that such networks enhance geographical externalities in regions and improve productivity and environmental efficiency. These findings provide readers with guidelines regarding desirable regional economic policies for economies facing population decline.

Furthermore, the book provides readers with a platform from which to understand the effects of inter-regional networks from the perspective of passenger travel. Many studies on inter-regional networks have focused on the economic effects of logistics networks, centering on highways (e.g., Melo et al. 2016; Stelder 2016). Few studies have analyzed the economics of passenger travel using railways and airports alongside conventional road networks and highways. Analyses of the inter-regional movement of passengers not only deepen our knowledge of high-speed transportation networks but also bridge gaps in our knowledge of the network effects on passenger travel.

1.2 Structure of the Book

This book consists of three parts and 10 chapters.

Part I comprises Chaps. 2, 3, and 4. It reviews Japan's regional economic structure and analyzes its regional productivity dynamics. Chapter 2 examines Japan's regional economic systems and regional disparities in depth. In Japan, population migration continues to flow into the Greater Tokyo Area. According to the theory of agglomeration, the spatial concentration of economic activities in the Greater Tokyo Area should strengthen its increasing returns to scale and increase inter-regional disparities in per capita gross value added (GVA). However, inter-regional disparities in per capita GVA have been shrinking over the long term, a phenomenon that conventional theories cannot explain satisfactorily. As a step toward understanding this phenomenon, this chapter analyzes the regional economic systems and regional disparities in per capita GVA since 1990 and identifies the socioeconomic determinants that have led to such regional convergence.

Chapter 3 focuses on regional productivity and confirms the regional convergence of productivity using a stochastic convergence model. It is necessary to improve total factor productivity (TFP) to enhance competitiveness, given the socioeconomic conditions amid globalization, population decline, and an aging society with falling birthrates. This chapter shows that TFP in Japan's regions has grown consistently since 1980. Notably, the results indicate that TFP increases along with the convergence of regional disparities. The results also show that geographic factors play an essential role in determining long-term growth in TFP.

Chapter 4 considers the determinants of regional TFP. This chapter focuses on the three main determinants, namely, social overhead capital, regional agglomeration, and industrial structure, and provides empirical evidence of their impacts on regional TFP growth. The results show that social overhead capital and regional agglomeration contribute to TFP growth by increasing both productivity and productive efficiency. Moreover, the chapter shows that productive efficiency in the manufacturing industry is high and that the geographic concentration of globally competitive manufacturers improves the efficiency of the regional economy. The results thus suggest that upgrading public infrastructure and forming regional agglomerations are crucial strategic measures for regional economic growth.

Part II comprises Chaps. 5, 6, and 7. This part focuses on inter-regional network economies as drivers of regional sustainability. Chapter 5 defines the inter-regional network economies and evaluates them. This chapter quantifies the effects of "borrowed size," which defines how inter-regional networks enable small cities to grow faster than large ones (Alonso 1973). The results show that the impact of inter-regional networks on TFP growth is significant across Japan and that the geographical range of agglomeration economies is expanding through the development of high-quality transportation networks. The results suggest that high-quality transportation networks are a potential driver for the achievement of regional sustainability.

Chapter 6 assesses the impact of inter-regional networks on regional disparities in per capita GVA. Despite the continuing concentration of economic activities in the Greater Tokyo Area, no sustained expansion of regional disparities has been observed. The chapter shows that improved inter-regional networks have been the driving force behind the strengthening of productivity in local areas. Furthermore, the formation of inter-regional networks significantly reduces regional disparities. Thus, the results provide evidence that high-quality transportation networks can help to drastically reduce regional disparities in Japan's economy.

Chapter 7 proposes a new approach for the evaluation of inter-regional network economies. The proposed approach allows us to measure economies of scale and technological progress, separately, even under imperfect competition. This chapter measures the level of economies of scale in Japan's regions through the proposed approach and investigates inter-regional network economies. The chapter also assesses how the opening of the *Linear-Chuo Shinkansen*, a new magnetic levitation train, impacts the productivity of various regions in Japan. The results show that Japan's current national land plan has the potential to revitalize regional economies.

Part III comprises Chaps. 8, 9, and 10. It focuses on energy conservation as another driver of regional sustainability. Chapter 8 analyzes the impact of regional agglomeration on energy intensity, defined as energy consumption divided by the GVA. In industrialized countries, balancing reductions in greenhouse gas emissions with the promotion of regional economic growth has become a critical policy agenda. This chapter analyzes the role of regional agglomeration as a factor in energy conservation. The results show that population concentration in large metropolitan areas leads to an improvement in energy intensity. In contrast, population dispersion in local areas exacerbates the energy intensity. These results suggest it is necessary to promote the geographical concentration of the population to improve the efficiency of nationwide energy usage.

Chapter 9 defines energy efficiency indices based on the stochastic frontier approach as a desirable energy conservation measure. Using energy efficiency indices, this chapter examines whether regional agglomeration and inter-regional networks are drivers that increase productivity and improve energy efficiency in the regional economy. The results reveal a threshold for the agglomeration effect on energy efficiency and show that a scale of agglomeration that exceeds the threshold is necessary for the effect to occur. The results also show that the formation of inter-regional networks is effective in improving energy efficiency. The results suggest that improving energy efficiency requires a regional policy that strengthens inter-regional networks.

Chapter 10 examines whether improvements in inter-regional networks change the energy consumption pattern of a region and whether there is a modal shift from passenger vehicles to railways for inter-regional travel. An energy demand analysis for the passenger vehicle sector reveals that the modal shift from passenger vehicles to railways may be accelerated. This chapter shows that upgrading inter-regional networks reduces the energy consumption of the passenger vehicle sector. The chapter also shows that the opening of the *Linear-Chuo Shinkansen* has the potential to change regional energy consumption patterns. This provides significant evidence that supports the policy direction of Japan's national land plan.

1.3 Contributions of the Book

The most noteworthy feature of Japan's regional economic system is that the monocentric concentration in the Greater Tokyo Area progresses in tandem with a reduction in regional disparities. Conventional theories cannot fully explain this phenomenon. This book elucidates this phenomenon from the viewpoint of inter-regional networks based on the concept of the "borrowed size" effect (Alonso 1973). Local areas can "borrow" the agglomeration economies of the Greater Tokyo Area by using a high-quality transportation network system. This enables local regions to grow beyond the Greater Tokyo Area, thus shrinking inter-regional disparities. However, authoritative studies have not demonstrated these dynamics (e.g., Fujita et al. 2004). The results in this book provide a potential explanation for this paradox.

Another contribution of this book is that it provides several applications of analytical methods such as the stochastic convergence model for inter-regional disparities, the partial adjustment model for the dynamics of productivity, and the stochastic frontier model for production activity and energy demand patterns. Cross-sectional and panel data models are conventionally used to verify reductions in regional disparities (Magrini 2004). Previous studies have focused on static analysis, dynamic analyses that consider the behavioral mechanisms of economic agents have rarely been conducted. In general, firms make location decisions based on historical and geographical factors (McCann 1998). In this book, it is assumed that the performance of the regional economy depends on behavioral mechanisms based on adaptive expectations.

This book also introduces indicators for measuring the strength of inter-regional networks. Market expansion in other regions is believed to improve the market potential in the home region. Conventional indicators evaluate the sizes of economic activities in other regions, such as population and GVA, depending on the fixed physical distance (Hansen 1959; Batty 2009). This book uses travel time distance to evaluate the inter-regional distance from the perspective of passenger travel accurately. Passenger vehicles, railways, and aviation are all used for inter-regional travel. The shortest travel time distance is calculated using these transportation means to evaluate the strength of inter-regional networks. These indicators make it possible to measure inter-regional network economies accurately from the perspective of passenger travel.

Moreover, the Solow residual approach using the cost share is used to assess economies of scale and inter-regional network economies. Conventional Solow residual approaches assume perfect competition and constant returns to scale. However, in Japan, most firms face imperfect markets and price markups (Nishimura et al. 1999; Okada 2005; Kiyota et al. 2009). Furthermore, the assumption of constant returns-to-scale production technology is not always supported in Japanese studies (Nakajima et al. 1998). Therefore, conventional Solow residual approaches cannot correctly identify inter-regional network economies in Japan. The cost-share approach used in this book resolves this concern.

In addition, this book identifies how inter-regional networks impact energy conservation. Conventional discussions on inter-regional network externalities have been limited to productivity effects; whether inter-regional networks have routes that affect energy conservation remains unclear. This book shows that improving inter-regional networks facilitates the modal shift from passenger vehicles to railways and, consequently, improves efficiency in energy usage. In many countries, these findings on the impact of inter-regional networks on energy conservation are not considered in regional policies. In this sense, this book provides readers with insights into the new role played by inter-regional networks that are not fully understood.

Finally, this book confirms the validity of the national land policy. Japan's national land plan aims to overcome the nation's population decline by creating a land structure that promotes human interactions beyond regions.[2] This would be achieved by forming regional agglomeration and high-speed transportation networks through the *Linear-Chuo Shinkansen* project. This book shows that accelerating regional agglomeration would help enhance regional productivity and sustainability. The upgrading of inter-regional networks would enable local areas to become more competitive than large metropolitan areas, thereby reducing productivity disparities. Furthermore, the creation of regional agglomeration and inter-regional networks would not only enhance productivity but also help solve global environmental problems by improving the efficiency of energy usage. These findings strongly support the validity of the national land plan in Japan.

Several countries have a national land structure similar to that of Japan. The United Kingdom and South Korea, for example, also feature a monocentric concentration of economic activities. Japan's experience in formulating regional policies aimed at balancing economic growth with regional disparity reduction will, thus, provide valuable insights to such countries. The results of the study in this book, therefore, provide a valuable reference for regional economic policies in other countries.

1.4 Notes on the Book

1.4.1 Geographical Units and Data for Analysis

The last section describes several notes related to the book's overall analysis. The first discussion relates to the validity of the prefecture as a geographical unit of analysis. Figures 1.1 and 1.2 show maps of prefectures and the division of regions in Japan.

Administrative areas, such as municipalities (cities and towns), are often established based on historical and natural conditions. As a result, administrative areas tend to deviate from the geographical range of actual economic activities. For example, many residents of suburban cities commute to adjacent large metropolitan cities. The urban functions of suburban cities are thus considered being integrated with those of their larger neighbors. In other words, the scope of economic activity exceeds the scope of administrative areas. In particular, the spatial spillovers of economic activities have a massive impact at the municipal level. The effects of urban agglomeration will be overestimated if spatial autocorrelations are not adequately controlled. However, it is not easy to quantify the dynamic states of commuting migration between administrative areas precisely.[3]

---

[2]See Appendix for details on Japan's national land plan.

[3]In Japan, there is a study on the optimal urban area setting based on this background (Kanemoto and Tokuoka 2002). For the database, see http://www.csis.u-tokyo.ac.jp/UEA/index_e.htm (Accessed January 2021).

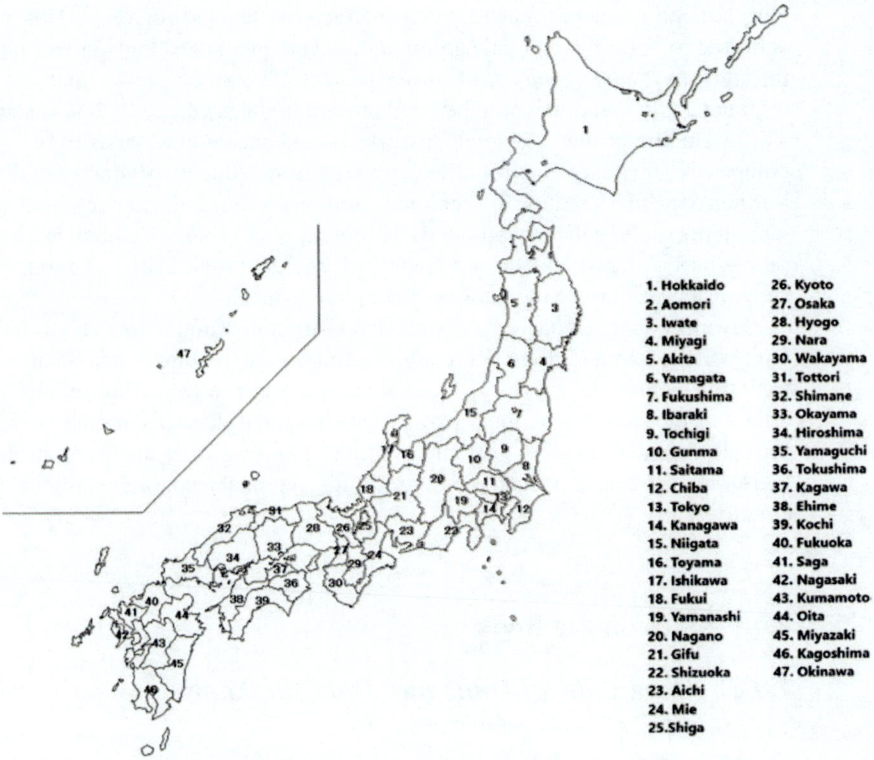

Fig. 1.1 Prefectures in Japan

Naturally, inter-regional network economies are not limited to urban or metropolitan areas but extend over a broad region. Since conventional studies have supposed that urban agglomeration has manifested only in urban areas, the scope of external economies has tended to be limited to municipalities. However, the concept of inter-regional networks allows this external effect, which is far from being limited to urban areas, the possibility to extend more broadly (Burger and Meijers 2016; Camagni et al. 2016; Meijers et al. 2016). The effect of urban agglomeration extends into a broader area by connecting each urban area with an inter-regional network. In this case, if the geographical area for analysis is limited to municipalities, the effect of the inter-regional network will be underestimated. Hence, a more accurate evaluation of inter-regional network economies requires a broader area than urban areas as the analysis target.

Furthermore, in Japan, the city, town, and village alone cannot be considered a unit of evaluation for assessing regional policy from a macroscopic perspective. Japan's regional industrial policy is usually implemented at the prefectural or regional level, which includes several prefectures. That is, analyses at the prefectural or regional level not only ensure consistency with regional industrial policy but also enable an accurate assessment of policies, such as a reduction in regional disparities.

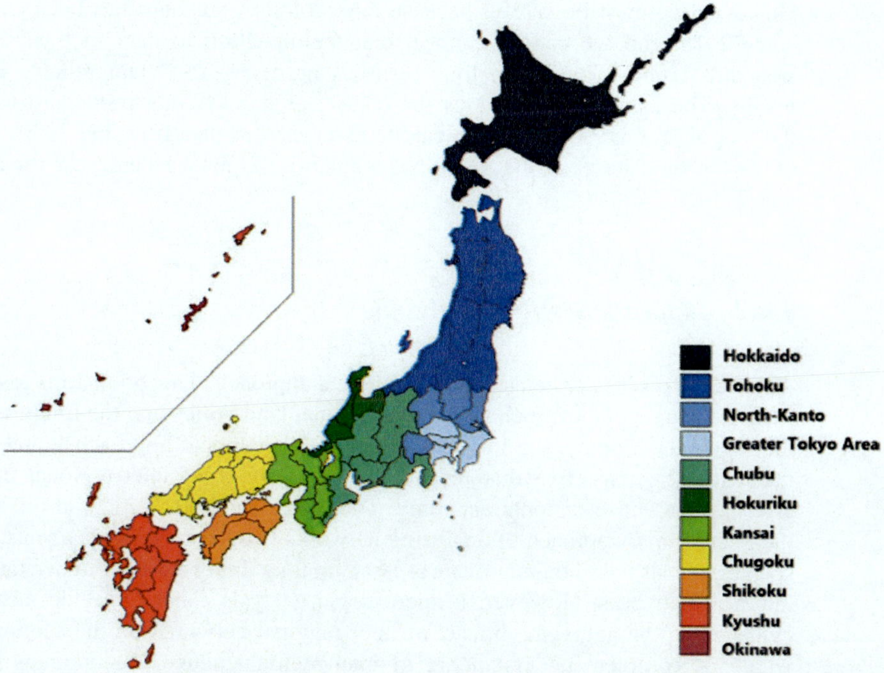

Fig. 1.2 Division of regions in Japan. Note: The regional classification is as follows: Hokkaido (Hokkaido), Tohoku (Aomori, Iwate, Miyagi, Akita, Yamagata, Fukushima, and Niigata), North Kanto (Ibaraki, Tochigi, Gunma, and Yamanashi), Greater Tokyo Area (Saitama, Chiba, Tokyo, and Kanagawa), Hokuriku (Toyama, Ishikawa, and Fukui), Chubu (Nagano, Gifu, Shizuoka, Aichi, and Mie), Kansai (Shiga, Kyoto, Osaka, Hyogo, Nara, and Wakayama), Chugoku (Tottori, Shimane, Okayama, Hiroshima, and Yamaguchi), Shikoku (Tokushima, Kagawa, Ehime, and Kochi), Kyushu (Fukuoka, Saga, Nagasaki, Kumamoto, Oita, Miyazaki, and Kagoshima), and Okinawa (Okinawa)

In particular, most official data on production and energy use are available at the national and prefectural levels but not at the municipal level. For example, data on private and social capital stock are not measured at the municipal (or urban, metropolitan) level, which makes it extremely difficult to measure economic performance at the municipal (or urban, metropolitan) level precisely. By using official data at the prefectural level, we can accurately evaluate the productivity and environmental efficiency of regional economies.[4]

Finally, the data used in this book cover research up to 2014. Currently, the available data on Japan's regional economic activities cover research until 2018.

---

[4]Based on the similar background, the Research Institute of Economy, Trade and Industry (RIETI) has been developing a regional economic database at the prefectural level, which is named "R-JIP." The database can be viewed at https://www.rieti.go.jp/en/database/r-jip.html (accessed January 2021).

However, we must be careful because the 2008SNA standard has been employed since 2015, and we cannot connect data before 2006 to data in the 2008SNA standard. Using a long-term time series is necessary to obtain reliable analysis results. Thus, this book employs the dataset of the 1993SNA standard to utilize the long-term time series, which can be connected to data from the 1990s and the 2000s. In the dataset of the 1993SNA standard, the most recent year for the data was 2014.

1.4.2 Approaches for Analysis

The second discussion relates to an analytical approach. This book aims to contribute to regional policies, such as Japan's national land policy and the future vision of the regional economy. To this end, the book's analytical approach is based on a macroscopic perspective that reveals the externalities of inter-regional networks affecting the entire regional economy. Therefore, this book's method differs from the microscopic approach of analyzing networks between economic agents. Microscopic analysis based on microdata is essential for gaining a deeper understanding of interfirm networks. However, a microscopic analysis cannot provide meaningful evidence on the aggregate impact of inter-regional networks on the economy as a whole. A complete understanding of inter-regional network economies requires macroscopic and microscopic analyses.

This book considers the macroscopic effects of inter-regional interactions on knowledge transmission. In the microscopic analysis of interfirm transaction networks, human mobility is known to be essential for knowledge production activities. For example, studies on knowledge spillover have shown that application patents tend to cite patents from geographically close organizations and that geographic clusters of firms enable knowledge spillovers (Jaffe et al. 1993; Griffith et al. 2011). Microstudies in Japan also clarify that the geographic proximity of firms and human mobility stimulates knowledge-creating activities (Bernard et al. 2019; Inoue et al. 2019). These studies suggest that regional agglomeration and transportation networks are connected to large metropolitan areas. This book's understanding of inter-regional networks from a macroscopic perspective reinforces the findings of microscopic analyses of interfirm networks.[5]

Japan's markets are forecasted to shrink as the population declines. To overcome this market contraction, new goods and services must be created through innovation. In the manufacturing industry, collaboration with the service industry progresses in product planning, design, marketing, and quality control. The service industry is also related to the development of industrial products; innovation in the medical care

[5]The computable general equilibrium analysis is another approach of macroscopic analysis. See Rokicki et al. (2020) for an up-to-date study on computable general equilibrium model on inter-regional networks.

industry is realized through collaboration with the manufacturing industry in areas such as advanced medicine, software development, and education. The relationship between these industrial linkages and inter-regional networks is thus an important research topic, but it is not covered in this book. These research topics represent promising future research agendas.[6]

1.4.3 On Regional Hierarchy

The third discussion relates to the regional system from the perspective of hierarchy. The theory of agglomeration explains that the cumulative growth of a region is linked to the construction of multitiered spatial systems, based on the rational behavior of economic agents (Fujita and Thisse 2002). Spatial economics posits that goods and services have critical distances depending on their degree of differentiation, thereby creating a multi-hierarchical spatial system. The development of a high-quality transportation infrastructure reduces transport costs; the critical distance of goods in each industry would be expanded, in turn encouraging the centralization of economic activity.

A regional hierarchy has been formed in Japan, with the Greater Tokyo Area as the summit (Fujita and Tabuchi 1997; Fujita et al. 2004). The development of high-quality transportation networks has reduced transport costs and increased accessibility to the Greater Tokyo Area. At the same time, the agglomeration of knowledgeable workers in the Greater Tokyo Area has helped accumulate intellectual capital, create innovation, and increase economic growth. Until the 1980s, the Greater Tokyo Area had a positive feedback mechanism of agglomeration, and strong economic growth in Tokyo became the driving force behind Japan's economy. In the 1990s, however, economic concentration in the Greater Tokyo Area led to congestion costs and soaring land prices, strengthening external diseconomies.

Porter (2000) critically discusses the monocentric concentration of economic activity in the Greater Tokyo Area from a political perspective. He argues that Japan's socioeconomic systems are centralized, meaning that the central government tends to intervene in competition and that such geographic patterns come at the expense of productivity. His theory of competition does not suggest that agglomeration economies benefit all industries; it argues that agglomeration regions should be specialized at the cluster level to realize sustainable growth. One question that follows Porter's argument is whether regional economies that specialize in specific strategic industries are more productive and stable than regional economies with a diversified industrial structure. To the best of our knowledge, this question has not yet been definitively answered. However, this book does not discuss the hierarchy of

---

[6]There are plentiful of studies on interfirm collaboration and innovation in Japan. For example, see Iino et al. (2021) for an up-to-date study on global interfirm research collaboration network based on the microstudy.

regions in conjunction with agglomeration and inter-regional networks. It may be essential to examine their economic effects from the perspective of economic efficiency, stability, and risk dispersion to determine the most desirable national land structure. We aim to pursue this research agenda in the future.

Appendix: Japan's National Land Plan

This book considers research agendas related to Japan's national land plan. Therefore, we must briefly summarize the national land plan for readers unfamiliar with its content.

Japan's national land plan is a long-term, comprehensive spatial plan for the use, development, and conservation of land at a national level. Since the formulation of the First Comprehensive National Development Plan in 1962, Japan's postwar national land planning has been based on the Comprehensive National Land Development Act and has been revised to resolve various issues throughout the years.

Japan's government formulated its current national land plan in 2015 (MLIT 2015). The latest national land planning period is 10 years. The latest national land plan defines its basic concept as the creation of a "country that promotes interaction." The term "interaction" here means the inter-regional movement of humans, goods, money, and information arising from inter-regional cooperation relationships. Dynamic interactions between regions, which occur through inter-regional networks, are considered crucial for regional sustainable development.

Providing services efficiently amid a population decline requires maintaining the size of regional markets via networking. There are two critical points in network formation. The first point is the individuality of each region as an economic entity. Differences in individuality arise when regions independently identify their local resources and refine their attractiveness. This difference in individuality creates interactions among regions that become the source of regional vitality. Through these efforts, Japan aims to create a national land structure that increases the productivity and efficiency of the nation as a whole by providing high-quality services efficiently and creating new value, even in the face of its population decline.

The second point for networking is the installation of the *Linear-Chuo Shinkansen,* a new high-speed transportation system. The *Linear-Chuo Shinkansen* is a 438-kilometer Shinkansen line connecting Tokyo, Nagoya, and Osaka. It is scheduled to open in 2027 between Tokyo and Nagoya and in 2045 between Nagoya and Osaka (see Fig. 1.3). The superconducting maglev system with a maximum speed of 505 km/h plans to connect Tokyo and Nagoya in about 40 minutes and Tokyo and Osaka in about an hour. The opening of the *Linear-Chuo Shinkansen* will significantly reduce travel time. With this shortened travel time, Japan's major metropolitan areas will be able to work closely together as an integrated economic zone, creating a world-class "super-mega-region" on an unparalleled economic scale. This dramatic reduction in travel time is expected to stimulate increased face-to-face communication between economic agents. When the *Linear-Chuo*

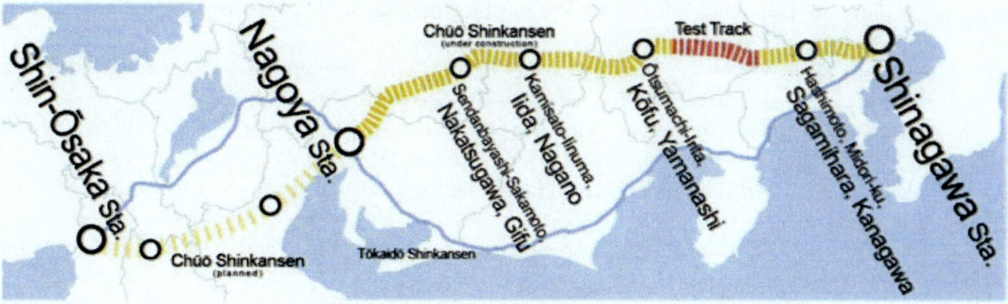

Fig. 1.3 Route of the *Linea-Chuo Shinkansen* in Japan. Source: Wikipedia (Accessed August 2020)

Shinkansen connects Tokyo, Nagoya, and Osaka with approximately a one-hour traveling time between them, information exchanges are expected to increase, and new joint research, development, and innovation may be pursued among collaborating firms.

References

Alonso W (1973) Urban zero population growth. Daedalus 102(4):191–206

Batty PWJ (2009) Accessibility: in search of a unified theory. Environ Plann B 36:191–194

Bernard AB, Moxnes A, Saito YU (2019) Production networks, geography, and firm performance. J Polit Econ 127(2):639–688

Burger MJ, Meijers EJ (2016) Agglomerations and the rise of urban network externalities. Pap Reg Sci 95(1):5–15

Camagni R, Capello R, Caragliu A (2016) Static vs. dynamic agglomeration economies: spatial context and structural evolution behind urban growth. Pap Reg Sci 95(1):133–158

Capello R (2016) Regional economics (second edition). Routledge, Abingdon

Carlino G, Kerr WR (2015) Agglomeration and innovation. In: Duranton G, Henderson JV, Strange W (eds) Handbook of regional and urban economics, vol 5A. Elsevier, Amsterdam, pp 349–404

Combes PP, Gobillon L (2015) The empirics of agglomeration economies. In: Duranton G, Henderson JV, Strange W (eds) Handbook of regional and urban economics, vol 5A. Elsevier, Amsterdam, pp 247–348

Fujita M, Mori T, Henderson JV, Kanemoto Y (2004) Spatial distribution of economic activities in Japan and China. In: Henderson JV, Thisse JF (eds) Handbook of regional and urban economics, vol 4. Elsevier, Amsterdam, pp 2911–2977

Fujita M, Tabuchi T (1997) Regional growth in postwar Japan. Reg Sci Urban Econ 27(6):643–670

Fujita M, Thisse J (2002) Economics of agglomeration. Cambridge University Press, Cambridge

Griffith R, Lee S, Van Reenen J (2011) Is distance dying at last? Falling home bias in fixed–effects models of patent citations. Quant Econ 2(2):211–249

Hansen WG (1959) How accessibility shapes land use. J Am I Planners 25:73–76

Iino T, Inoue H, Saito YU, Todo Y (2021) How does the global network of research collaboration affect the quality of innovation? Jpn Econ Rev 72:5–48

Inoue H, Nakajima K, Saito YU (2019) Localization of collaborations in knowledge creation. Ann Reg Sci 62(1):119–140

Jaffe AB, Trajtenberg M, Henderson R (1993) Geographic localization of knowledge spillovers as evidenced by patent citations. Q J Econ 108(3):577–598

Kanemoto Y, Tokuoka K (2002) Proposal for the standards of metropolitan areas of Japan. J Appl Reg Sci 7:1–15. (in Japanese)

Kiyota K, Nakajima T, Nishimura KG (2009) Measurement of the market power of firms: the Japanese case in the 1990s. Ind Corp Change 18(3):381–414

Magrini S (2004) Regional (di)convergence. In: Henderson JV, Thisse JF (eds) Handbook of regional and urban economics, vol 4. Elsevier, Amsterdam, pp 2741–2796

McCann P (1998) The economics of industrial location: a logistics-costs approach. Springer, Berlin, Heidelberg

McCann P (2013) Modern urban and regional economics, 2nd edn. Oxford University Press, Hampshire

Meijers E, Burger MJ, Hoogerbrugge MM (2016) Borrowing size in networks of cities: City size, network connectivity and metropolitan functions in Europe. Pap Reg Sci 95(1):181–198

Melo PS, Graham DJ, Levinson D, Aarabi S (2016) Agglomeration, accessibility and productivity: evidence for large metropolitan areas in the US. Urban Stud 54(1):179–195

MLIT (2015) National Spatial Strategy (National Plan). http://www.mlit.go.jp/common/001127196.pdf. Accessed January 2021

Nakajima T, Nakamura M, Yoshioka K (1998) An index number method for estimating scale economies and technical progress using time-series of cross-section data: sources of total factor productivity growth for Japanese manufacturing, 1964–1988. Jpn Econ Rev 49(3):310–334

Nishimura K, Ohkusa Y, Ariga K (1999) Estimating the markup over marginal cost: a panel analysis of Japanese firms 1971–1994. Int J Ind Organ 17(8):1077–1111

Okada Y (2005) Competition and productivity in Japanese manufacturing industries. J Jpn Int Econ 19(4):586–616

Porter ME (2000) Location, competition, and economic development: local clusters in a global economy. Econ Dev Q 14(1):5–34

Porter ME, Van der Linde C (1995) Toward a new conception of the environment competitiveness relationship. J Econ Perspect 9(4):97–118

Rokicki B, Haddad EA, Horridge JM, Stępniak M (2020) Accessibility in the regional CGE framework: the effects of major transport infrastructure investments in Poland. Transportation. https://doi.org/10.1007/s11116-019-10076-w

Rosenthal S, Strange W (2004) Evidence on the nature and sources of agglomeration economies. In: Henderson JV, Thisse JF (eds) Handbook of regional and urban economics, vol 4. Elsevier, Amsterdam, pp 2119–2171

Stelder D (2016) Regional accessibility trends in Europe: road infrastructure, 1957–2012. Reg Stud 50(6):983–995

Part I
Regional Economic Structure and Productivity

Chapter 2
Regional Economic Structure in Japan

Abstract This chapter provides an overview of the regional economic structure. Japan continues to experience migration and a spatial concentration of economic activities in the Greater Tokyo Area. The theory on agglomeration economies explains that this population inflow enhances the Greater Tokyo Area's increasing returns to scale. In other words, as population inflow in the Greater Tokyo Area increases its economies of scale, the gaps in the economic performance between the Greater Tokyo Area and local areas are expected to widen, and the regional disparities in gross value added (GVA) per capita should expand. However, regional disparities in GVA per capita have been shrinking rather than expanding since the 1990s. Conventional theories do not explain this phenomenon well. This chapter provides evidence of economic growth in local areas and the potential for economic advance. Notably, this chapter reveals that social overhead capital, industrial structure, and fiscal transfer have enhanced the economic power of local areas and helped reduce regional disparities. Japan's experiences provide valuable insights into regional development policies aimed at achieving compatibility between economic growth and equitability.

Keywords Fiscal transfer · Industry structure · Regional economic structure · Regional disparity · Social overhead capital

2.1 Introduction

Regional disparities are of significant concern not only for the central government but also for local government policymakers as regional equality, especially in per capita income levels, and the efficiency of the national economy has a trade-off relationship (Richardson 1979). Promoting spatial agglomeration in a specific region strengthens the region's economy and enhances efficiency. In contrast, it becomes difficult to achieve sustainable growth in other regions because of the outflow of workers and capital. This results in an uneven geographical distribution of economic activities that increase regional inequality. That is, pursuing efficiency to increase

A. Otsuka, *A New Driver of Regional Sustainability in Japan*, New Frontiers in Regional Science: Asian Perspectives 54,
https://doi.org/10.1007/978-981-16-3709-4_2

national economic growth should lead to uneven regional performance and inequality.

In Japan, the greatest spatial concentration of economic agents is in the Greater Tokyo Area, with a positive population inflow. Agglomeration theories explain that this population inflow enhances the Greater Tokyo Area's increasing returns to scale. In other words, as population inflow into the Greater Tokyo Area increases its economies of scale, the gaps in the economic performance between the Greater Tokyo Area and local areas are expected to widen, and the regional disparities in gross value added (GVA) per capita should expand. However, as will become apparent in the following sections, regional disparities in GVA per capita have been shrinking rather than expanding since the 1990s.[1] Conventional theories do not explain this phenomenon well.

This chapter focuses on this paradox and reviews Japan's regional economic structure between the 1990s and the 2000s. Clarifying the mechanisms that enable compatibility between economic growth and reductions in regional disparities allows us to provide policy suggestions for countries with monocentric land structures. This chapter considers the potential factors that have enabled local areas to catch up with the Greater Tokyo Area. This chapter discusses three factors, specifically social overhead capital (SOC), industrial structure, and fiscal transfer from the central to the local government.

The development of SOC enhances regional competitiveness, thereby improving the economic performance of local areas. The sharing of SOC among firms can reduce fixed costs in production and increase productivity. As discussed in Chap. 4, it is well known that postwar SOC investments in Japan have contributed to improving regional productivity. Moreover, recent studies show that the upgrading of SOC, such as highways, high-speed railways, and airports, may have expanded the geographic scope of agglomeration economies. Local areas can grow by "borrowing" the functions of large metropolitan areas through SOC.[2] Japan's SOC investment may not only strengthen the production capacity of industries but also expand the geographical scope of agglomeration economies and help increase regional productivity.

In addition to the SOC, the industrial structure needs to be considered as a second factor. Japan's manufacturing industry is highly productive and has a significant export industry. Empirical studies have found that regions with a spatial concentration in the manufacturing industry are highly competitive and productive (Otsuka et al. 2010; Otsuka and Goto 2015a). Therefore, the location of manufacturing industries may have helped enhance regional competitiveness.

---

[1]In a Japan's newspaper, there is an article that the regional disparity in Japan peaked in the 1960s and has been on a downward trend from 1970s up to now. (The Nikkei: Nihon Keizai Shimbun on October 23, 2020)

[2]This effect can be explained as the effect of "borrowed size" (Alonso 1973). See Part II (Chaps. 5, 6, and 7) for borrowed size effect in detail.

We also need to consider fiscal transfers from the central government to the local government as a third factor. The local allocation tax, a fiscal transfer, is allocated from the central to local governments in order to guarantee the financial resources of each region and to balance financial power levels between regions. A local allocation tax is allocated excessively to regions with a weak economic base and inadequate fiscal income and is under-allocated to regions with a solid economic base and relatively high fiscal income. In other words, the local allocation tax is inherently designed to mitigate regional disparities in financial strength.

This chapter examines whether these factors have increased the feasibility of economic catch-up. To the best of our knowledge, no study has systematically considered Japan's regional economic structure between the 1990s and the 2000s. Hence, this chapter provides an insight into Japan's recent experiences with global readers. This chapter is structured as follows. Section 2.2 provides an overview of Japan's regional economic structure and evidence of economic catch-up in local areas. Section 2.3 validates the theories on regional disparities for Japan. Section 2.4 focuses on SOC, industrial structure, and fiscal transfer as determinants of regional disparities in GVA per capita. Section 2.5 summarizes the conclusions and discusses the future research agenda.

2.2 Regional Economic Structure

First, we review Japan's regional economic structures. This section explores the geographical distribution of GVA and the population. It then describes regional disparities in GVA per capita.[3,4]

Table 2.1 lists the top five regions by share of GVA and population in 2014. Tokyo is the leading player in both aspects, accounting for 18.46% of all GVA. Osaka's share of total GVA is 7.29%, roughly 10 percentage points lower than that of Tokyo. This implies an excessive geographical concentration of about 20% of Japan's economy in Tokyo. By contrast, Tokyo accounts for 10.13% of Japan's total

---

[3]The GVA for each prefecture is based on the gross regional product in the *Annual Report of Prefectural Accounts* (Cabinet Office) and is deflated by the value-added deflator reported in the *System of National Accounts* (Cabinet Office). Hence, the GVA in this chapter refers to real gross value added.

[4]Regional economic disparities are often discussed in the context of labor income disparities. Income represents the disposable income earned by workers living in the area. Workers who live in other areas are involved in production activities in areas that have a massive net inflow via commuting, such as Tokyo; thus, such an area has more economic power than what is assessed by disposable labor income. In other words, evaluating regional economic power by labor income makes it impossible to evaluate economic power accurately in areas that have a massive net inflow of commuting. As GVA represents the scale of production activity that has occurred in that region, GVA is preferable for an accurate assessment of the economic strength of a region. Of course, if the movement of commuters can be accurately controlled, it is also useful to discuss regional disparities based on labor income data.

Table 2.1 Top five prefectures by GVA share and population share in 2014

GVA			Population		
Prefecture		Percentage share	Prefecture		Percentage share
1	Tokyo	18.46	1	Tokyo	10.13
2	Osaka	7.29	2	Kanagawa	7.07
3	Aichi	7.13	3	Osaka	6.86
4	Kanagawa	5.87	4	Aichi	5.76
5	Saitama	4.05	5	Saitama	5.67
	Total	42.79		Total	35.50

Source: Calculations based on the *Annual Report on Prefectural Accounts* (Cabinet Office) and *Basic Resident Registers* (Ministry of Internal Affairs and Communications)

Table 2.2 Gini coefficients and coefficient of variation (CV) in 2014

	47 prefectural regions		46 prefectural regions (excl. Tokyo)	
	Gini coefficient	CV	Gini coefficient	CV
GVA	0.514	1.382	0.439	0.941
Population	0.447	0.978	0.418	0.883

Source: Calculations based on the *Annual Report on Prefectural Accounts* (Cabinet Office) and *Basic Resident Registers* (Ministry of Internal Affairs and Communications)

population, while Kanagawa is ranked second for population size at 7.07%, which is close to Tokyo's population. This emphasizes the remarkable concentration of economic activity in Tokyo relative to the demographic distribution.

Table 2.2 illustrates the geographical distribution distortion of both GVA and the population. Based on the Gini coefficient and the coefficient of variation (CV) values calculated for the 47 prefectures, GVA exceeds the population, indicating that the regional disparities in economic activities are higher than those in demography. Excluding Tokyo, both the Gini coefficient and CV values are smaller than they are when all 47 prefectures are considered in the calculation, indicating that Tokyo strongly influences Japan's regional disparity levels.

Figure 2.1 shows the net inflow of population into the Greater Tokyo Area, Chubu, Kansai, and local areas. A monocentric concentration of the population in the Greater Tokyo Area has developed since the 1980s. Population migration from local areas to the Greater Tokyo Area began reaccelerating in the 2000s. Overall, we can confirm a significant geographical concentration of the population in the Greater Tokyo Area.[5]

Figure 2.2 shows the time series of the percentage shares of GVA and population in the Greater Tokyo Area and local areas. In the Greater Tokyo Area, the share of GVA declined between 1990 and 1996 remained stable. In 2014, the share of GVA in the Greater Tokyo Area was 32.2%, which is slightly lower than what it was in 1990. By contrast, the share of the population in the Greater Tokyo Area rose from 25.5% in 1990 to 27.7% in 2014, indicating that its population concentration is

[5]See Appendix 1 for further considerations of the monocentric structure in Japan's national land.

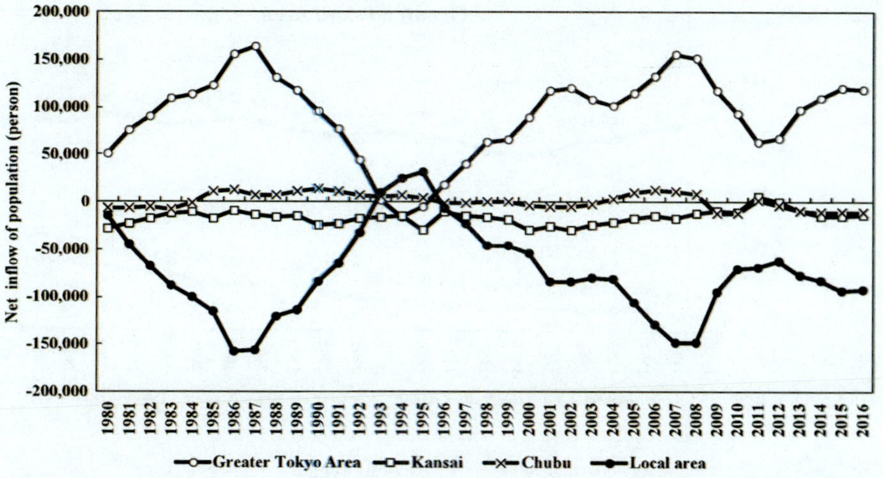

Fig. 2.1 Internal migration in Japan. Source: Calculations based on the *Annual Report on Internal Migration in Japan* (Ministry of Internal Affairs and Communications). Note: The regional classifications in this figure are as follows: Greater Tokyo Area (Saitama, Chiba, Tokyo, and Kanagawa), Chubu (Nagano, Gifu, Shizuoka, Aichi, and Mie), Kansai (Shiga, Kyoto, Osaka, Hyogo, Nara, and Wakayama), and local areas (Hokkaido, Aomori, Iwate, Miyagi, Akita, Yamagata, Fukushima, Niigata, Ibaraki, Tochigi, Gunma, Yamanashi, Toyama, Ishikawa, Fukui, Tottori, Shimane, Okayama, Hiroshima, Yamaguchi, Tokushima, Kagawa, Ehime, Kochi, Fukuoka, Saga, Nagasaki, Kumamoto, Oita, Miyazaki, Kagoshima, and Okinawa)

increasing. This suggests that productivity in the Greater Tokyo Area is likely declining since the share of production activity has not increased as much as the population share.

In contrast, the share of GVA in local areas increased from 1990 to 1994 and has leveled off since, while the population share in local areas declined from 44.9% in 1990 to 42.5% in 2014. In local areas, the reduction in the share of the population was dominant relative to the share of the production activity; hence, productivity may have increased. In other words, it is likely that the significant geographical concentration of the population in the Greater Tokyo Area, which progressed after the 1990s, did not lead to an increase in productivity in the Greater Tokyo Area. Conversely, in local areas, productivity is increasing despite population decline, suggesting that economic power has steadily increased in these areas.

Based on the conventional theory on agglomeration, we can easily imagine that the Greater Tokyo Area continues to grow through the economic benefits provided by population concentration, for instance, economies of agglomeration. However, this has not always been the case in Japan. Table 2.3 shows the growth trends of GVA per capita by region. Taking 1990 as the base year (1990 = 100), the Greater Tokyo Area and Kansai are below 100 as of 2014. These areas are experiencing significant economic stagnation due to the economic recession caused by the collapse of the asset-inflated bubble economy in 1991 and of Lehman Brothers in 2008. Furthermore, the 2014 GVA per capita levels of the Greater Tokyo Area and Kansai

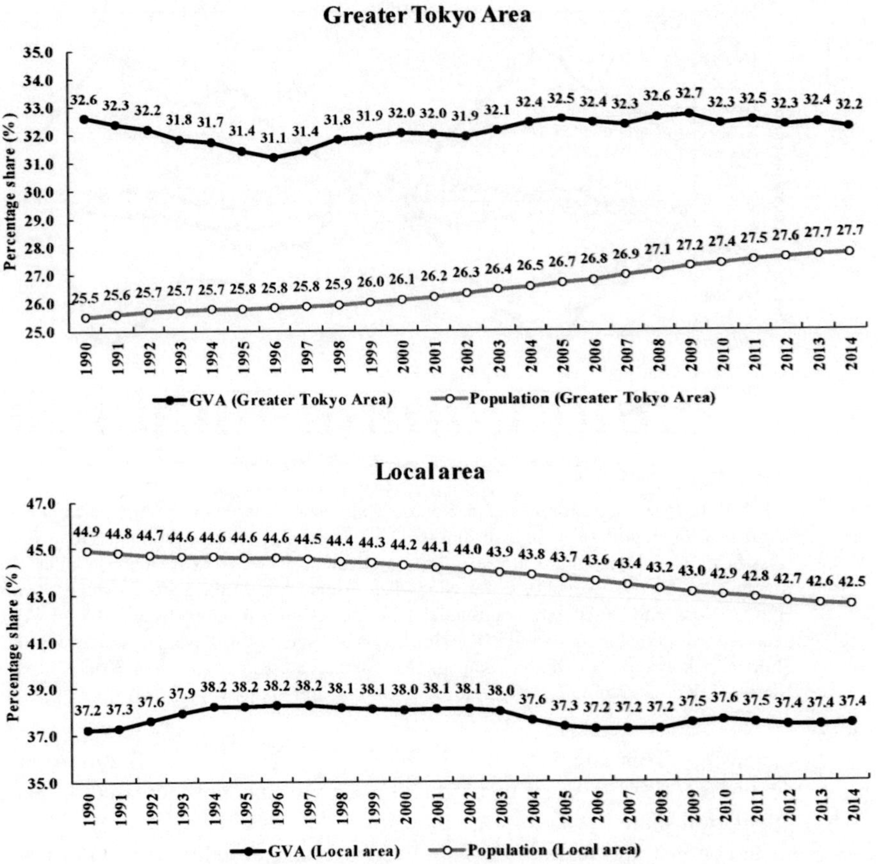

Fig. 2.2 The trends in percentage share of GVA and population. Source: Calculations based on the *Annual Report on Prefectural Accounts* (Cabinet Office) and *Basic Resident Registers* (Ministry of Internal Affairs and Communications). Note: The regional classifications in this figure are as follows: Greater Tokyo Area (Saitama, Chiba, Tokyo, and Kanagawa) and local areas (Hokkaido, Aomori, Iwate, Miyagi, Akita, Yamagata, Fukushima, Niigata, Ibaraki, Tochigi, Gunma, Yamanashi, Toyama, Ishikawa, Fukui, Tottori, Shimane, Okayama, Hiroshima, Yamaguchi, Tokushima, Kagawa, Ehime, Kochi, Fukuoka, Saga, Nagasaki, Kumamoto, Oita, Miyazaki, Kagoshima, and Okinawa)

have not recovered to their level in 1990. Meanwhile, the economic strength of local areas has recovered since the beginning of the 2000s, with their GVA per capita growing faster than the national average.

Figure 2.3 shows the time-series changes in the CV of GVA per capita. The CV declined sharply between 1990 and 1995, before increasing temporarily in 2005. However, it declined again from 2005 to 2014, with the 2014 levels well below the 1990 levels. This CV trend indicates that the regional disparities in GVA per capita have been shrinking over the long term.

Table 2.3 Growth trend of GVA per capita by Japan's regions (1990 = 100)

Region	1990	1995	2000	2005	2010	2014
Hokkaido	100	101	98	99	99	102
Tohoku	100	103	104	105	105	115
North Kanto	100	96	96	99	105	112
Greater Tokyo Area	100	92	93	95	92	95
Chubu	100	98	100	107	104	113
Hokuriku	100	99	101	104	104	107
Kansai	100	97	93	94	94	98
Chugoku	100	98	98	104	104	111
Shikoku	100	103	105	105	110	116
Kyushu	100	100	101	104	108	110
Okinawa	100	95	96	97	99	105
National	100	97	97	100	99	104

Source: Calculations based on the *Annual Report on Prefectural Accounts* (Cabinet Office) and *Basic Resident Registers* (Ministry of Internal Affairs and Communications)
Note: See Fig. 1.2 in Chap. 1 for the regional classification

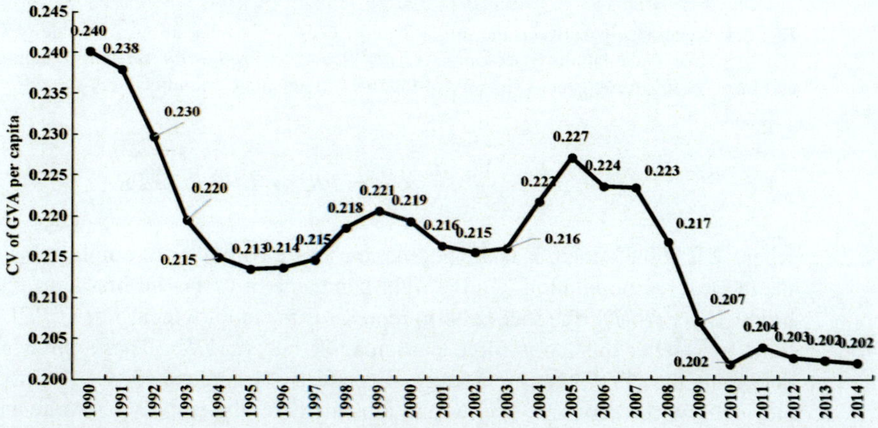

Fig. 2.3 Trend in GVA per capita disparities among Japan's regions. Source: Calculations based on the *Annual Report on Prefectural Accounts* (Cabinet Office) and *Basic Resident Registers* (Ministry of Internal Affairs and Communications)

Figure 2.4 plots the relationship between the initial levels of GVA per capita and GVA per capita growth from 1990 to 2014. Based on the negative correlations observed in the figure, the higher the GVA per capita level in 1990, the lower the GVA per capita growth rate. Conversely, the lower the GVA per capita level in 1990, the higher the GVA per capita growth rate, indicating that areas with lower GVA per capita may be catching up with areas with higher GVA per capita.

To explore the potential of economic catching up deeply, we confirm the determinants of the GVA per capita after the 1990s. The GVA per capita (VP) can be broken into three elements, as shown in Eq. (2.1):

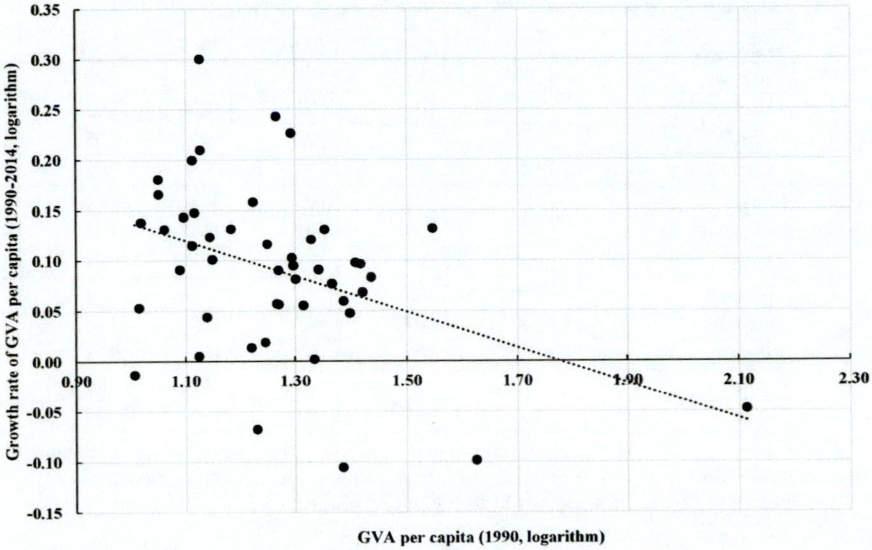

Fig. 2.4 Relationship between the initial level of GVA per capita and growth rate of GVA per capita. Source: Calculations based on the *Annual Report on Prefectural Accounts* (Cabinet Office) and *Basic Resident Registers* (Ministry of Internal Affairs and Communications)

$$VP \equiv \frac{V}{P} = \frac{V}{L} \times \frac{L}{N} \times \frac{N}{P} = PRD \times EPR \times LFPR, \tag{2.1}$$

where V is value added, P is the population, L is the number of employees, and N is the labor force population. On the right-hand side of (2.1), the first term represents productivity (*PRD*), the second term represents the employment rate (*EPR*), and the third represents the labor force participation rate (*LFPR*). These three elements determine the GVA per capita level. If productivity is elevated, GVA per capita is elevated. As the economy booms and jobs increase, the employment rate and GVA per capita increase. The entry of young people, homemakers, and the elderly into labor markets increases the labor force participation rate and GVA per capita.

Taking the logarithm of Eq. (2.1) yields the following equation:

$$lnVP = lnPRD + lnEPR + lnLFPR. \tag{2.2}$$

Variance decomposition of Eq. (2.2) yields the following:

$$\begin{aligned} var(VP) &= var(PRD) + var(EPR) + var(LFPR) \\ &\quad + 2[cov(PRD, EPR) + cov(PRD, LFPR) + cov(EPR, LFPR)]. \end{aligned} \tag{2.3}$$

Eq. (2.3) shows that the variance in GVA per capita can be decomposed into the variance and covariance of its determinants. Table 2.4 presents the decomposition

Table 2.4 Variance decomposition of GVA per capita

Variable	1990	1995	2000	2005	2010	2014
var (PRD)	53.3	45.7	40.1	47.7	49.5	52.1
var (EPR)	24.3	29.4	26.6	22.6	23.5	23.1
var (LFPR)	6.9	6.9	6.6	4.8	5.2	7.5
covariance	15.5	17.9	26.7	24.9	21.8	17.3

Source: Calculations based on the *Annual Report on Prefectural Accounts* (Cabinet Office), *Basic Resident Registers* (Ministry of Internal Affairs and Communications), and the *Labor Force Survey* (Ministry of Internal Affairs and Communications)

results of the volatility in GVA per capita based on Eq. (2.3). In 1990, the *PRD* accounted for more than 50% of the *VP* change, which declined through 2000 and rose thereafter. In contrast, the impact of employment was smaller than that of productivity; variability in *EPR* accounted for approximately 20% of the total volatility, while variability in *LFPR* accounted for less than 10%, indicating that the most significant determinant of GVA per capita volatility was productivity.

Furthermore, to assess the growth contribution of each determinant to GVA per capita by region, we decompose the growth of GVA per capita.

By adding a subscript for time t to Eq. (2.1) yields the following:

$$VP_t = PRD_t \times EPR_t \times LFPR_t. \tag{2.4}$$

Taking the logarithms on both sides of Eq. (2.4) and deriving the difference from time $t - 1$ yield the following:

$$ln\,\frac{VP_t}{VP_{t-1}} = ln\,\frac{PRD_t}{PRD_{t-1}} + ln\,\frac{EPR_t}{EPR_{t-1}} + ln\,\frac{LFPR_t}{LFPR_{t-1}}. \tag{2.5}$$

To focus on the time changes in GVA per capita, multiplying weight w on both sides of (2.5) yields the following identical equation:

$$\Delta VP_t = w_t\,ln\,\frac{PRD_t}{PRD_{t-1}} + w_t\,ln\,\frac{EPR_t}{EPR_{t-1}} + w_t\,ln\,\frac{LFPR_t}{LFPR_{t-1}}, \tag{2.6}$$

where

$$w_t = \frac{VP_t - VP_{t-1}}{lnVP_t - lnVP_{t-1}}.$$

Equation (2.6) shows that time changes in GVA per capita can be evenly decomposed into three components: changes in productivity (*PRD*), employment rate (*EPR*), and labor force participation rate (*LFPR*).

Figure 2.5 illustrates the results of decomposing the GVA per capita growth for each region based on Eq. (2.6). In Japan as a whole, productivity declined significantly between 1990 and 1995 and has been trending upward since then. The

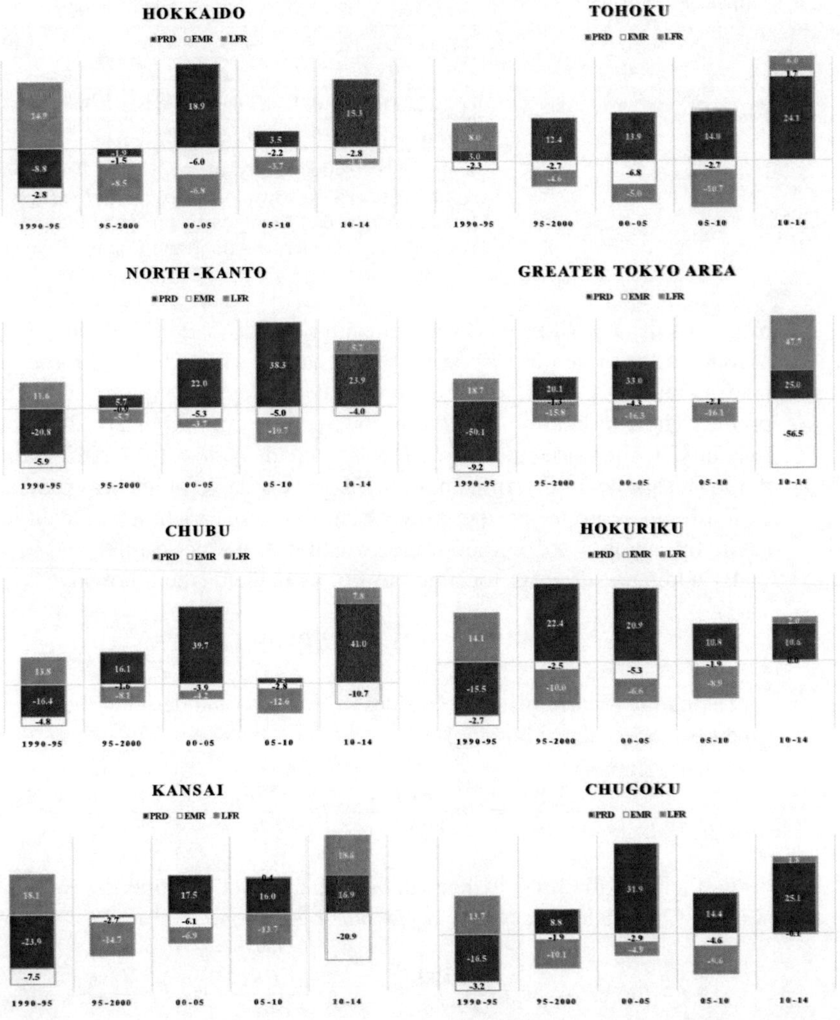

Fig. 2.5 Decomposition of GVA per capita growth in Japan's regions. Source: Calculations based on the *Annual Report on Prefectural Accounts* (Cabinet Office), *Basic Resident Registers* (Ministry of Internal Affairs and Communications), and the *Labor Force Survey* (Ministry of Internal Affairs and Communications). Note: See Fig. 1.2 in Chap. 1 for the regional classification

increase in productivity between 2000 and 2005 is particularly remarkable. The movement of the Greater Tokyo Area is similar to that of Japan as a whole. After productivity recovered in 1995, it experienced a significant drop in the latter half of the 2000s, presumably due to the economic recession caused by the collapse of Lehman Brothers in 2008. Unlike the Greater Tokyo Area, local areas saw a significant increase in productivity in the 2000s. In Tohoku, North Kanto, Chugoku,

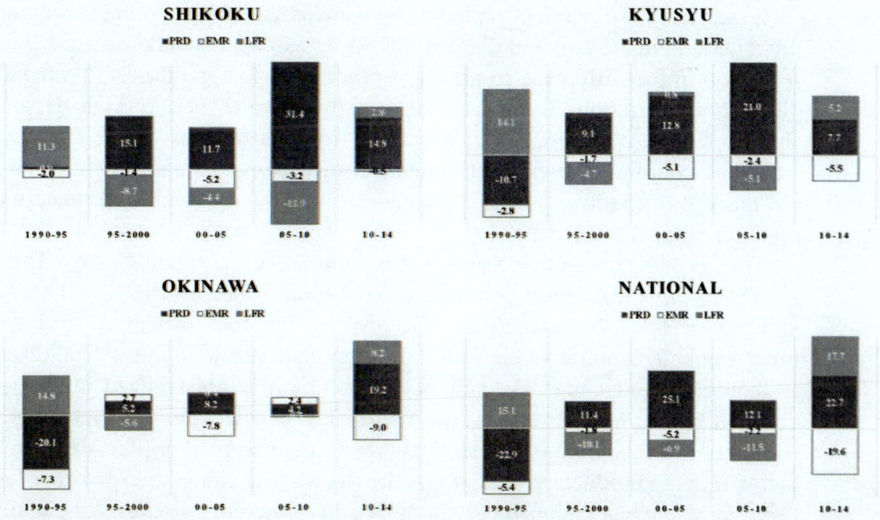

Fig. 2.5 (continued)

Shikoku, and Kyushu, productivity increased significantly in the late 2000s. In many local areas, the productivity increase exceeded that of the Greater Tokyo Area. Therefore, it is highly probable that the regional disparities in GVA per capita narrowed because local economic recoveries outperformed those of the Greater Tokyo Area, suggesting that local areas are catching up with it.

2.3 Theories on Regional Disparities

There are two perspectives on regional disparities in GVA per capita.[6] The first perspective is based on neoclassical theory, which explains that market mechanisms reduce regional disparities (Barro and Sala-i-Martin 2004). This theory highlights the roles of labor input, capital input, and technological progress in the process of economic growth. Constant returns to scale are assumed, and free inter-regional movements of the production factors decrease regional disparities. The theory states that due to the equalization in the capital-labor ratio between regions, the inter-regional disparities in production factor prices diminish, and those in GVA per capita also decrease.[7]

[6]See Appendix 2 for a textbook description of the two perspectives on regional disparities.

[7]An empirical assessment of the neoclassical theory has been conducted in many countries and many regions. However, it should be noted that the implications of convergence between nations usually differ from those of convergence between regions. Notably, empirical evaluations depend on the indicators and periods selected. Exploring several handbooks would reveal fruitful findings on regional disparities in developed and developing countries (e.g., Magrini 2004).

If the market mechanism explained by neoclassical theory is functioning in Japan, the reduction in the regional disparity in GVA per capita should be explained by the reduction in the difference in prices of production factors, that is, the reduction in population migration from local areas to the Greater Tokyo Area. However, as shown in Fig. 2.1, population migration from local areas to the Greater Tokyo Area has continued despite the reduction in regional disparities. In other words, the market mechanism assumed by neoclassical theory cannot adequately explain regional disparities in Japan.[8]

The second perspective is based on cumulative causation theory. This theory highlights the role of the export industry as a source of economic growth (Armstrong and Taylor 2000; Capello 2016). The positive feedback mechanisms of economic growth enable cumulative economic development, resulting in regional disparities.[9] It should be noted that the cumulative causation is not realized in the world of constant or decreasing returns assumed in the neoclassical theory because in the economy assumed by the neoclassical theory, the marginal product decreases for an increase in the production factors. In other words, the cumulative growth of regional economies can be explained only in the world of increasing returns as mentioned by Kaldor (1966). Therefore, in this theory, economies of scale play a significant role in the variation of regional disparities. The empirical findings are shown in Chap. 7, and we can confirm the size of economies of scale in Japan's regions.

Table 2.5 presents the scale parameters (γ) computed for Japan's regions.[10] The parameter of economies of scale in the Greater Tokyo Area has been 1.366 since the 2000s, which is higher than the level in the 1990s. Only the Greater Tokyo Area and Okinawa have seen an increase in economies of scale during this period owing to their increased spatial population concentration; the agglomeration economies have strengthened in both regions. By contrast, in most local areas, economies of scale have declined significantly, with the most significant reductions in Tohoku, Shikoku, Chugoku, and Hokkaido.

Figure 2.6 plots the dynamic relationship between the regional average of economies of scale (γ) and the CV of GVA per capita. The relationship was negative in the 1990s; that is, the regional disparities in GVA per capita decreased along with the increase in economies of scale. However, this correlation has been positive since the

---

[8]One possibility for the continuation of the population inflow to the Greater Tokyo Area is that the real wage gap between regions may not have narrowed because labor demand in Tokyo had increased significantly relative to the increase in labor supply. An official data showed that job openings in local areas increased under the Abe administration (2012–2020), but so did job openings in Tokyo (see Appendix 3).

[9]Empirical models on the cumulative causation theory are provided by Dixon and Thirlwall (1975a, b) based on the idea of cumulative growth developed by Kaldor (1975). The model is characterized by the inclusion of a positive feedback mechanism expressed as Verdoorn's law. This mechanism signifies that the growth of regional economies is a cumulative process because the expansion of production leads to increases in productivity.

[10]See Chap. 7 for calculation procedures on the scale parameters by regions.

Table 2.5 Economies of scale in Japan's regions

Region	Level of economies of scale (γ)		Variation rate (%)
	1990s	After 2000s	
Hokkaido	0.917	0.912	−0.49
Tohoku	1.021	1.013	−0.69
North Kanto	1.102	1.101	−0.09
Greater Tokyo Area	1.358	1.366	0.60
Chubu	1.161	1.160	−0.08
Hokuriku	1.088	1.086	−0.21
Kansai	1.246	1.246	−0.06
Chugoku	1.111	1.105	−0.55
Shikoku	1.116	1.109	−0.63
Kyushu	1.099	1.097	−0.25
Okinawa	1.161	1.167	0.54
National	1.140	1.138	−0.21

Notes: (1) Economies of scale are calculated based on Model C (Table 7.4) in Chap. 7
(2) See Fig. 1.2 in Chap. 1 for the regional classification

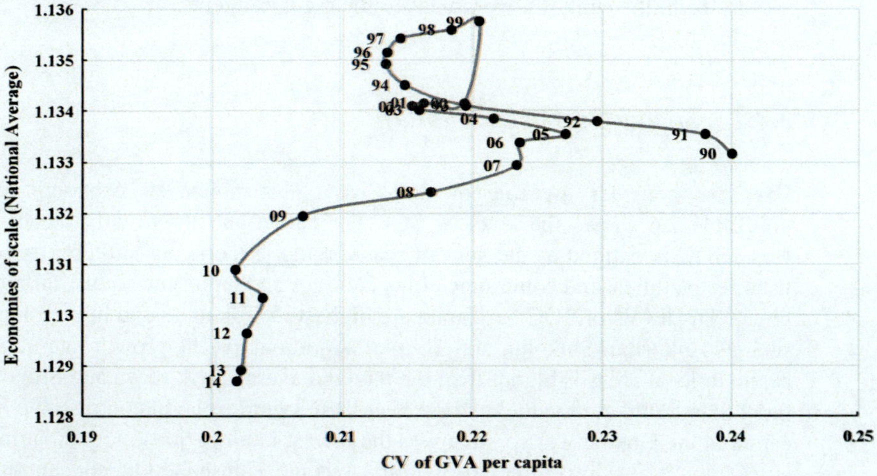

Fig. 2.6 Dynamic relationship between economies of scale and CV of GVA per capita (1990–2014). Source: Calculations based on the *Annual Report on Prefectural Accounts* (Cabinet Office), *Basic Resident Registers* (Ministry of Internal Affairs and Communications), and the estimates of economies of scale. Note: Economies of scale are calculated based on Model C (Table 7.4) in Chap. 7

2000s, with a decline in the regional average economies of scale and shrinking regional disparities in GVA per capita.

There are two routes for realizing increasing returns to scale in regional economies. The first is the increasing returns of production technologies at the firm level. Second, even if the firms' production technologies yield constant returns to scale, the geographical externalities can generate increasing returns to scale in the region overall.[11] In a case, such as in Japan with a monocentric land structure, if the cumulative causation theory holds, then the relatively high level of economies of scale in a region, like the Greater Tokyo Area, should guarantee its cumulative growth, leading to an increase in regional disparities. However, the results show that the enhancement in the economies of scale in the Greater Tokyo Area has not led to increased regional disparities in GVA per capita. Therefore, it can be concluded that the economies of scale are not the primary source of the variation of regional disparities and that the cumulative causation theory has also not functioned in Japan overall.

2.4 Determinants of Economic Catching Up

As the next step to explore the potential drivers of catching up in the regional economy, we consider the determinants of catching up in regional economies. This section focuses on the three factors of SOC, industrial structure, and fiscal transfer from the central government to local governments.

2.4.1 *Social Overhead Capital*

First, we consider the role of SOC as a determinant of economic catching up. Table 2.6 shows the level of SOC per capita and its growth rate by region. Here, SOC is defined as the sum of roads, ports, airports, agriculture, forestry and fisheries facilities, and communications facilities and represents industrial infrastructure.[12] The levels of SOC per capita are highest in Hokkaido and high in local areas such as Hokuriku, Shikoku, and Tohoku. Additionally, the growth rate of SOC per capita in local areas is higher than the national average: Okinawa and Shikoku have more than doubled in value in 2014 over their 1990 levels. In contrast, the SOC per capita in the Greater Tokyo Area was the lowest in all periods, while that in Kansai and Chubu is also lower than the national average. Consequently, concentrated SOC investments in local areas are likely to increase their GVA per capita through the strengthening of external economies.

Figure 2.7 plots the dynamic relationship between SOC per capita and GVA per capita over the 1990–2014 period, showing a positive correlation. In other words, the

---

[11]Originally, Chipman (1970) proved that external economies for economic agents can be internalized at the aggregate level and expressed as economies of scale. For the context of agglomeration economies, see Otsuka (2017).

[12]The concept of SOC is defined by Hirschman (1958) and is generally consistent with concepts such as "public capital," "public infrastructure," and "government capital."

Table 2.6 SOC per capita in Japan's regions

Region	1990		2000		2014	
	(million yen/person)	Ratio to 1990 (1990 = 100)	(million yen/person)	Ratio to 1990 (1990 = 100)	(million yen/person)	Ratio to 1990 (1990 = 100)
Hokkaido	4.680	(100)	6.679	(143)	8.039	(172)
Tohoku	3.153	(100)	4.470	(142)	5.372	(170)
North Kanto	2.020	(100)	2.836	(140)	3.445	(171)
Greater Tokyo Area	1.482	(100)	1.873	(126)	2.030	(137)
Chubu	1.989	(100)	2.885	(145)	3.474	(175)
Hokuriku	2.972	(100)	4.373	(147)	5.610	(189)
Kansai	1.637	(100)	2.421	(148)	2.918	(178)
Chugoku	2.798	(100)	4.003	(143)	4.853	(173)
Shikoku	2.786	(100)	4.427	(159)	5.579	(200)
Kyushu	2.448	(100)	3.634	(148)	4.540	(185)
Okinawa	2.000	(100)	3.304	(165)	4.327	(216)
National	2.197	(100)	3.110	(142)	3.670	(167)

Source: Calculations based on the estimates of SOC by the Central Research Institute of Electric Power Industry
Note: See Fig. 1.2 in Chap. 1 for the regional classification

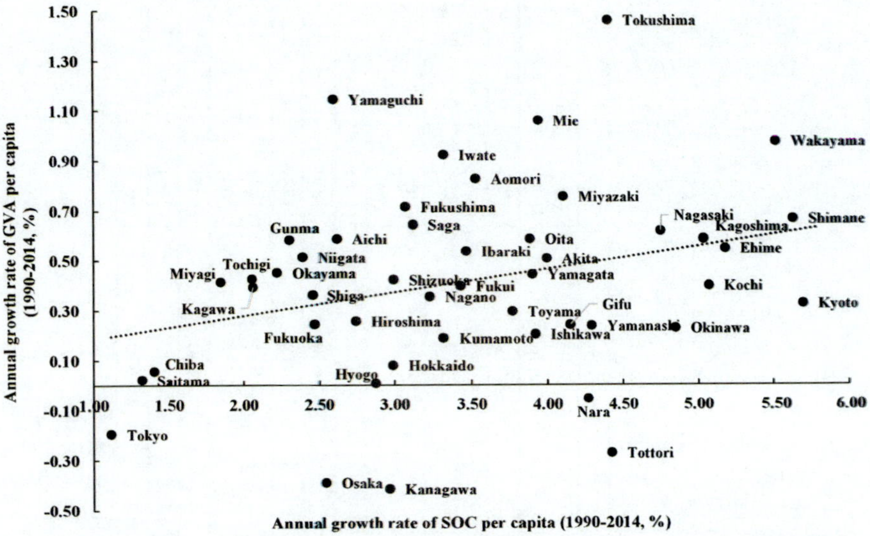

Fig. 2.7 Dynamic relationship between SOC per capita and GVA per capita. Source: Calculations based on the *Annual Report on Prefectural Accounts* (Cabinet Office), *Basic Resident Registers* (Ministry of Internal Affairs and Communications), and the estimates of SOC by the Central Research Institute of Electric Power Industry

higher the SOC per capita, the higher the GVA per capita. In Wakayama and Tokushima, the SOC per capita has increased significantly, resulting in an increase in GVA per capita. Conversely, Tokyo's SOC per capita and GVA per capita have declined. The increased productivity of local areas due to SOC investments may be contributing to the economic catching up of local areas.[13]

Japan's high-speed transportation infrastructure is built around Tokyo as a hub at the center of highways, high-speed railways, and air roads. The high-speed transportation infrastructure that was developed from the 1990s to the 2000s shortened the travel time to Tokyo considerably. This shortening may have facilitated access to Tokyo's giant markets and significantly increased the GVA per capita in local areas. Figure 2.8 plots the relationship between the shortening of travel time to Tokyo and the growth rates of GVA per capita. A definite positive correlation is observed; the correlation coefficient is 0.41 and is statistically significant. We see that GVA per capita is rising sharply in areas where the travel time to Tokyo has been dramatically shortened, and this effect is more substantial in areas further away from Tokyo than it is in areas adjacent to Tokyo. Local areas such as Tokushima, Yamaguchi, Shimane, Aomori, and Iwate have been highly effective in reducing travel time. Thus, the development of high-speed transportation infrastructure was likely the

[13]Otsuka and Goto (2015b) clarify that SOC works as an external economy and boosts regional productivity by enhancing agglomeration economies.

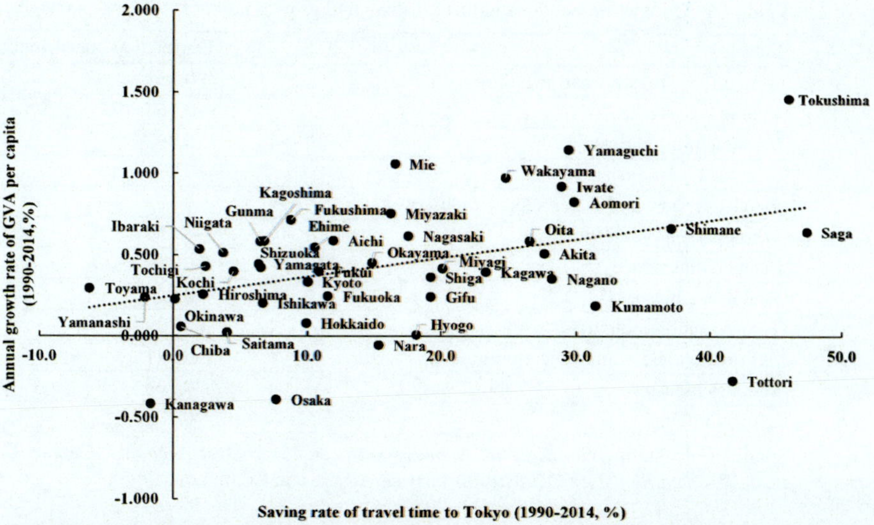

Fig. 2.8 Dynamic relationship between travel time savings to Tokyo and GVA per capita. Source: Calculations based on the *Annual Report on Prefectural Accounts* (Cabinet Office), *Basic Resident Registers* (Ministry of Internal Affairs and Communications), and the *National Integrated Transport Analysis System* (Ministry of Land, Infrastructure, Transport and Tourism)

driving force behind the drastic productivity increase in local areas further from Tokyo. This suggests the possible realization of inter-regional network economies.[14]

2.4.2 Industrial Structure

Next, we discuss the roles of the industrial structure as determinants of economic catching up. Table 2.7 reports the correlation coefficients between the industrial share and the growth rate of GVA per capita for each region. The correlation coefficient between the manufacturing industry share and GVA per capita growth rate is high at 0.392, implying that regions specializing in manufacturing have higher growth rates of GVA per capita. Conversely, regions specializing in tertiary industries, such as financial insurance, real estate, and services, have lower growth rates of GVA per capita. Morikawa (2011) notes that Japan is increasingly trending toward a service economy and that the service industry enjoys economies of scale as agglomeration economies. As shown in Table 2.5, only the Greater Tokyo Area and Okinawa, which are specialized in the services industry, enjoy increasing returns to scale. That is, his findings can only be applied to these two regions. However, economies of scale in other regions have been declining. Thus, economies of scale in

[14]This finding also suggests that inter-regional network economies exceed the agglomeration shadow effect in Japan. See Part II (Chaps. 5, 6, and 7) for discussions on this topic.

Table 2.7 Correlation between industrial share and growth rate of GVA per capita

Industry	Correlation coefficient (in 2014)
Agriculture, forestry, and fisheries	0.331
Mining	0.164
Manufacturing industry	0.392
Construction industry	0.281
Electricity, gas, and water supply industry	0.181
Wholesale and retail business	−0.458
Financial insurance	−0.359
Real estate business	−0.621
Transportation industry	−0.129
Information and communication industry	−0.541
Services industry	−0.269
Official affairs	0.198

Source: Calculations based on the *Annual Report on Prefectural Accounts* (Cabinet Office) and *Basic Resident Registers* (Ministry of Internal Affairs and Communications)

the services industry do not lead to an increase in the GVA per capita in local areas; therefore, the reasons for local areas' economic catch-up cannot be fully explained by the location of the services industry.

Figure 2.9 plots the relationship between the location quotient (*LQ*) of the manufacturing industry and the growth rate of GVA per capita.[15] The figure shows a clear upward-right relationship. In other words, the growth rate of GVA per capita is higher in regions specializing in the manufacturing industry. For example, the location of the manufacturing plant is concentrated in Mie. Growth in GVA per capita is also remarkable in this region. Similar trends are observed in Tokushima and Yamaguchi. These regions are not metropolitan areas but local areas. This finding suggests that the location of manufacturing industries is one of the driving forces behind the economic catching up.

Figure 2.10 plots the time-series relationship between the labor productivity of the manufacturing industry and the CV of GVA per capita. It shows a clear negative correlation, indicating that elevated productivity in the manufacturing industry influences CV reduction. The productivity growth of the manufacturing industry is believed to have strengthened the economic power of local areas, allowing them to catch up with large metropolitan areas. This suggests that the manufacturing industry's location must be considered in the analysis of Japan's regional disparities.

[15]The location quotient is an index that represents the concentration and specialization of an industry. The location quotient LQ_{ij} of industry i in region j is defined as follows:

$LQ_{ij} = \frac{L_{ij}/\sum_i L_{ij}}{\sum_j L_{ij}/\sum_i \sum_j L_{ij}}$, where L_{ij} is the employment in industry i and region j. Therefore, the numerator reflects the employment share of industry i in region j, and the denominator expresses the employment share of industry i nationwide. If this value exceeds 1, it signifies that the employment share of industry i in that region is higher than the nationwide share.

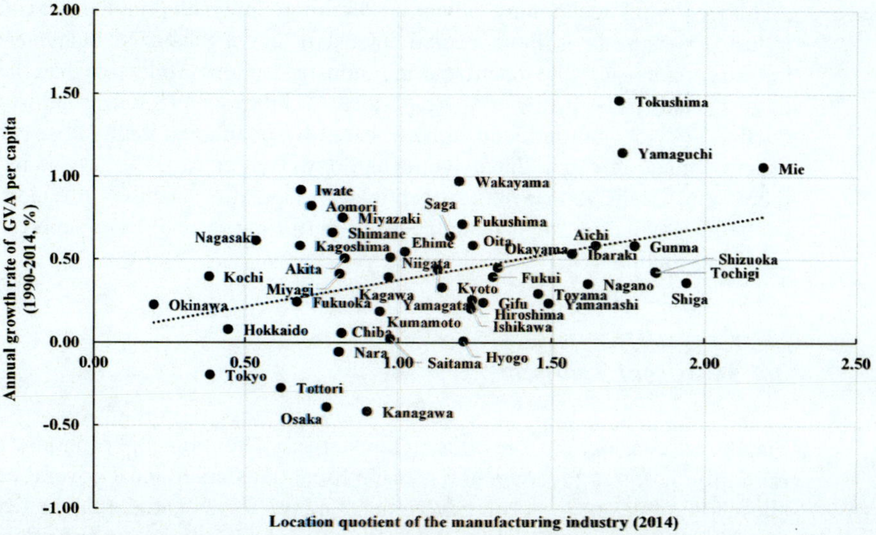

Fig. 2.9 Relationship between location quotient of the manufacturing industry and the annual growth rate of GVA per capita. Source: Calculations based on the *Annual Report on Prefectural Accounts* (Cabinet Office) and *Basic Resident Registers* (Ministry of Internal Affairs and Communications). Note: See footnote 15 for the definition of the location quotient

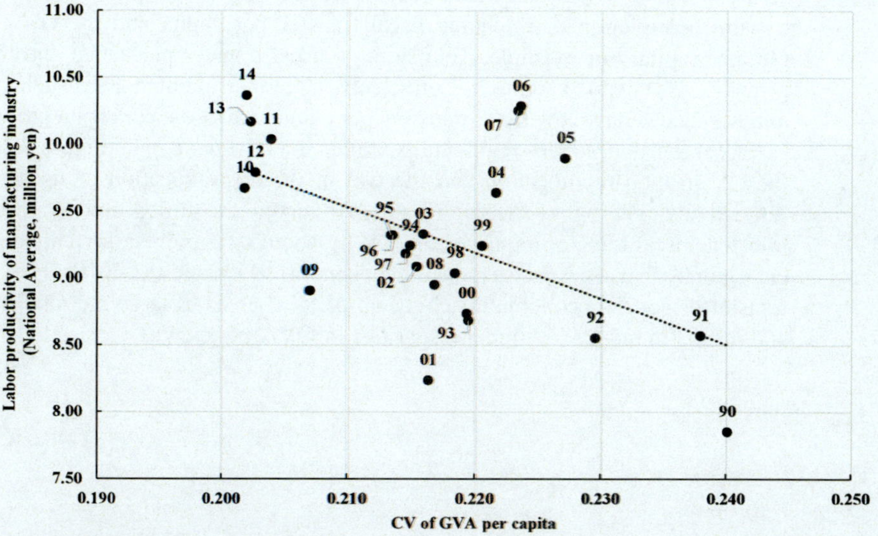

Fig. 2.10 Dynamic relationship between labor productivity of manufacturing industry and CV of GVA per capita (1990–2014). Source: Calculations based on the *Annual Report on Prefectural Accounts* (Cabinet Office), *Basic Resident Registers* (Ministry of Internal Affairs and Communications), and the *Nikkei Economic Electronic Databank System*

Labor-saving technology advances are more prevalent in the manufacturing industry because it is more capital intensive and mechanized than the services industry. As a result, the manufacturing industry is more productive than the service industry and leads to higher wages. Moreover, the manufacturing industry's production activities are unlikely to be affected by population decline because of the progress made in capital-intensive technology. By contrast, the service industry is more labor intensive and thus susceptible to population decline. In regions with a declining population, high manufacturing performance may have suppressed economic stagnation.

2.4.3 *Fiscal Transfer*

Finally, we consider the role of fiscal transfer as a determinant of economic catching up. Japan's central government has made fiscal transfers to local governments. The allocation of taxes to local governments plays an essential role in decreasing financial disparities among local governments and adjusting government finances.[16] The taxes allocated to local governments are financial resources that local public entities can use for any purpose they choose. In this sense, the fiscal transfer becomes a central system for securing financial resources for local governments.

Regions receiving large local allocation tax grants can invest in infrastructure to strengthen their fiscal and economic capacities. Figure 2.11 reveals the positive dynamic correlation between the fiscal transfer per capita and the GVA growth rate per capita. For example, Tokushima's fiscal transfer per capita and the GVA growth rate per capita are high. Conversely, large metropolitan areas such as Tokyo and Kanagawa have low fiscal transfers per capita and GVA per capita growth rates.

Fiscal transfer reduces regional disparities in GVA per capita. Figure 2.12 shows the CV in the pre-allocation and the CV in the post-allocation of fiscal transfer, respectively. The figure shows that the CV curves are shifted downward by fiscal transfer. Fiscal transfer improves the CV by about 0.02 points; the reducing effects on regional disparities are sustained between the 1990s and the 2010s. Hence, fiscal transfer drives the economic catching up of local areas to large metropolitan areas and results in reduced regional disparities in GVA per capita.

[16]The Local Allocation Tax Act determines the total amount of tax allocation from the national to local governments. The act establishes the framework of tax allocation that gives a specific ratio of national taxes to local governments from the general account. The size of the fiscal transfer received by the local government as a whole was 25 trillion yen in 2016, accounting for 30% of the total revenue of the local government.

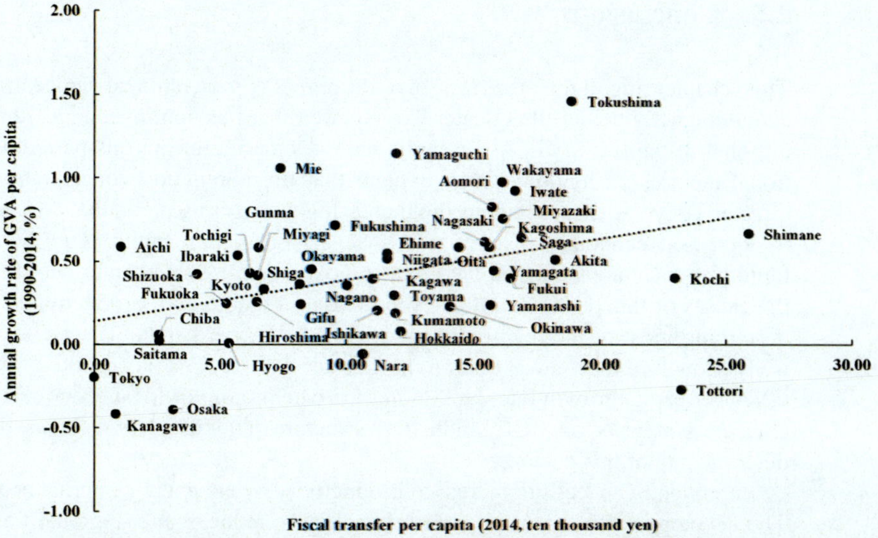

Fig. 2.11 Relationship between the fiscal transfer per capita and the annual growth rate of GVA per capita. Source: Calculations based on the *Annual Report on Prefectural Accounts* (Cabinet Office), *Basic Resident Registers* (Ministry of Internal Affairs and Communications), and the *Nikkei Economic Electronic Databank System*

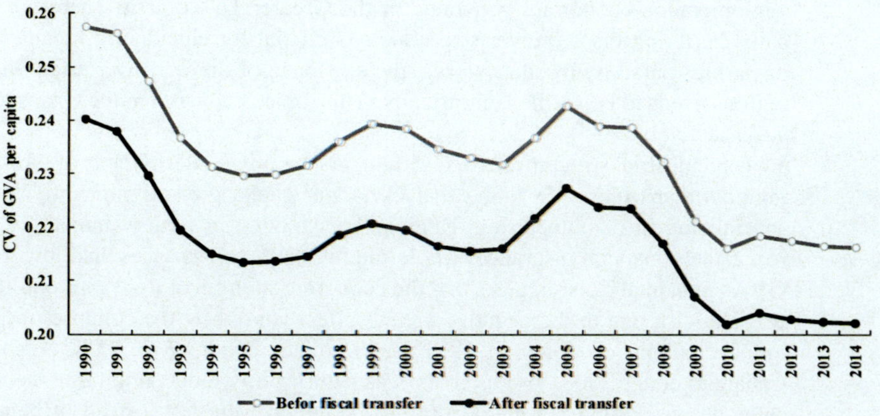

Fig. 2.12 The trends of CV before and after fiscal transfer. Source: Calculations based on the *Annual Report on Prefectural Accounts* (Cabinet Office), *Basic Resident Registers* (Ministry of Internal Affairs and Communications), and the *Nikkei Economic Electronic Databank System*

2.5 Conclusions

This chapter highlights the fact that despite the geographical concentration of economic activities in the Greater Tokyo Area that has continued since the 1990s, regional disparities in GVA per capita have decreased during this period. Conventional theories on agglomeration explain that the population concentration in the Greater Tokyo Area strengthens the increasing returns to scale in that area and leads to increased economic disparities. However, GVA per capita is growing more rapidly in local areas than in the Greater Tokyo Area. This chapter has shown that the causes of this phenomenon are productivity related, with productivity volatility describing most of the regional disparities in GVA per capita. The higher productivity growth in local areas than in the Greater Tokyo Area has resulted in a higher GVA per capita growth rate, facilitating the catching up of local economies. In this chapter, we focus on SOC, industrial structure, and fiscal transfer as the main determinants of this catch-up.

Improved SOC leads to increased productivity by enhancing external economies. The development of transportation infrastructure reduces inter-regional travel time distances and expands the scope of knowledge spillovers, which is a benefit of agglomeration economies. As mentioned, Japan's high-speed transportation network was constructed using the Greater Tokyo Area as a hub. As a result, the development of a high-speed transportation network has shortened travel time to the Greater Tokyo Area. These networks may allow local areas to borrow the benefits of agglomeration economies generated in the Greater Tokyo area. Therefore, empirically clarifying the borrower size effects is crucial for elucidating Japan's regional disparities paradox. In other words, the existence of the borrower effect in Japan's regions needs to be verified empirically. This topic is covered in the Chaps. 5, 6, and 7, respectively.

The industrial structure and fiscal transfers are other determinants of the shrinking regional disparities. We found that GVA per capita grew significantly in regions specializing in manufacturing. Regions specializing in tertiary industries, such as real estate, financial insurance, wholesale retailing, and services, had low growth in GVA per capita. This suggests that the economic strength of large metropolitan areas was sluggish due to the negative wealth effect caused by the collapse of the asset-inflated bubble economy in 1991 and Lehman Brothers in 2008. According to Caballero et al. (2008), productivity was significantly reduced in large metropolitan areas because zombie firms needing to be culled were left instead of being eliminated. Even in the 2000s, productivity in large metropolitan areas did not return to the level of the 1990s. However, in local areas, after experiencing the industry's hollowing out in the 1990s, manufacturing plants returned to Japan in the 2000s with stable economic levels. Productivity growth in regions specializing in manufacturing exceeded that of large metropolitan areas.

Fujita and Tabuchi (1997) point out that the shift in Japan's industrial structure from the heavy and chemical industry to the high-tech and the services industry was responsible for the excess concentration of economic agents in the Greater Tokyo

Area. Indeed, the trend toward a service economy has strengthened economies of scale in the Greater Tokyo Area but has not led to an increase in regional disparities in GVA per capita. Instead, the enhanced productivity of the manufacturing industry is likely to have contributed to a reduction in regional disparities in GVA per capita. Fiscal transfer from the central government is a crucial source of funding for building such an industrial base, strengthening the fiscal capacity of local governments, and enabling them to invest in infrastructure effectively. However, it has also been reported to exacerbate the cost efficiency of local governments in Japan (Ogawa and Tanahashi 2008; Otsuka et al. 2014; Hayashi 2017). Therefore, the impact of fiscal transfers on regional economic performance should also be analyzed from a multifaceted perspective in further research.

As mentioned in the introduction, the efficiency of economic activity and equitability have a trade-off relationship. Neoclassical economists have argued that regional policies that promote the development of underdeveloped areas distort the efficient allocation of resources and hinder national economic development (Higgins 1992). On the other hand, if the government allocates investment to highly productive regions, the national economy will grow faster, but regional income inequality will increase. Development in more developed regions is a source of further growth, and measures for reducing regional inequality are not offered when the domestic economy is performing well (Hewings 1978). However, Japan's experience teaches us that the implementation of appropriate regional policies can reconcile economic growth and equitability, specifically through the distribution of SOC investment, industrial structure, and fiscal transfers to local governments. Economic growth and equitability are made compatible by redistributing the benefits of economic growth gained by the excess concentration of economic agents in the Greater Tokyo Area to local areas. In Chaps. 3 and 4, we consider the role of productivity and SOC that led to the economic catch-up of local areas in depth.

Appendix 1: Measurement of the Mono-/Polycentricity of Japan's National Land Structure

In Appendix 1, following many previous studies (Meijers 2008, Meijers and Burger 2010, Wang et al. 2020), we measure the monocentricity/polycentricity of Japan's national land structure based on the population rank-size distribution of prefectures as follows:

$$\ln(Rank - 1/2) = a - b \cdot \ln(SIZE) + \varepsilon,$$

where *Rank* is the rank of prefectures according to their population. To mitigate potential sample size bias in the Pareto exponent, 1/2 is subtracted from *Rank* (Gabaix and Ibragimov 2011). *SIZE* represents the population level in the prefecture. Coefficient b is the Pareto exponent, which represents the magnitude of

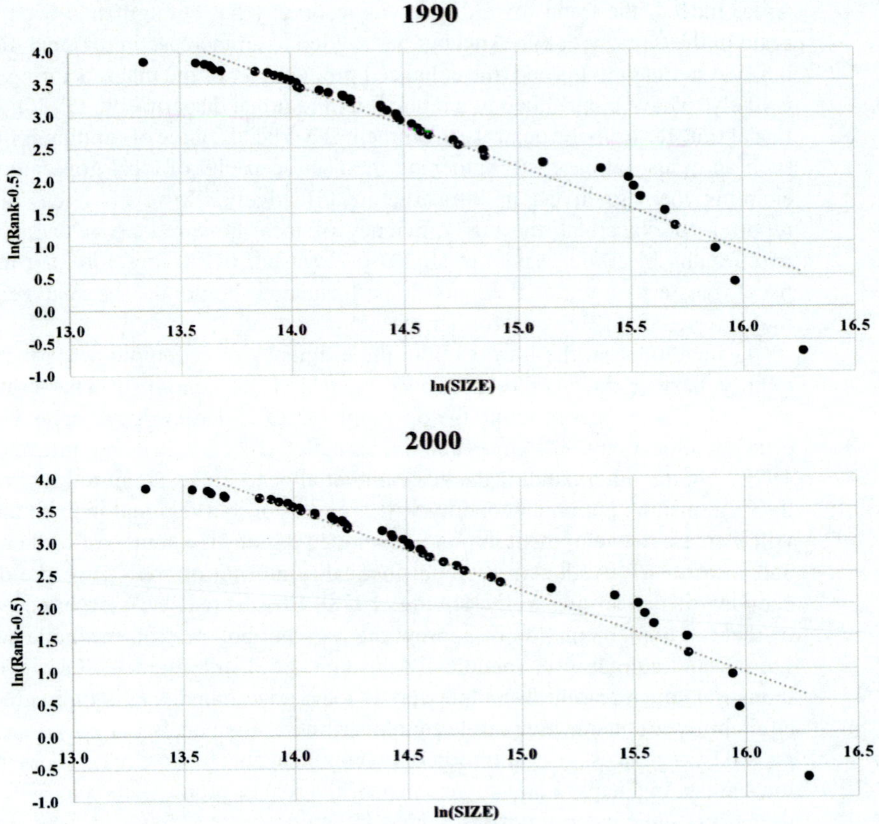

Fig. 2.13 Relationship between prefectural population size and its rank. Source: Calculations based on *Basic Resident Registers* (Ministry of Internal Affairs and Communications)

polycentricity. The higher the absolute value of the Pareto exponent (b), the more polycentric the national land structure. a and $\boldsymbol{\varepsilon}$ are the constant and error terms, respectively.

Figure 2.13 shows the relationship between the prefecture's population size and its ranking from 1990 to 2014. From the figure, we can observe a negative correlation. Also, the slope of the regression line becomes gentle a bit over time.

Table 2.8, which is the estimated results on the Pareto exponent (b), shows that the absolute value of b decreases over time since 1990. The results indicate that Japan's national land structure has been becoming monocentric modestly.

Appendix 2: Conventional Theories on Regional Economic Disparities

This appendix briefly reviews two theories on regional disparities in GVA per capita. The first perspective is that of the neoclassical theory, which explains that market mechanisms reduce regional disparities. This theory highlights the roles of labor input, capital input, and technological progress within the process of economic growth. Constant returns to scale are assumed, and free inter-regional movements of the production factors work to decrease regional disparities. The second perspective is that of the theory of cumulative causation. This theory highlights the role of the export industry as a source of economic growth. Increasing returns to scale are assumed, and the positive feedback mechanisms of economic growth enable cumulative economic development, resulting in widened regional disparities.

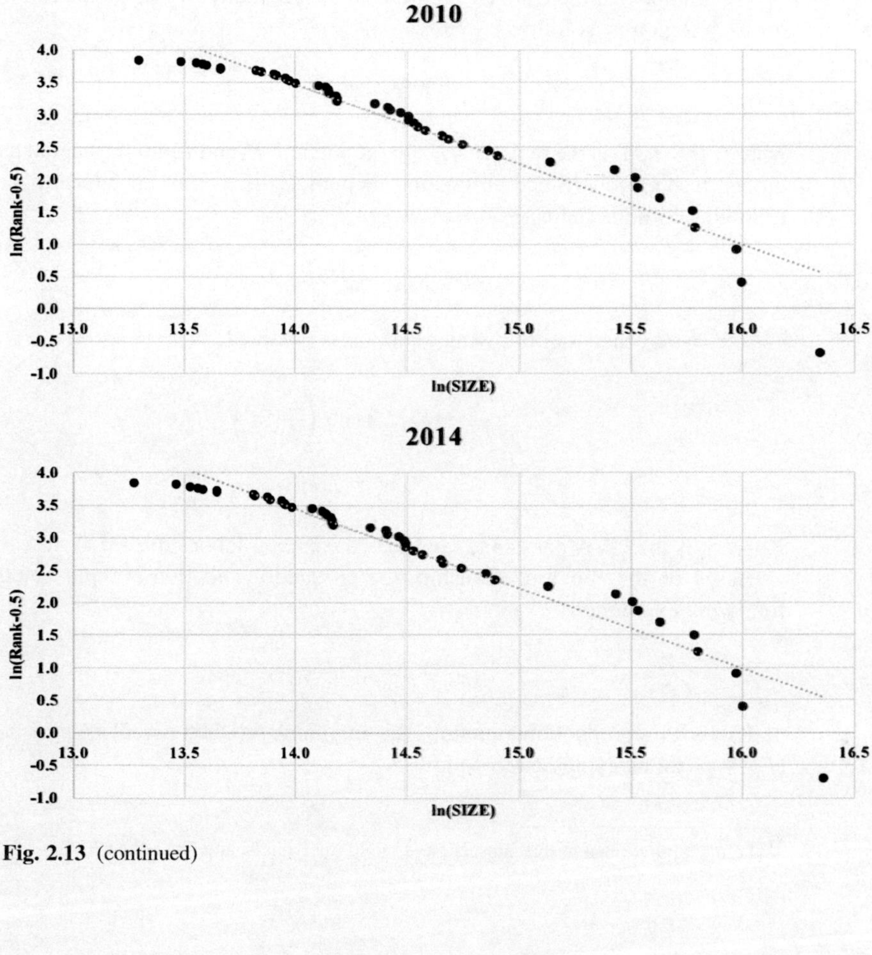

Fig. 2.13 (continued)

Table 2.8 Estimation results on the Pareto exponent

	1990		2000		2010		2014	
a	21.752	**	21.380	**	20.795	**	20.600	**
	(0.792)		(0.804)		(0.761)		(0.748)	
b	1.304	**	1.277	**	1.238	**	1.226	**
	(0.055)		(0.055)		(0.052)		(0.052)	
Adjusted R-squared	0.925		0.920		0.924		0.924	

Notes: (1) ** and * indicate significance at the 1% and 5% levels, respectively
(2) The values in parentheses indicate standard errors

Neoclassical Theory

The first perspective on regional disparities, the neoclassical theory, assumes a production structure of constant returns to scale. A competitive equilibrium ensures that the value of marginal products is equal to the factor price. Each production factor moves freely between regions according to the factor price.

We assume that there are two regions in the economy.[17] The production function for each region is as follows:

$$Y_i = f(K_i, L_i),$$

where i ($i = a, b$) is the region, Y_i is the output, and K_i and L_i are the capital and labor inputs, respectively. Since production technology is a constant return to scale, the following formula holds:

$$\lambda f(K_i, L_i) = f(\lambda K_i, \lambda L_i).$$

If $\lambda = 1/L_i$, then the following equation is obtained:

$$\frac{1}{L_i} \cdot f(K_i, L_i) = f\left(\frac{K_i}{L_i}, 1\right),$$

$$\therefore\ y_i = f(k_{i.})$$

where y_i is the GVA per capita, and k_i is the capital-labor ratio.

Based on the above relationship, the production function is represented by the following expression:

$$Y_i = L_i \cdot f(k_i).$$

Under this production function, the marginal productivity of capital and labor (F_K, F_L) can be expressed as follows:

[17]The model described in this subsection is based on Yamada and Tokuoka (2007).

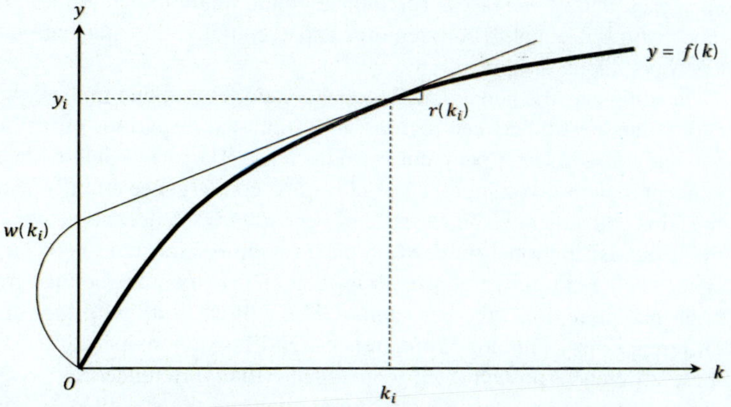

Fig. 2.14 Neoclassical growth model

$$F_K = \frac{\partial Y_i}{\partial K_i} = \frac{\partial Y_i}{\partial k_i} \cdot \frac{\partial k_i}{\partial K_i} = f'(k_i),$$

$$F_L = \frac{\partial Y_i}{\partial L_i} = f(k_i) + L_i \cdot \frac{\partial f}{\partial k_i} \cdot \frac{\partial k_i}{\partial L_i} = f(k_i) - k_i \cdot f'(k_i).$$

Based on an assumption of perfect competition, the following relationship holds:

$$F_K = r(k), \; F_L = w(k),$$

where r is the return on capital, and w is the wage rate.

Recall that the tangential equation at point k_i on function $f(x)$ can be expressed by the following equation:

$$y - f(k_i) = f'(k_i)(x - k_i).$$

After reformulating this equation, we obtain the following equation:

$$y = f'(k_i) \cdot x + [f(k_i) - k_i \cdot f'(k_i)].$$

The marginal productivity of capital input is the slope of the tangent; thus, $F_K = f'(k_i)$. The marginal productivity of labor input is an intercept of the tangent at the vertical axis; thus, $F_L = f(k_i) - k_i \cdot f'(k_i)$. Figure 2.14 illustrates this situation.

If there is a difference in the capital-labor ratio k_i between the two regions, then there is also a regional difference in GVA per capita y_i. For example, if $k_b < k_a$ and $y_b < y_a$, then the condition of the competitive equilibrium ensures $w_b < w_a$ and $r_a < r_b$. In this case, because there is a regional difference in the factor price, each production factor will move between regions according to the factor price. That is, if workers move from Region b to Region a, then capital moves from Region a to Region b. This results in a decrease in k_a and an increase in k_b. Therefore, y_a

decreases, and y_b increases. The inter-regional migration continues until the capital-labor ratio k_i is equal in both regions, and eventually, the inter-regional disparities in GVA per capita disappear.

In summary, the neoclassical model concludes that due to the equalization in the capital-labor ratio between regions, inter-regional disparities in factor prices diminish, and those in GVA per capita also decrease (Barro and Sala-i-Martin 2004). This concept includes two approaches: (1) sigma convergence and (2) beta convergence. In sigma convergence, the variance of per capita GVA decreases over time. Based on the neoclassical model framework, each region is expected to converge to a steady-state level. Beta convergence posits that if low-income regions grow faster than high-income regions, the per capita GVA will catch up with high-income regions. Differences in technology, preferences, and institutions persist across regions, but these differences are expected to be smaller than differences across countries. If the regional economic structures are not similar and the steady-state level is different, they are not expected to converge to the same level. This is denoted as "conditional convergence."

Cumulative Causation Theory

The second perspective on regional disparities is the theory of cumulative causation. This theory shows the potential for increasing regional disparities. The basic scheme of this theory is shown in Fig. 2.15.

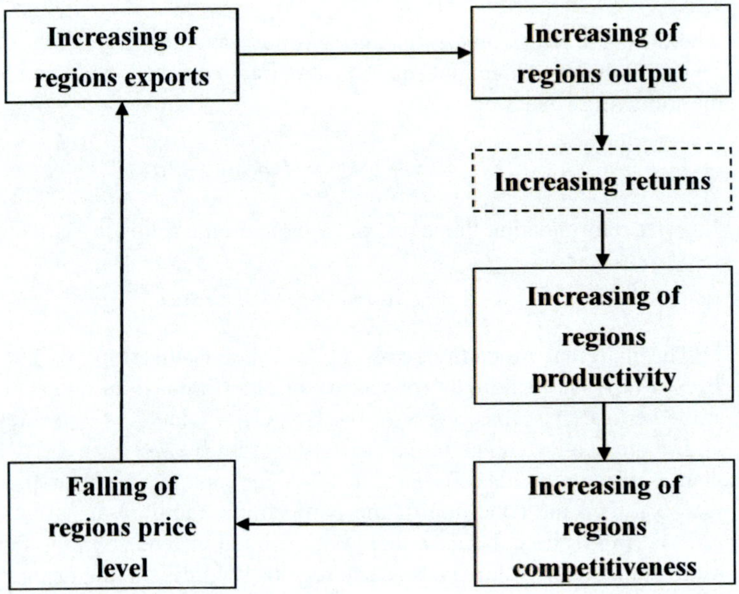

Fig. 2.15 Mechanism of cumulative growth

First, the production of the export industry expands given the increase in nationwide demand. This expansion in production leads to increased productivity in the industry by inducing capital investment and research and development (R&D) spending. If this increase in productivity exceeds the increase in production costs, the competitiveness of the industry increases, thereby resulting in further expansion in regional exports.

A model for this theory is provided by Dixon and Thirlwall (1975a, b) and is based on the idea of cumulative growth developed by Kaldor (1975).[18]

As a starting point for the model, we assume that the productivity growth rate, q, is determined by the one-period lag in output growth rate, y_{-1}:

$$q = a + \lambda y_{-1}, (\lambda > 0), \tag{2.7}$$

where a is the autonomous productivity growth, and λ is a constant known as the "Verdoorn coefficient." This relationship expresses Verdoorn's law (Verdoorn 1949) whereby the higher the output growth rate, the higher the productivity increase.

The second component of the model argues that the rate of change in local export prices (p) is defined as the rate of change in labor costs (w) minus the rate of growth in productivity (q):

$$p = w - q. \tag{2.8}$$

Here, it is assumed that any increase in production costs leads to an increase in cost inflation and that any increase in productivity reduces cost inflation. The increase in production costs is also assumed to be determined by nationwide factors and is treated as an exogenous variable.

The third component argues that the growth rate of exports, x, depends on the rate of change in the price of export goods (p), the rate of change in the price of export goods in other regions (p_f), and the rate of change in income in other regions (z). Thus, the export function of a region is defined by the following expression:

$$x = b_0 p + b_1 p_f + b_2 z, \tag{2.9}$$

where b_0 and b_1 are price elasticities of demand, and b_2 is the income elasticity of world demand.

[18] The model described in this subsection is based on Armstrong and Taylor (2000).

The final component argues that the local output growth rate y depends on the export growth rate x:

$$y = \gamma x, \tag{2.10}$$

where γ is the responsiveness of output growth to the growth in exports.

Substituting Eqs. (2.7), (2.8), and (2.9) for Eq. (2.10) yields the following equation:

$$y = \gamma\left[-b_0(w-a) + b_1 p_f + b_2 z\right] + \gamma b_0 \lambda y_{-1}$$

or, more simply,

$$y = \alpha_0 + \alpha_1 y_{-1},$$

where $\alpha_0 = \gamma[-b_0(w-a) + b_1 p_f + b_2 z]$, and $\alpha_1 = \gamma b_0 \lambda$. The growth becomes stable when $\alpha_1 < 1$ and unstable when $\alpha_1 > 1$.

The model is characterized by the inclusion of a positive feedback mechanism expressed as Verdoorn's law. Thus, if the Verdoorn coefficient λ is positive, then cumulative causality is established. In other words, the growth of regional economies is a cumulative process because the expansion of production leads to increases in productivity. However, in this model, Verdoorn's law treats the path by which productivity growth depends on production growth as a black box. Therefore, the model does not explain any determinants of regional economic growth. The export industry is the only source of regional economic growth, and the potential for productivity improvement in any local industries is ignored.

As mentioned in the main text, it should be noted that this cumulative causation is not realized in the world of constant or decreasing returns assumed in the neoclassical theory because in the economy assumed by the neoclassical theory, the marginal product decreases as the input of production factors increases. In other words, the cumulative growth of regional economies can only be explained in the world of increasing returns.

Appendix 3: Active Job Openings to Applicants Ratio by Prefecture

The Abe administration (2012–2020) in Japan has identified the lack of jobs in local areas as a cause of the monocentric concentration of the population in Tokyo and has implemented regional policies to encourage job creation in local areas. The Abe administration's regional policies have been effective in creating jobs in the local areas for 2012–2019, and the number of jobs in many local areas increased significantly (Fig. 2.16). However, the number of job openings in Tokyo also increased significantly, and as a result, this did not lead to a decrease in migration from local

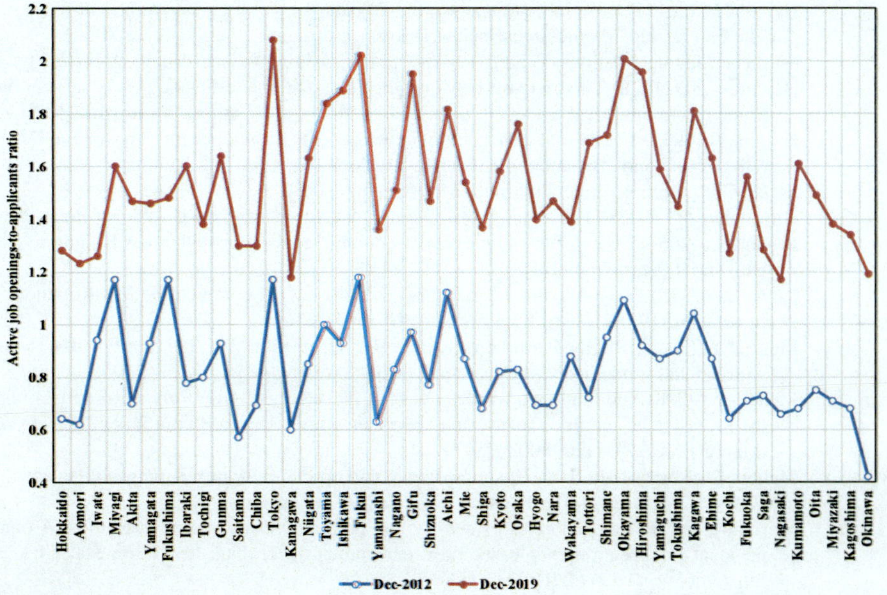

Fig. 2.16 Active job openings to applicants ratio by prefecture under the Abe administration. Source: Calculations based on *Employment Referrals for General Workers* (Ministry of Health, Labour and Welfare)

areas to Tokyo. After 2020, we have to note whether the impact of COVID-19 will change the pattern of population migration between Tokyo and the local areas.

References

Alonso W (1973) Urban zero population growth. Daedalus 102(4):191–206

Armstrong H, Taylor J (2000) Regional economies and policy, 3rd edn. Blackwell, Cornwall

Barro R, Sala-i-Martin X (2004) Economic growth, 2nd edn. MIT Press, Cambridge, Massachusetts

Caballero RJ, Hoshi T, Kashyap AK (2008) Zombie lending and depressed restructuring in Japan. Am Econ Rev 98(5):1943–1977. https://doi.org/10.1257/aer.98.5.1943

Capello R (2016) Regional economics (2nd edn.). Routledge, Abingdon

Chipman JS (1970) External economies of scale and competitive equilibrium. Q J Econ 84 (3):347–385. https://doi.org/10.2307/1879425

Dixon RJ, Thirlwall AP (1975a) Regional growth and unemployment in the United Kingdom. Macmillan, London

Dixon RJ, Thirlwall AP (1975b) A model of regional growth rate differences on Kaldorian lines. Oxford Econ Pap 27(2):201–214

Fujita M, Tabuchi T (1997) Regional growth in postwar Japan. Reg Sci Urban Econ 27(6):643–670. https://doi.org/10.1016/S0166-0462(96)02167-9

Gabaix X, Ibragimov R (2011) Rank− 1/2: A simple way to improve the OLS estimation of tail exponents. J Bus Econ Stat 29(1):24–39. https://doi.org/10.1198/jbes.2009.06157

Hayashi M (2017) Using DEA to analyze the efficiency of welfare offices and influencing factors: The case of Japan's municipal public assistance programs. In: Tone K (ed) Advances in DEA theory and applications: With extensions to forecasting models. Wiley, Hoboken, pp 300–314

Hewings GJD (1978) The trade-off between aggregate national efficiency and interregional equity: Some recent empirical evidence. Econ Geogr 54:254–263. https://doi.org/10.2307/142839

Higgins B (1992) Equity and efficiency in development: Basic concepts. In: Savoie DJ, Brecher I (eds) Equity and efficiency in economic development: Essays in Honour of Benjamin Higgins. McGill-Queen's University Press, Montreal, pp 21–50

Hirschman AO (1958) The strategy of economic development. Yale University Press, New Haven

Kaldor N (1966) Causes of the slow rate of economic growth in the United Kingdom. Cambridge University Press, Cambridge

Kaldor N (1975) Economic growth and the Verdoorn law: A comment on Mr. Rowthorn's article. Econ J 85(340):891–896. https://doi.org/10.2307/2230633

Magrini S (2004) Regional (di)convergence. In: Henderson JV, Thisse JF (eds) Handbook of regional and urban economics, vol 4. Elsevier, Amsterdam, pp 2741–2796

Meijers E (2008) Summing small cities does not make a large city: Polycentric urban regions and the provision of cultural, leisure and sports amenities. Urban Stud 45(11):2323–2342. https://doi.org/10.1177/0042098008095870

Meijers EJ, Burger MJ (2010) Spatial structure and productivity in US metropolitan areas. Environ Plan A 42(6):1383–1402. https://doi.org/10.1068/a42151

Morikawa M (2011) Economies of density and productivity in service industries: An analysis of personal service industries based on establishment-level data. Rev Econ Stat 93(1):179–192. https://doi.org/10.1162/REST_a_00065

Ogawa H, Tanahashi K (2008) Effect on new public management: data envelopment analysis. Gov Audit Rev 15:47–62

Otsuka A (2017) A new perspective on agglomeration economies in Japan. Springer, Singapore

Otsuka A, Goto M (2015a) Regional policy and the productive efficiency of Japanese industries. Reg Stud 49(4):518–531

Otsuka A, Goto M (2015b) Agglomeration economies in Japanese industries: the Solow residual approach. Ann Regional Sci 54(2):401–416

Otsuka A, Goto M, Sueyoshi T (2010) Industrial agglomeration effects in Japan: Productive efficiency, market access, and public fiscal transfer. Pap Reg Sci 89(4):819–839. https://doi.org/10.1111/j.1435-5957.2010.00286.x

Otsuka A, Goto M, Sueyoshi T (2014) Cost-efficiency of Japanese local governments: Effects of decentralization and regional integration. Reg Stud Reg Sci 1(1):207–220

Richardson HW (1979) Aggregate efficiency and interregional equity. In: Folmer H, Oosterhaven J (eds) Spatial inequalities and regional development. Martnus Nijhoff, The Hague, pp 161–183

Verdoorn PJ (1949) Fattori the regolano lo sviluppo della produttività del lavoro, L'Industria, 1:3–10. English Translation by A.P. Thirlwall, 'Factors governing the growth of labour productivity', in D. Ironmonger, J.O.N. Perkins, T. van Hoa (eds), National Income and Economic Progress, London: Macmillan Press, 1988, pp. 199–207. Reprinted in L.L. Pasinetti (1993), Italian Economic Papers, vol. II, Bologna: Il Mulino, New York and Oxford: Oxford University Press, pp. 59–68

Wang Y, Sun B, Zhang T (2020) Do polycentric urban regions promote functional spillovers and economic performance? Evidence from China Reg Stud Doi. https://doi.org/10.1080/00343404.2020.1841147

Yamada H, Tokuoka K (eds) (2007) Introduction to regional and urban economics, 2nd edn. Tokyo, Yuhikaku Publishing Company Limited. (in Japanese)

Chapter 3
Regional Productivity and Convergence

Abstract This chapter measures the total factor productivity (TFP) in Japan's regions and clarifies whether a convergence of TFP disparities has been observed since 1980. Japan's regional economies face global competition amid the challenges of a declining and aging population. Given these economic conditions, the Japanese government has sought to boost TFP to enhance sustainability in regional economies. This chapter measures TFP using Japanese regional data. Most of Japan's studies measure TFP at the national level; few studies attempt TFP analysis in a regional context. Therefore, this chapter contributes to TFP research in the context of regional economies. Furthermore, this chapter introduces a stochastic convergence model to verify the regional convergence. In Japan's study, cross-sectional studies show regional convergence, while some time-series studies do not show convergence. Therefore, another objective of this chapter is to provide additional evidence to supplement the discussions of previous studies. The results of this chapter reveal that Japan's TFP has not only continually increased over the study period but has also reduced regional disparities. Furthermore, the results show that TFP converged to each region's steady-state level rather than the national level. These results suggest the significance of regional production environments and provide policy implications for regional economies.

Keywords Convergence · Regional disparity · Stochastic convergence model · Total factor productivity (TFP)

3.1 Introduction

The source of competitiveness in Japan's regional economies has shifted in recent years from comparative advantages to competitive advantages (Porter 1998; Ishikura et al. 2003). From the postwar high-growth period to the mid-1980s, the advantages

This chapter is based on Otsuka and Goto (2016).

A. Otsuka, *A New Driver of Regional Sustainability in Japan*, New Frontiers in Regional Science: Asian Perspectives 54,
https://doi.org/10.1007/978-981-16-3709-4_3

of production costs, such as low labor and location costs, were significant factors that affected the competitiveness of regional economies. Industrial agglomeration could offer low-input prices, provided each region with a comparative advantage, and helped foster regional economic growth. However, globalization since the mid-1990s has exposed Japan's manufacturing firms to fierce global competition, and many manufacturing production bases moved to Southeast Asia and China. This relocation of manufacturing plants increased the hollowing out of regional industries. Moreover, from this period, Japan's regions have begun to face a declining and aging population. Under growing unfavorable conditions, scholars highlighted improved productivity as a necessary condition for achieving regional sustainability. For example, Porter (1990) and Krugman (1991) note the significance of innovation for sustainable growth because innovation fosters a region's ability to provide goods and services that can withstand global competition, highlighting the fact that innovation is a more critical element than comparative advantage. Notably, Porter (1990) argues that the success of innovation largely depends on the regional production environment promoting interfirm competition and cooperation. It also leads to regional sustainability in the context of the industrial cluster.

In considering regional productivity, we must focus on the dynamism of total factor productivity. However, macroscopic studies on regional productivity have focused on trends in labor productivity because it is simple to calculate and helps capture production performance under specific conditions (Barro and Sala-i-Martin 1995). Labor productivity is measured as output per unit of labor and is commonly known as "factor productivity." If the composition of inputs is approximately the same among different economic agents, labor productivity can be used as a measure to compare the overall productivity of these agents. Alternatively, if the technology used in different economic agents or at varying periods is assumed to be the same, this indicator is a valid measure of productivity. Practically, however, industrial structures and input compositions differ across regions and periods. For example, regions with capital-intensive industries that adopt technologies that require substantial capital expenditure tend to obtain higher levels of labor productivity. In such cases, even if labor productivity is higher than average, it is difficult to discern whether it is a result of efficient labor or merely a high capital-labor ratio. Therefore, measuring productivity using various input factors, labor, and capital is essential for examining overall regional productivity or regional competitiveness. This explains why TFP is preferable to the factor productivity used in many previous studies.

This chapter focuses on TFP and has two primary objectives. First, we measure TFP using Japanese regional data. Most of Japan's studies measure TFP on a national level; relatively few studies attempt TFP analysis in the regional context (Nemoto and Goto 2005; Goto et al. 2018; Tokui 2018). Therefore, this chapter contributes to TFP research in the context of regional economies. Second, this chapter clarifies whether TFP growth in Japan converged and, if it did, whether the convergence proceeded at the national or regional level. Barro and Sala-i-Martin (1995) consider the regional disparity in labor productivity in Japan through a cross-sectional analysis. Kawagoe's (1999) and Togo's (2002) studies based on time-series analyses are critical to this discussion. Togo's (2002) study on regional disparities in labor productivity from the 1980s to the 1990s does not show convergence. Therefore, the second objective of this chapter is to provide additional evidence to supplement the discussions of previous studies.

The remainder of this chapter is organized as follows. Section 3.2 measures TFP using regional-level data from Japan. We analyzed regional productivity variation to clarify whether TFP growth converges among regions. Section 3.3 introduces a stochastic convergence model and verifies the regional convergence of TFP. Finally, Sect. 3.4 concludes the chapter.

3.2 Total Factor Productivity

3.2.1 Methods of Measurement

To measure TFP, this study adopts the method used by Good et al. (1997) and Aw et al. (2001). The method is characterized by nonparametric estimates of TFP that use the disparity in production activities between economic agents. The method assumes a representative agent with average output and input at a certain point in time, and the TFP for each economic agent is calculated by referring to its disparity from the representative agent. Because the TFP of the representative agent fluctuates over time, this method facilitates a time-series comparison of TFP.

The relative TFP level of region j ($j = 1, \cdots, N$) for time t ($t = 1, \cdots, P$) or $lnTFP_{jt}$ is expressed as follows:

$$\begin{aligned} ln\, TFP_{jt} = &\left(ln\, Y_{jt} - \overline{ln\, Y_t}\right) + \sum\nolimits_{s=1}^{t}\left(\overline{ln\, Y_s} - \overline{ln\, Y_{s-1}}\right) \\ &- \left[\sum\nolimits_{i=1}^{n}\frac{1}{2}\left(S_{ijt} + \overline{S_{it}}\right)\left(ln\, X_{ijt} - \overline{ln\, X_{it}}\right)\right. \\ &\left. + \sum\nolimits_{s=1}^{t}\sum\nolimits_{i=1}^{n}\frac{1}{2}\left(\overline{S_{is}} + \overline{S_{is-1}}\right)\left(\overline{ln\, X_{is}} - \overline{ln\, X_{is-1}}\right)\right], \end{aligned} \tag{3.1}$$

where Y_{jt} represents the output of region j at time t, X_{ijt} is the input factor i ($i = 1, \cdots, n$) for region j at time t, and S_{ijt} is the cost share of input factor i in region j at time t. The overline above each symbol expresses the inter-regional average value of each variable. Eq. (3.1) shows that in addition to the comparable TFP level at a given point in time and a given region, it is possible to measure the regional TFP level by considering the TFP level change in a time series.

The first line of Eq. (3.1) consists of two parts that measure regional output. The first part expresses the regional output in time t as a deviation from the mean output in that year, thus reflecting information on the cross-sectional distribution of output. The second part sums the changes in the mean output across all years, which effectively captures the shift in the output distribution over time by chain-linking the movement in the output reference point. The next line in Eq. (3.1) performs the same operation for each input X_i. The inputs are summed using a combination of the input cost share for region S_{ijt} and the average revenue share $\overline{S_{is}}$ in each year as weights. The index provides a measure of the proportional difference in TFP for region j in year t relative to the hypothetical region in the base period. We used 1980 as the base period.

The following equation defines the national-level TFP in time t as the weighted average of each region's TFP:

$$ln\,TFP_t = \sum\nolimits_{j=1}^{47} \boldsymbol{\theta}_{jt}\, ln\,TFP_{jt}, \tag{3.2}$$

where $lnTFP_{jt}$ is the TFP level of region j at time t, and weight $\boldsymbol{\theta}_{jt}$ is the j's share of the output of region j at the national level.

3.2.2 Data

We measure Eqs. (3.1) and (3.2) using Japanese prefecture-level data covering 30 years from 1980 to 2010. Since there are many regional statistics, we need to compile the dataset from various sources. The dataset is compiled mainly from the *Annual Report on Prefectural Accounts*, prepared by the Cabinet Office.

To measure the TFP index, the output for each prefecture is measured as the gross regional product adjusted by the value-added deflator reported in the *System of National Accounts* (SNA). The inputs include capital and labor used for production.

Capital input is the private capital stock multiplied by the capital utilization ratio. The private capital stock is drawn from the private capital stock series estimated by the Central Research Institute of Electric Power Industry. The private capital stock series is calculated from gross investment by applying the benchmark year method.[1] The capital utilization ratio is the reciprocal of the capital coefficient, which we calculate using the national-level values of the prefectures' gross product and capital stock. The temporal variability in the logarithmic value of the capital coefficient reciprocal shows a constant gradient over the long term because of the use of capital-intensive technology. We calculated the deviation in this temporal variability and used it as the capital utilization ratio.[2,3]

[1]The same approach (benchmark year method) has been adopted to estimate capital stock by the Cabinet Office (see *Private Sector Capital Stock Statistics*).

[2]We expect that variations in the logarithm of the inverse of the capital coefficient $ln(Y/K)$ have a constant slope over time under a production system employing capital-using technology in the long term. However, the value fluctuates every year in an observed dataset. Hence, we assume that the fluctuations in $ln(Y/K)$ can be attributed to a change in capital utilization, as well as a time trend. Based on that assumption, a proxy of the capital utilization rate can be measured with a residual error term ($\boldsymbol{\varepsilon}$) in the regression $ln(Y/K) = \boldsymbol{\alpha} + \boldsymbol{\beta}T + \boldsymbol{\varepsilon}$, where T is a time trend, and $\boldsymbol{\beta}$ is a time-invariant slope of $ln(Y/K)$.

[3]From the estimation procedure of the capital utilization ratio, we can remove the effect of variation in capital stock caused by the national economic cycle to a certain extent. However, the removal of variation will not extend to economic activities at the regional level.

We obtain labor input by multiplying the hours worked by the number of employees. Data for employees in each region were obtained from the *Annual Report on Prefectural Accounts* (Cabinet Office). The hours worked are estimated using the following procedure based on data from the *Monthly Labor Survey* (Ministry of Health, Labor, and Welfare). First, we extract the survey's index of hours as national-level data. Second, we calculate the rate of deviation from the national level of the actual hours worked for each prefecture. Third, the deviation rate is multiplied by the obtained national-level value to construct an index of the hours worked for each prefecture.

In the calculation of the cost share of each input factor, the total cost is defined as the total value of capital and labor costs. The cost shares (s_K, s_L) of capital and labor inputs are subsequently established by dividing the total cost by the cost of each input factor.

Capital cost is the variable obtained by multiplying the private capital stock by the capital service price. The capital service price is calculated using the following equation:

$$\text{Capital service price} = \frac{p_K(r + d)}{(1 - \tau)},$$

where p_K is the capital goods price, which is a deflator for private fixed capital investment derived from the *Annual Report on Prefectural Accounts* (Cabinet Office); r represents the average contract interest rate on loans and discounts published by the Bank of Japan; d represents the depreciation rate, calculated by dividing the depreciation cost by capital stock; and τ is the corporate tax rate (withholding portion). For labor cost, we adopt employee compensation from the *Annual Report on Prefectural Accounts* (Cabinet Office).

3.2.3 Measurement Results

Table 3.1 shows the trend in Japan's TFP level calculated using Eq. (3.2). Although variations are observed in national-level TFP throughout the observation period, there is a long-term upward trend. TFP increased throughout the measurement period. Relative to the TFP in 1980, TFP increased threefold in 2010.

Here, we focus on the variation in TFP growth over time. We use the method of Foster et al. (2001), who analyze variations in TFP growth in periods by measuring them as the variation in TFP between year t and the base year ($t - \tau$) and decomposing it into three effects.[4] τ is fixed with a specific value, such as 10 or 20.

[4]In calculating TFP by using firm- or plant-level data, the entry and exit effects are considered in addition to the within, between, and covariance effects (Foster et al. 2001).

Table 3.1 Trends in Japan's TFP levels

Year	TFP (index)	Growth (1980 = 100)
1980	0.0973	100
1981	0.1002	103
1982	0.1029	106
1983	0.1035	106
1984	0.1031	106
1985	0.1447	149
1986	0.1519	156
1987	0.1748	180
1988	0.1945	200
1989	0.2090	215
1990	0.2357	242
1991	0.2422	249
1992	0.2409	247
1993	0.2405	247
1994	0.2387	245
1995	0.2479	255
1996	0.2676	275
1997	0.2618	269
1998	0.2615	269
1999	0.2824	290
2000	0.2971	305
2001	0.2989	307
2002	0.3209	330
2003	0.3255	334
2004	0.3267	336
2005	0.3362	345
2006	0.3387	348
2007	0.3445	354
2008	0.3210	330
2009	0.3134	322
2010	0.3236	332

Within effect: This is defined as the sum of the weighted average value of TFP growth achieved in each region at time t. The weight $\theta_{jt-\tau}$ is given by the output share of region j for time $t-\tau$, where $t-\tau$ is the base year for the measurement. The within effect is expressed as follows, where P is the last year of the measurement:

$$\sum_{j=1}^{47} \theta_{jt-\tau} \Delta lnTFP_{jt}. \quad (t = 1, \cdots, P).$$

Between effect: This is defined as the weighted sum of regional differences in TFP level for time $t-\tau$. The effect is measured as the deviation of the TFP from its inter-region average $\overline{ln\,TFP_{t-\tau}}$. The weight $\Delta\theta_{jt}$ is given by the change in the output share for each region and time. The between effects are expressed as follows:

Table 3.2 Decomposition results of TFP growth in Japan

		Contribution of each effect		
	Annual average TFP growth rate total (%)	Within effect (%)	Between effect (%)	Covariance effect (%)
Period	(Total) = (a) + (b) + (c)	(a)	(b)	(c)
1980s (1980–1990)	1.384	1.311	0.039	0.033
	[100.0]	[94.8]	[2.9]	[2.4]
1990s (1990–2000)	0.614	0.623	−0.022	0.013
	[100.0]	[101.5]	[−3.6]	[2.1]
2000s (2000–2010)	0.265	0.237	0.021	0.007
	[100.0]	[89.4]	[8.0]	[2.6]
All periods (1980–2010)	0.754	0.728	0.014	0.012
	[100.0]	[96.5]	[1.9]	[1.6]

Note: The values in square brackets are the contribution rates (% share)

$$\sum_{j=1}^{47} \boldsymbol{\Delta\theta}_{jt}(\ln TFP_{jt-\tau} - \overline{\ln TFP_{t-\tau}}).\ (t = 1, \cdots, P).$$

Covariance effect: This is defined as the sum of the product of TFP growth ($\boldsymbol{\Delta lnTFP_{jt}}$) and the change in output share ($\boldsymbol{\Delta\theta_{jt}}$) for each region and time. The covariance effects are expressed as follows

$$\sum_{j=1}^{47} \boldsymbol{\Delta\theta}_{jt}\boldsymbol{\Delta} lnTFP_{jt}.\ (t = 1, \cdots, P).$$

In summary, the within effect attributes the national-level TFP growth to each region's productivity growth under the assumption that the regional weight is fixed for the benchmark period. The between effects focus on the inter-temporal output expansion in each region as a driver of national-level TFP growth. The covariance effect attributes national-level TFP growth to increased productivity and the expansion of the relative output share in each region. If the between and covariance effects are large, this implies that regions with high productivity increased their output levels and, therefore, that regional disparities in productivity expanded during this period.

Table 3.2 presents the results of the decomposition analysis for the national-level annual TFP growth rates from 1980 to 2010. The annual TFP growth rate was 1.384% in the 1980s. In the 1990s, however, the growth rate slowed to 0.614% and declined further in the 2000s, during which the average annual growth rate was 0.265%. From this table, we identify the following characteristics concerning the TFP growth rate:

First, the most significant determinant describing TFP growth was the *within effect* over the whole period. In the 1980s, the effect explained approximately 94.8% of TFP growth, which strengthened in the 1990s. In particular, the TFP growth rate was fully explained by the within effect in the 1990s, whereas the *between* and *covariance effects* were weak, as was the negative effect on TFP growth observed for the *between effect*. In the 2000s, however, the *within effect* weakened (89.4%), while the *between effect* strengthened (8.0%), with a positive effect on TFP growth.

Second, the *between* and *covariance effects* increased TFP by only 0.039% and 0.033% annually on average, respectively, in the 1980s, and the effects decreased by −0.022% and 0.013%, respectively, in the 1990s. These negligible effects on TFP growth continued in the 2000s. Throughout the measurement period, the impacts of the *between* and *covariance effects* on TFP growth were 0.014% and 0.012%, respectively. Consequently, the contribution rate of the *between effect* for the entire observation period was 1.9%, and the impact of the *covariance effect* was 1.6%. These results show that there is only a slight growth impact on TFP, even when the output share expands. Thus, for regions with high productivity, there was a small impact on TFP via an increase in output share.

Observing the three effects on TFP growth is essential to verify whether TFP disparities between regions occur. If the *within effect* is relatively large, regional disparities in TFP growth have not expanded. On the other hand, when the *between* and *covariance* effects were relatively significant, regional disparities have expanded. Therefore, our results show that the TFP disparity between regions did not increase over the study period.

We now examine the TFP trends for each prefecture. Table 3.3 lists the top five regions based on TFP. In 1980, large metropolitan areas such as Tokyo, Osaka, and Kanagawa were ranked high. The position of Tokyo remained unchanged from 1980 to 2010. However, the second and subsequent positions changed significantly. The ranking of Osaka, Japan's second-largest prefecture, fell over time. Instead, regions specializing in the manufacturing industry, such as Shiga and Chiba, rose in the rankings. In particular, there was an incredibly substantial increase in these 2000s in the prefectures.

We can confirm that the difference between the first and the second places gradually narrowed in the table. In 1980, the difference between top and second was about 0.2 percentage points, whereas the difference in 2010 was only 0.15 percentage points. The difference between the maximum and minimum values also gradually decreased, from 0.608 percentage points in 1980 to 0.512 percentage points in 2010. This suggests that inter-regional disparities in TFP are shrinking.

Figure 3.1 depicts the relationship between regional TFP levels in 1980 and the growth rates from 1980 to 2010 for each prefecture. In 1980, TFP was high in large metropolitan areas such as Tokyo and Osaka. Until 2010, however, regions with high TFP shifted from large metropolitan areas to local areas. Throughout the observation period, Shiga showed the highest increase in TFP, followed by Fukui and Wakayama. In contrast, the TFP growth rates in Tokyo and Osaka did not increase significantly. TFP growth progressed remarkably in local areas relative to large metropolitan areas such as Tokyo and Osaka.

Table 3.3 Top 5 prefectures in regional TFP

	Prefecture	1980		Prefecture	1990		Prefecture	2000		Prefecture	2010
1	Tokyo	0.402	1	Tokyo	0.514	1	Tokyo	0.578	1	Tokyo	0.592
2	Osaka	0.211	2	Kanagawa	0.339	2	Shiga	0.396	2	Shiga	0.446
3	Kanagawa	0.164	3	Osaka	0.315	3	Kanagawa	0.365	3	Kanagawa	0.392
4	Kyoto	0.151	4	Nara	0.307	4	Osaka	0.331	4	Chiba	0.343
5	Okinawa	0.133	5	Shiga	0.295	5	Chiba	0.317	5	Osaka	0.323
	Max-Min	0.608		Max-Min	0.569		Max-Min	0.538		Max-Min	0.512

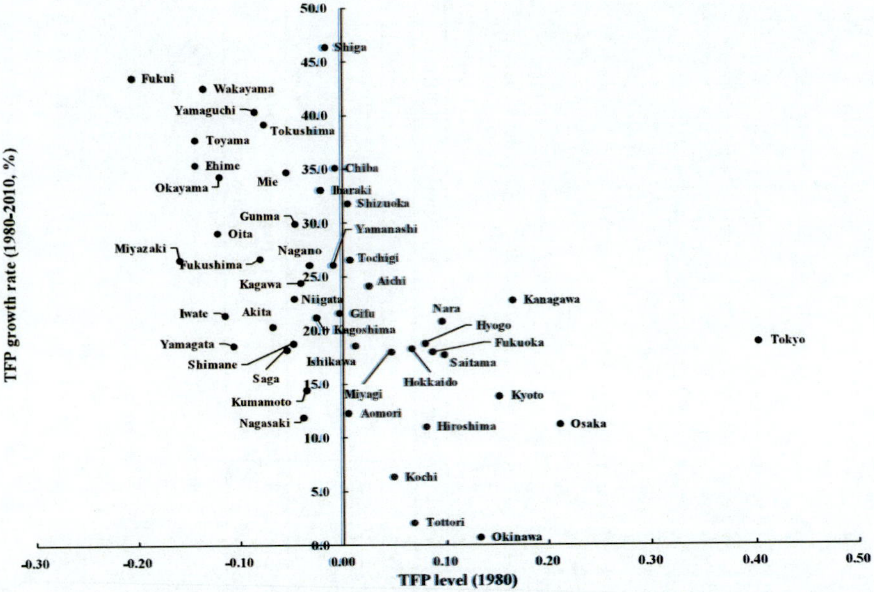

Fig. 3.1 Relationship between regional TFP levels and TFP growth rate

One cause of the drop in TFP growth in Tokyo is the shift in the industrial structure. From 1980 to 2010, the manufacturing industry in Tokyo continued to decline while the non-manufacturing industries became significantly concentrated. In the meantime, during the economic downturn of the 1990s and 2000s, the TFP growth of non-manufacturing industries fell significantly relative to that of the manufacturing industry (Otsuka et al. 2010; Otsuka and Goto 2015). Therefore, it is considered that the TFP growth rate in Tokyo that was concentrated in the non-manufacturing industries decreased.

These results partially reflect the fact that the policy measures associated with regional revitalization efforts implemented from the 1970s to the 2000s, in which public investments aimed at establishing production infrastructure in local areas were prioritized and led to higher production activities in the local manufacturing industries. Moreover, in existing cluster districts in large metropolitan areas, external diseconomies, such as sharply rising land prices, congestion costs, and environmental pollution, may have adversely affected production activities in urban non-manufacturing industries.

3.3 Statistical Test on Regional Convergence

Neoclassical theory assumes that each region's productivity converges at each region's steady-state level. The methods used to test conditional convergence are broadly classified into cross-sectional and time-series analyses. The former method was represented by Barro and Sala-i-Martin (1995). Cross-sectional analysis tests examine whether there is a negative correlation between the initial level and the rate of change in economic performance indexes, such as gross national product (GNP) per capita. Time-series analysis tests the stationarity of convergence and focuses on whether the effect of a shock on economic performance, which follows a stochastic process, is temporary or permanent. The conditions of convergence are as follows: (a) The shock is temporary, and (b) an economy showing lower economic performance in the initial stages has a growth rate higher than that of an economy showing superior economic performance in the initial stages.

Cross-sectional analysis cannot differentiate between the short-term dynamic transition process and the long-term stationary state for economic performance. This is a problem because even if convergence can be acknowledged, there is no way to investigate whether convergence is stationary in the long term. Thus, this study applies the time-series method to test the convergence of TFP among regions.

3.3.1 *Stochastic Convergence Model*

Dowrick and Nguyen (1989) and Bernard and Jones (1996) examine productivity convergence using a stochastic model. These studies adopt the stochastic convergence model to analyze national-level productivity convergence using OECD data. For example, Bernard and Jones' (1996) model considers the difference between each country's TFP and the TFP of the representative country as a stochastic variable and tests whether the stochastic variable is stationary. If the stochastic variable is stationary, then each country follows the asymptotic growth rate of the world economy. However, Bernard and Jones (1996) did not test for conditional convergence. To ascertain whether the neoclassical theory has been established in Japan's regional economy, this study extends their research by adopting a test for conditional convergence. Each region has a unique stationary level of convergence under the application of the stochastic model.

First, the TFP level of region j ($j = 1, \cdots, N$) in time t ($t = 1, \cdots, P$) is expressed as follows:

$$ln\, TFP_{jt} = \gamma_j t + \lambda ln F_{jt} + \varepsilon_{jt}, \tag{3.3}$$

where γ_j is an exogenous variable that expresses the rate of technological progress in region j, and F_{jt} is a catching-up variable of region j at time t. Thus, λ is a parameter that expresses the catching-up speed. If $\lambda > 0$, then a catching-up effect exists, and if

$\lambda = 0$, then the catching-up effect does not exist. $\boldsymbol{\varepsilon}_{jt}$ expresses the random error term of the dispersion with variance $\boldsymbol{\sigma}_{\varepsilon}^2$ and an average of 0.

This study formulates the inter-temporal path of the catching-up variable $\overline{TFP}_{jt-1}$ $(\equiv \frac{F_{jt}}{F_{jt-1}})$ as the inverse of the TFP ratio, TFP of each region j ($j = 1, \cdots, N$) to that of the representative region ($j = 0$):

$$\overline{TFP}_{jt-1} \equiv \frac{1}{\frac{TFP_{jt-1}}{TFP_{0t-1}}}. \tag{3.4}$$

Equation (3.4) can be expressed in logarithm form:

$$ln\,\overline{TFP}_{jt-1} \equiv ln\,F_{jt} - ln\,F_{jt-1} \equiv ln\,TFP_{0t-1} - ln\,TFP_{jt-1}.$$

Accordingly, the following relationship is obtained for the TFP growth of region j:

$$ln\,\frac{TFP_{jt}}{TFP_{jt-1}} = \boldsymbol{\gamma}_j + \boldsymbol{\lambda}\,ln\,\frac{TFP_{0t-1}}{TFP_{jt-1}} + \widehat{\varepsilon}_{jt}, \tag{3.5}$$

if, however, $\widehat{\boldsymbol{\varepsilon}}_{jt} = \varepsilon_{jt} - \varepsilon_{jt-1}$.

In Eq. (3.5), the TFP growth rate for each region is expressed by the rate of technological progress and the catching-up effect variable. Hence, the inter-temporal path of region j's TFP level is expressed as follows:

$$ln\,TFP_{jt} = \boldsymbol{\gamma}_j + \boldsymbol{\lambda}\,ln\,\overline{TFP}_{jt-1} + ln\,TFP_{jt-1} + \widehat{\boldsymbol{\varepsilon}}_{jt}. \tag{3.6}$$

The inter-temporal path for the representative region is described as follows:

$$ln\,TFP_{0t} = \gamma_0 + ln\,TFP_{0t-1} + \widehat{\varepsilon}_{0t}. \tag{3.7}$$

Therefore, the inter-temporal path of the TFP catching-up effect in region j is derived as follows:

$$ln\,\overline{TFP}_{jt} \equiv ln\,TFP_{0t} - ln\,TFP_{jt} = (\gamma_0 - \boldsymbol{\gamma}_j) + (1 - \lambda)\,ln\,\overline{TFP}_{jt-1} + u_{jt}, \tag{3.8}$$

where the error term for u_{jt} $\left(u_{jt} = \widehat{\boldsymbol{\varepsilon}}_{0t} - \widehat{\varepsilon}_{jt}\right)$ is assumed to be independently distributed in relation to j and t. Using Eq. (3.8), we can test whether the term $ln\,\overline{TFP}_{jt}$, representing the relative difference in TFP for region j from a representative region, is stationary. If $\boldsymbol{\lambda} = 0$, then the stochastic process of $ln\,\overline{TFP}_{jt}$ can be interpreted as nonstationary. In this case, the productivity shock is permanent, and the catching-up effect does not exist because no stochastic convergence in the difference in TFP levels can be acknowledged. If $\boldsymbol{\lambda} > 0$, then the stochastic process of the difference in TFP levels between regions is interpreted as stationary. The shock to the region's productivity level is not permanent, suggesting that TFP convergence exists. In this case, the productivity of each region converges to an asymptotic growth rate.

3.3.2 Panel Unit Root Test

Now, we examine the stationarity of the TFP catching-up effect using the panel data unit root test. For the test, the following formula is assumed for a certain y_{jt}:

$$y_{jt} = \rho_j y_{jt-1} + X'_{jt}\delta + \varepsilon_{jt}. \tag{3.9}$$

Here, j ($j = 1, \cdots, N$) represents the cross section, and t ($t = 1, \cdots, P$) is the observation period. X_{jt} is an exogenous variable in which a fixed effect is included. ρ_j is an autoregressive coefficient, and δ is a coefficient that should be estimated. The error term ε_{jt} is assumed to be independently distributed in relation to j and t. In this case, if $|\rho_j| < 1$, y_{jt} is weakly stationary. If $|\rho_j| = 1$, then the unit root exists for y_{jt}. The methods of Levin et al. (2002) and Im et al. (2003) were used for the test. Both methods used the following formula:

$$\Delta y_{jt} = \alpha y_{jt-1} + \sum\nolimits_{L=1}^{p_j} \beta_{jL} \Delta y_{jt-L} + X'_{jt}\delta_j + \varepsilon_{jt}. \tag{3.10}$$

Levin et al. (2002) assume a common unit root, and Im et al. (2003) assume an individually different unit root; the degree of the lag variables is assumed to vary depending on the cross-section items. The null hypothesis, $\alpha = 0$ ($\rho = 1$), indicates that the deviation in the productivity level of the relevant and representative regions is a nonstationary process that possesses drift terms. The alternative hypothesis, $\alpha < 0$ ($\rho < 1$), indicates that the deviation in productivity is a stationary process, which means that convergence is achieved.

Table 3.4 shows the results of the test statistics. The test rejects the null hypothesis $\alpha = 0$; thus, the null of "TFP of all regions with a unit root" is rejected. This suggests that the TFP levels in the regions converge and that the productivity of each region converges to an asymptotic level.

Table 3.4 Results of panel unit root test

Method of panel unit root tests	Statistics [prob.]		Individual effects	Cross section	Obs.
Levin, Lin, and Chu	−3.5741	**	Present	47	1363
	[0.00]				
Im, Pesaran, and Shin	−1.8081	**	Present	47	1363
	[0.04]				

Notes: (1) ** and * indicate significance at the 1% and 5% levels, respectively. (2) The values in square brackets indicate p-values

This study also examines the existence of conditional convergence, or the individual effect, in line with the method used by Dolado et al. (1990). Specifically, the unit root test is conducted using a model that initially assumes individual effects. If the test rejects the existence of the unit root, then the test completes. However, if the test does not reject the unit root, the estimation is repeated using a model that does not assume individual effects, and a procedure for performing a unit root test is adopted. According to the test results, the model that assumes individual effects is adopted because the test rejects the existence of the unit root. The TFP levels of the regions in Japan converge to an asymptotic level in each region rather than to an average level of regions. This result supports the conditional convergence hypothesis.

3.4 Conclusions

In this chapter, we measured TFP in Japan using regional data and elucidated whether TFP growth in Japan was accompanied by a convergence of regional disparities. This chapter also examines the impacts of the three determinants of TFP growth: within, between, and covariance effects. The results showed that TFP increased over the long term (30 years) from 1980 to 2010 and that the impacts on TFP of the between and covariance effects were minor. Additionally, the results suggested that TFP did not grow in conjunction with economic expansion, which was achieved by the concentration of production in specific regions such as large metropolitan areas. This finding is consistent with Porter's (1998) argument that amid exposure to globalized economic activity, economies of scale facilitated by agglomeration in large metropolitan areas do not have substantial impacts on sustained national TFP growth.

Moreover, we confirmed that the TFP levels in each region converged throughout the observation period. The results show that the TFP of each region converged to a steady state in each region. Although this finding of conditional convergence cannot necessarily be compared with the results of other studies because of differences in the objects of analysis and the methods employed, the results of this chapter conflict with Kawagoe (1999) and Togo's (2002) results and support those of Barro and Sala-i-Martin (1995). Kawagoe (1999) and Togo (2002), which are comparatively short-term data analyses in the economic expansion phase of the 1980s and the 1990s, show an expansion of regional disparities. However, Barro and Sala-i-Martin (1995) show that inter-regional disparities shrink when using long-term data. Our results are similar to those of Barro and Sala-i-Martin (1995) because we also use long-term data covering 30 years.

Our finding on the conditional convergence of TFP suggests that the creation and accumulation of unique knowledge in each region is an essential element for the sustainability of regional economies. This finding is consistent with Otsuka et al. (2010), who show that a region's unique technological progress explains the majority of regional economic growth. This highlights the importance of region-specific production environments (milieu), such as public infrastructure, facilities, and entrepreneurship. This conclusion suggests the necessity of extensive research exploring the potential relationships between region-specific elements and TFP growth. Thus, Chap. 4 considers the regional determinants of TFP growth in depth.

Finally, it should be noted that this chapter considered regional convergence without using any spatial econometric or spatial panel methods capable of identifying convergence clubs or spatial spillovers. The analysis of spatial convergence is of interest to many scholars (e.g., Rey and Montouri 1999; Egger and Pfaffermayr 2006; Fingleton and López-Bazo 2006). Considering the spatial effect in the stochastic convergence model is a crucial extension of this study.

References

Aw BY, Chen X, Roberts MJ (2001) Firm-level evidence on productivity differentials and turnover in Taiwanese manufacturing. J Dev Econ 66(1):51–86

Barro RJ, Sala-i-Martin X (1995) Economic growth. McGraw-Hill Incorporated, New York

Bernard AB, Jones CI (1996) Productivity across industries and countries: Time series theory and evidence. Rev Econ Statistics 78(1):135–146

Dolado JJ, Jenkinson T, Sosvilla-Rivero S (1990) Cointegration and unit roots. J Econ Surv 4 (3):250–273

Dowrick S, Nguyen DT (1989) OECD comparative economic growth 1950–85: Catch-up and convergence. Am Econ Rev 79(5):1010–1030

Egger P, Pfaffermayr M (2006) Spatial convergence. Pap Reg Sci 85(2):199–215

Fingleton B, López-Bazo E (2006) Empirical growth models with spatial effects. Pap Reg Sci 85 (2):177–198

Foster L, Haltiwanger J, Krizan CJ (2001) Aggregate productivity growth: Lessons from microeconomic evidence. In: Hulten CR, Dean ER, Harper MJ (eds) New development in productivity analysis. The University of Chicago Press, Chicago, pp 303–372

Good DH, Nadiri MI, Sickles RC (1997) Index number and factor demand approaches to the estimation of productivity. Handbook Appl Econ Microecon 2:14–80

Goto M, Atris AM, Otsuka A (2018) Productivity change and decomposition analysis of Japanese regional economies. Reg Stud 52(11):1537–1547

Im KS, Pesaran MH, Shin Y (2003) Testing for unit roots in heterogeneous panels. J Econ 115:53–74

Ishikura Y, Fujita M, Maeda M, Kanai K, Yamasaki A (2003) Strategy for cluster initiatives in Japan. Yuhikaku Publishing Company Limited, Tokyo. (in Japanese)

Kawagoe M (1999) Regional dynamics in Japan: A reexamination of Barro regressions. J Jpn Int Econ 13(1):61–72

Krugman P (1991) Geography and trade. MIT Press, Cambridge

Levin A, Lin CF, Chu CSJ (2002) Unit root tests in panel data: Asymptotic and finite-sample properties. J Econ 108(1):1–24

Nemoto J, Goto M (2005) Productivity, efficiency, scale economies and technical change: A new decomposition analysis of TFP applied to the Japanese prefectures. J Jpn Int Econ 19(4):617–634

Otsuka A, Goto M (2015) Regional policy and the productive efficiency of Japanese industries. Reg Stud 49(4):518–531

Otsuka A, Goto M (2016) Total factor productivity and the convergence of disparities in Japanese regions. Ann Reg Sci 56(2):419–432

Otsuka A, Goto M, Sueyoshi T (2010) Industrial agglomeration effects in Japan: Productive efficiency, market access, and public fiscal transfer. Pap Reg Sci 89(4):819–839

Porter ME (1990) The competitive advantage of nations. Free Press, New York

Porter ME (1998) On competition. Harvard Business School Press, Cambridge

Rey SJ, Montouri BD (1999) US regional income convergence: A spatial econometric perspective. Reg Stud 33(2):143–156

Togo K (2002) Productivity convergence in Japan's manufacturing industries. Econ Lett 75 (1):61–67

Tokui J (2018) Regional productivity differences in Japan: Industry-level studies based on the R-JIP database. University of Tokyo Press, Tokyo. (in Japanese)

Chapter 4
Regional Productivity and Determinants

Abstract This chapter considers the determinants of Japan's regional TFP. An increase in TFP can be achieved through two paths: The first is a shift in the production frontier, which amounts to an increase in output for a given input volume (productivity effect). The second is an approach to the production frontier by ensuring that outputs are closer to the production frontier levels for a given input volume (productive efficiency effect). The elements of external economies, such as social overhead capital (SOC) and regional agglomeration, affect both. From these two paths, this chapter clarifies the roles played by SOC and regional agglomeration in increasing regional sustainability by using the stochastic frontier model of the TFP index. The empirical analysis using Japan's regional data provides the following evidence. First, SOC investment contributes to TFP growth and, more importantly, has a productivity effect and productive efficiency effect, mainly in local areas. Second, regional agglomeration underpins the TFP growth in large metropolitan areas. Third, the productive efficiency effect is high in regions specializing in internationally competitive manufacturing industries. It is concluded that providing high-quality public infrastructure and enhancing regional productivity are essential strategies for the government to consider in its efforts to achieve sustainable regional growth.

Keywords Agglomeration economies · Productive efficiency · Social overhead capital (SOC) · Stochastic frontier analysis (SFA) · Total factor productivity (TFP)

4.1 Introduction

The declining birthrate and aging society that Japan is facing are leading to serious concerns about regional sustainability. Declining trends in the working-age population and household savings are already evident in Japan's regions. If not

This chapter is based on Otsuka (2017).

A. Otsuka, *A New Driver of Regional Sustainability in Japan*, New Frontiers in Regional Science: Asian Perspectives 54,
https://doi.org/10.1007/978-981-16-3709-4_4

accompanied by an increase in total factor productivity (TFP), reductions in production factors will depress the potential growth rate of regional economies. Therefore, it is necessary to perform structural reforms of regional economic systems, such as the reallocation of economic resources employed in low-productivity sectors to high-productivity sectors.

An increase in TFP can be achieved through two paths: The first is a shift in the production frontier, which amounts to an increase in output for a given input volume (productivity effect). The second is an approach to the production frontier by ensuring that outputs are closer to the production frontier levels for a given input volume (productive efficiency effect). The elements of external economies, such as social overhead capital (SOC) and regional agglomeration, affect both.

SOC is defined as the public capital formed by annual investments in critical facilities and services for the entire national economy, including agriculture, forestry and fisheries facilities, roads, harbors, airports, communications, parks, water supply and sewerage systems, social insurance and welfare facilities, schools, hospitals, as well as soil, water control, and conservation facilities.[1] SOC is well known to function as an external economy (Ashauer 1989). Firms located in regions with high-quality public infrastructure can achieve shorter travel times, reduced transport costs, and increased transport volumes. Public infrastructure that supports industrial activities, such as roads, harbors, and airports, accounts for more than 50% of the total in Japan. The development of public infrastructure improves regional productive ability, allowing regions to procure inputs and utilize production facilities more effectively, thus producing goods at lower costs. Most studies in Japan have demonstrated that a region with high-quality SOC enjoys a TFP boost (Mera 1973; Merriman 1990; Yamano and Ohkawara 2000; Shioji 2001; Kataoka 2005). SOC not only enhances a firm's production ability but also strengthens regional TFP, thus leading to increased sustainability.

Furthermore, regional agglomeration—the tendency for populations, firms, or industries to cluster—improves TFP and leads to an increase in regional sustainability. Agglomeration economies constitute cost savings and increased productivity obtained when firms are spatially agglomerated (Marshall 1890). It is well known that firms in high-density areas benefit from external economies.[2] If firms are spatially agglomerated, the knowledge generated by one can easily spill over to others through channels such as face-to-face communication and the movement of skilled workers among firms. Thus, agglomeration economies help improve TFP by creating knowledge and its resultant spillover in agglomerated areas (Fujita and Thisse 2002; Carlino and Kerr 2015).

---

[1] The concept of SOC is defined by Hirschman (1958) and is generally consistent with concepts such as "public capital," "public infrastructure," and "government capital."

[2] Many empirical studies indicate that agglomeration economies contribute to enhancing regional productivity and global competitiveness (e.g., Eberts and McMillen 1999; Rosenthal and Strange 2004; Combes and Gobillon 2015).

This chapter focuses on TFP determinants in regional economies and clarifies the roles played by SOC and regional agglomeration in increasing regional sustainability by using the stochastic frontier model of the TFP index. This chapter's contributions to this research are threefold.

First, we analyze productivity effects (shift in the production frontier) and productive efficiency effects (ascending along an existing production frontier) simultaneously. Conventional studies focus on detecting the productivity effect of SOC and agglomeration externalities (e.g., Kanemoto et al. 1996; Mizutani and Tanaka 2010). Since the 2010s, studies have focused on the productive efficiency effect (e.g., Otsuka et al. 2010; Fritsch and Slavtchev 2011; Ke and Yu 2014; Otsuka and Goto 2015a; Tsekeris and Papaioannou 2017). However, to the best of our knowledge, no attempt has been made to understand the effect of these external economies on TFP in terms of both productivity and productive efficiency effects simultaneously.

Second, using the TFP index, this chapter tackles the endogeneity problem that occurs in productivity analyses. Most studies on SOC and regional agglomeration use the production function (Rosenthal and Strange 2004; Combes and Gobillon 2015). This approach leads to an endogeneity problem that generates estimation bias (Ciccone and Hall 1996; Ciccone 2002; Henderson 2003; Rosenthal and Strange 2004; Graham 2009; Graham et al. 2010; Combes and Gobillon 2015).[3] The TFP index approach does not specify the production function form, with specific factors representing the externalities. Therefore, this approach can mitigate the endogeneity problem when evaluating external economies (Otsuka and Goto 2015b).

Third, this chapter controls the influence of industrial structure on productive efficiency. As described in Chap. 2, in Japan, most competitive manufacturing industries are located in local areas, and the productive efficiency in these regions is expected to be high. Conversely, in the service industry, numerous industry types are labor intensive, and because labor productivity is low, the productive efficiency in the region specialized in the service industry is expected to be low. Therefore, this chapter evaluates the determinants of TFP in Japan's regional economies by controlling for industrial structure.

The remainder of this chapter is structured as follows. Section 4.2 describes the stochastic frontier model of the TFP index used for the empirical analysis and explains the study's data. Section 4.3 presents and discusses the estimation results. Section 4.4 concludes the chapter and provides policy suggestions.

[3]When estimating the agglomeration effect from a production function, the general assumption that the error term is distributed independently from the regression variables is applied. The presence of endogeneity could violate this assumption because it implies that the element increasing the agglomeration effect is associated with productivity and may thus be an endogenous variable. See Sect. 3.3 in Chap. 7 for further discussions on this concern.

4.2 Methods

4.2.1 Stochastic Frontier Model of the TFP Index

For the TFP measurement, we used the method described in Chap. 3, which is the nonparametric measurement method of Good et al. (1997) and Aw et al. (2001). This method assumes a typical economy with an average output and input size at a certain point in time. It calculates the TFP of each economy as a disparity relative to a typical economy. The TFP of a typical economy changes over time; therefore, this method allows a time-series comparison of TFP.

The TFP of region j ($j = 1, \cdots, N$) at time t ($t = 1, \cdots, P$) is measured using Eq. (4.1) in the form of a comparison with the average TFP level

$$
\begin{aligned}
ln\,TFP_{jt} = & \left(ln\,Y_{jt} - \overline{ln\,Y_t}\right) + \sum\nolimits_{s=1}^{t}\left(\overline{ln\,Y_s} - \overline{ln\,Y_{s-1}}\right) \\
& - \left[\sum\nolimits_{i=1}^{n}\frac{1}{2}\left(S_{ijt} + \overline{S_{it}}\right)\left(ln\,X_{ijt} - \overline{ln\,X_{it}}\right)\right. \\
& \left. + \sum\nolimits_{s=1}^{t}\sum\nolimits_{i=1}^{n}\frac{1}{2}\left(\overline{S_{is}} + \overline{S_{is-1}}\right)\left(\overline{ln\,X_{is}} - \overline{ln\,X_{is-1}}\right)\right],
\end{aligned}
\tag{4.1}
$$

where Y_{jt} represents the output of region j at time t, X_{ijt} is the input factor i ($i = 1, \cdots, n$) for region j at time t, and S_{ijt} is the cost share of input factor i in region j at time t. The overline above each symbol expresses the inter-regional average value of each variable. Equation (4.1) shows that in addition to the comparable TFP level at a given point in time and a given region, it is possible to measure the regional TFP level by considering the TFP level change in a time series.

As the determinants model of the TFP index, we use stochastic frontier analysis (SFA) and gross accounting decomposition. This approach allows us not only to identify the determinants of productive efficiency but also to measure the size of the determinants' contributions to TFP growth.

The underlying determinants model of the TFP index has the following logarithmic linear form:

$$
ln\,TFP_{jt} = \boldsymbol{\beta}_G\,ln\,G_{jt} + \boldsymbol{\beta}_D\,ln\,D_{jt} + \boldsymbol{\alpha}_j + v_{jt} - u_{jt}. \tag{4.2}
$$

Note that all the variables in Eq. (4.2) are expressed logarithmically. G is the SOC, and D is the population density as regional agglomeration. $\boldsymbol{\alpha}$ and $\boldsymbol{\beta}$ are estimation parameters. SOC and regional agglomeration increase TFP; specifically, when the productivity effect exists, the signs of $\boldsymbol{\beta}_G$ and $\boldsymbol{\beta}_D$ are positive. $\boldsymbol{\alpha}_j$ is the individual effect, which reflects the regional characteristics that cannot be expressed by explanatory variables.

The error term ($v_{jt} - u_{jt}$) comprises two parts: an observational error term (v_{jt}) and a managerial error associated with productive inefficiency (u_{jt}). The error term (v_{jt}) is assumed to be *i.i.d.* $N\left(0, \sigma_v^2\right)$ and independent of the managerial error term (u_{jt}) and all regressors of the proposed production function. u_{jt} is a non-negative random variable that is independently distributed as the truncation at zero of the $N(\mu, \sigma_u^2)$ distribution..

According to the specialization of Eq. (4.2), the level of productive efficiency TEF_{jt} is defined as the ratio of the TFP level (tfp_{jt}) on the frontier to the observed TFP level (TFP_{jt}):

$$TEF_{jt} = \frac{TFP_{jt}}{tfp_{jt}} = e^{-u_{jt}}. \tag{4.3}$$

Equations (4.2) and (4.3) provide the following growth accounting:

$$T\dot{F}P_{jt} = \beta_G \dot{G}_{jt} + \beta_D \dot{D}_{jt} + T\dot{E}F_{jt}, \tag{4.4}$$

where the dot on each variable indicates the percentage change. Because of the model structure, the estimated level of productive efficiency, TEF_{jt}, becomes a non-negative value with an upper limit of 1, as shown below:

$$TEF_{jt} = E(\exp(-u_{jt}) \mid v_{jt} - u_{jt}), \quad 0 < TEF_{jt} \leq 1. \tag{4.5}$$

We formulate the mean of productive inefficiency (μ_{jt}) as follows:

$$\mu_{jt} = \delta_0 - \sum\nolimits_Z \delta_Z \, ln \, Z_{jt}, \tag{4.6}$$

where Z represents the exogenous variables that explain productive efficiency, which are determinants of productive efficiency. The symbols δ are the parameters to be estimated.

After substituting Eq. (4.6) into Eq. (4.4), growth accounting is specified as follows:

$$T\dot{F}P_{jt} = \beta_G \dot{G}_{jt} + \beta_D \dot{D}_{jt} + \sum\nolimits_z \delta_z \dot{Z}_{jt}.$$

Therefore, the growth rate of an observed TFP ($T\dot{F}P_{jt}$) is measured as the sum of three components: (a) the productivity effect of SOC ($\beta_G \dot{G}_{jt}$), (b) the productivity effect of population density ($\beta_D \dot{D}_{jt}$), and (c) the rate of change in productive efficiency ($\sum_Z \delta_Z \dot{Z}_{jt}$). By incorporating an error term ($\dot{v}_{jt}$) into the TFP growth rate, we specify it as follows:

$$T\dot{F}P_{jt} = \beta_G \dot{G}_{jt} + \beta_D \dot{D}_{jt} + \sum\nolimits_z \delta_z \dot{Z}_{jt} + \dot{v}_{jt}. \tag{4.7}$$

4.2.2 Data

This study uses panel data pooled from 47 prefectures covering 1980 to 2010. In the measurement of the TFP index, the dataset on output and input was used in Chap. 3. In this study, SOC (*G*), population density (*D*), manufacturing industry ratio (*MR*), and service industry ratio (*SR*) were used as determinants of the TFP index.

SOC (*G*), which is public infrastructure, is the first determinant of productivity and productive efficiency. The data on SOC comes from the estimates of the Central Research Institute of Electric Power Industry, which has compiled annual SOC data since the 1970s. The estimation of SOC is carried out by accumulating the investment value related to improvements in public capital and deducting depreciation due to expired useful life. The investment value used as the basis for estimation was calculated using real values. The average useful life for each sector of public capital is set, and the value of depreciation is estimated based on the premise that the depreciation rate follows a gamma distribution.[4] The units of SOC data are presented as monetary amounts (JPY).

Population density (*D*), defined as the population density on habitable land, is the second determinant of productivity and productive efficiency. The denominator is the habitable land area (km^2), and the numerator is the population. Population and habitable land area data were extracted from the *Basic Resident Registers* and the *System of Social and Demographic Statistics*, respectively (Statistics Bureau, Ministry of Internal Affairs and Communications).

Population density has been used as a proxy index for agglomeration economies (Otsuka et al. 2010; Otsuka and Goto 2015a). Ciccone and Hall (1996) and Ciccone (2002) examine the role of density in agglomeration economies, showing that the relationship between productivity and density can be explained by agglomeration and diversity. Specifically, if employment density doubles, labor productivity increases by 5% to 6% due to agglomeration economies. Population density also has a positive correlation (0.78) with the diversity index, which is the inverse of the Herfindahl-Hirschman Index (*DIV*), with statistical significance at the 1% level.[5,6]

---

[4]See Hitomi and Hamagata (2008) for the detail calculation procedure on SOC data.

[5]*DIV* presents a measure of regional diversity in economic structures—by Duranton and Puga (2000) for example:

$$DIV_j = \frac{1}{\sum_{i=1}^{I} (S_{ij})^2}, \quad \text{where } S_{ij} = \frac{x_{ij}}{\sum_{i=1}^{I} x_{ij}}, i = 1, \ldots, I; j = 1, \ldots, J$$

S_{ij} reflects the employment share (x) of industry i in region j relative to total (national) employment for industry i or the concentration of industry i in region j relative to all regions. Therefore, DIV_j takes a value of 1 (the number of industries in a given industry classification) if industrial employment in region j is evenly distributed among all industries. In order to calculate the *DIV* index precisely, we must collect three- or four-digit industry classification data. However, these data have been published only at five-year intervals in Japan.

[6]The correlation coefficient is calculated based on the data of the three-digit industry classifications in 2010.

That is, given that economic structures are more diverse in more populated regions, population density is suitable as a proxy for agglomeration economies.

Finally, the manufacturing and service industry ratios (*MR* and *SR*) are introduced to control for the effect of regional industrial structure on productive efficiency. Ratios for the manufacturing and service industries are obtained by dividing their respective production values by the total prefectural production value. In both cases, data from the *Annual Report on Prefectural Accounts* (Cabinet Office) were used. The productive efficiency of Japan's manufacturing industry is high, while that of its non-manufacturing industry is low (Otsuka et al. 2010; Otsuka and Goto 2015a). This effect was controlled for in the present study.

Based on the above, this study assumes the following equation, vis-à-vis Eq. (4.5):

$$\mu_{jt} = \delta_0 - \delta_G \, ln \, G_{jt} - \delta_D \, ln \, D_{jt} - \delta_{MR} \, ln \, MR_{jt} - \delta_{SR} \, ln \, SR_{jt}, \qquad (4.8)$$

where δ is the parameter to be estimated. Note that if an explanatory variable improves the efficiency level, δ is positive.[7]

Table 4.1 shows the mean, standard deviation, minimum, and maximum values of the data as descriptive statistics at 10-year intervals. TFP increases consistently throughout the observation period. After rising sharply from the 1980s to the 1990s, the rate of increase slowed in the 2000s. Population density also increased from the 1980s to the 2000s. Population density fell slightly in 2000 but rose again in 2010. This is considered a consequence of the progress of the monocentric concentration in the Greater Tokyo Area. Social overhead capital increases steadily throughout the observation period, but its change over time diminishes. Large-scale investments in passenger infrastructure, such as railways and aviation facilities, were implemented during the observation period. The manufacturing industry ratio fell from 1980 to 2000 and then rose again in 2010. Despite the continuing hollowing out of the domestic industry, the manufacturing ratio increases on average. In contrast, changes in the service industry ratio were negligible throughout the observation period. Despite a shift in economic activity toward services, barely any difference was observed between the manufacturing and service industry ratios until 2010.

Table 4.2 presents the descriptive statistics for each region's TFP determinants. The SOC is high not only in large metropolitan areas, such as the Greater Tokyo Area, Kansai, and Chubu region, but also in local areas, such as Hokkaido, Tohoku, and Kyushu region. Notably, SOC has a high growth rate in local areas. This indicates that local areas have received more SOC investments than large metropolitan areas. While the population density in the Greater Tokyo Area is relatively high,

[7]For ease of understanding, we define the determinants of productive inefficiency as negative. Therefore, we expect the signs of δ to be positive. In other words, if the signs of δ are positive, as expected, the impact of each variable on productive inefficiency will be negative. In that sense, our setting does not contradict that of Otsuka (2017).

Table 4.1 Descriptive statistics

		Total factor productivity	Social overhead capital	Population density	Manufacturing industry ratio	Service industry ratio
		(index)	(million yen)	(persons/km^2)	(%)	(%)
		(*TFP*)	(*G*)	(*D*)	(*MR*)	(*SR*)
1980	Mean	−0.006	7,385,347	1276.3	21.6	23.1
	Standard deviation	0.109	7,255,505	1505.5	8.6	2.8
	Maximum	0.402	41,512,779	8371.9	43.7	29.4
	Minimum	−0.206	2,288,007	262.4	8.3	18.9
1990	Mean	0.120	12,092,645	1335.6	20.6	22.0
	Standard deviation	0.121	10,839,825	1573.9	7.2	2.8
	Maximum	0.514	58,171,387	8455.8	36.6	30.4
	Minimum	−0.055	3,821,977	259.3	6.4	16.4
2000	Mean	0.199	17,179,320	1350.2	19.4	23.9
	Standard deviation	0.100	14,128,891	1585.0	7.1	2.7
	Maximum	0.578	71,801,947	8412.9	33.6	32.5
	Minimum	0.040	5,829,801	259.5	6.1	18.7
2010	Mean	0.231	18,375,711	1359.6	22.4	23.8
	Standard deviation	0.101	14,305,476	1679.0	8.7	3.1
	Maximum	0.592	71,816,416	9065.6	42.6	33.3
	Minimum	0.080	6,653,443	248.6	3.9	17.8
1980–2010	Mean	0.135	14,189,249	1341.4	20.2	23.4
	Standard deviation	0.135	12,695,686	1575.9	7.5	2.9
	Maximum	0.662	72,474,451	9065.6	43.7	34.5
	Minimum	−0.206	2,288,007	248.6	3.8	16.0

it is low in local areas. In the Greater Tokyo Area, population concentration increased significantly during the observation period, while population agglomeration decreased in many local areas. This reveals an unbalanced allocation of SOC investment favoring sparsely populated local areas.[8]

[8]In Japan, public investment allocated to strengthening the production capacity also fulfills the role of income redistribution (Kanemoto et al. 1996; Yamano and Ohkawara 2000; Kataoka 2005). This is commonly known as the "simultaneity problem" (Hayashi 2003). Specifically, examining the productivity effect of SOC by region reveals that provincial regions with low productivity get more SOC allocated to them, meaning that the productivity effect is negatively biased. Therefore, determining the economic effects of SOC (productivity effect) accurately requires evaluating it based on the total amount rather than the per capita amount.

Table 4.2 Descriptive statistics of explanatory variables by region

	Social overhead capital (G)		Population density (D)		Manufacturing industry ratio (MR)		Service industry ratio (SR)	
	Mean	Annual growth rate (%)	Mean	Annual growth rate (%)	Mean	Annual growth rate (%)	Mean	Annual growth rate (%)
Hokkaido	51,834,001	3.33	258.9	−0.18	10.1	−1.31	25.3	−0.02
Tohoku	11,580,430	3.28	497.0	−0.20	14.9	0.69	23.2	0.14
North Kanto	9,721,581	3.41	799.1	0.20	27.1	0.75	21.7	0.19
Greater Tokyo Area	34,610,117	2.46	4577.9	0.57	20.1	−1.52	23.2	0.11
Chubu	16,246,869	3.09	1244.4	0.21	28.7	0.91	20.5	−0.15
Hokuriku	7,473,069	3.53	739.6	0.02	21.2	0.69	21.8	−0.06
Kansai	16,224,601	2.98	2408.9	0.12	24.3	−0.57	22.3	0.30
Chugoku	9,624,137	3.18	868.6	−0.11	22.0	−0.21	22.9	0.03
Shikoku	6,502,668	3.56	869.3	−0.11	18.4	−0.57	24.6	0.25
Kyushu	10,597,323	3.33	847.6	0.08	14.9	0.90	26.3	−0.04
Okinawa	7,357,110	5.16	1150.0	0.26	6.0	−2.51	31.2	0.70

Notes: (1) The values in the table are the values of the observation period (1980–2010)
(2) The values in the table are means of prefectures within each region
(3) See Fig. 1.2 in Chap. 1 for the regional classification

4.3 Results and Discussion

The estimation in the SFA model uses Battese and Coelli's Frontier Version 4.1 (Coelli 1996). Using this software package, it is possible to estimate a stochastic frontier model as the target of the panel data. Table 4.3 shows the estimation results. Model A expresses the result of the SFA model, and Model B expresses the results after a time effect is added.

First, the sign of parameter ($\boldsymbol{\beta_G}$), which expresses the productivity effect of SOC, is positive and statistically significant. Additionally, the sign of parameter ($\boldsymbol{\beta_D}$), which expresses the productivity effect of regional agglomeration, is positive and statistically significant. This shows that the productivity effect of SOC increases and, simultaneously, so does the productivity effect of regional agglomeration. Furthermore, as logarithmic values are taken for each variable, the size of each parameter expresses elasticity. The elasticities of SOC and population density are both around 0.3. This suggests that if SOC and population density were to increase by 1%, TFP would increase as much as 0.3%.

Next, observing the effect on the productive efficiency of SOC, the parameter $\boldsymbol{\delta_G}$ is significantly positive. Additionally, the population density and manufacturing industry ratio parameters ($\boldsymbol{\delta_D}$ and $\boldsymbol{\delta_{MR}}$) were significantly positive. This implies that SOC, population density, and manufacturing industry ratio contribute to

Table 4.3 Estimation results

	Model A			Model B		
Frontier function						
Constant (α)	0.3785	(0.0349)	**	0.3716	(0.0187)	**
β_G	0.3153	(0.0355)	**	0.2588	(0.0230)	**
β_D	0.2910	(0.0299)	**	0.2704	(0.0399)	**
Efficiency model						
Constant (δ_0)	0.2821	(0.0566)	**	0.2493	(0.1598)	*
δ_G	0.3591	(0.0259)	**	0.1799	(0.0266)	**
δ_D	0.1861	(0.0359)	**	0.0933	(0.0162)	**
δ_{MR}	0.1576	(0.0372)	**	0.2046	(0.0018)	**
δ_{SR}	−0.0606	(0.0404)	*	−0.2581	(0.0080)	**
Time effect	Excluded			Included		
σ^2	0.4283	(0.0180)	**	0.3678	(0.0329)	**
γ	0.0322	(0.0047)	**	0.0152	(0.0030)	**
Log-likelihood	−1376.53			−1325.78		
Observations	1457			1457		
Mean efficiency scores	0.7032			0.7319		

Notes: (1) ** and * indicate 1% and 5% significance levels, respectively
(2) The values in parentheses indicate standard errors
(3) The software used for the estimation is Frontier 4.1 (Coelli 1996)

increasing productive efficiency. Conversely, the parameter (δ_{SR}) of the service industry ratio is significantly negative, meaning that the higher the service industry ratio in a region, the lower its productive efficiency. This result is consistent with the results of previous studies (Otsuka et al. 2010; Otsuka and Goto 2015a).

Table 4.4 shows the levels of productive efficiency for the entire country and for the 11 regions, calculated using Eq. (4.5). The productive efficiency values of each region are expressed as the average of the prefectures in each region. For the observation period average, the Greater Tokyo Area was the most efficient, with a maximum efficiency value of 0.979, followed by Chubu (0.876). Therefore, productive efficiency is high in regions with megacities. This tendency is the same as that observed for the regional differences in TFP levels. The productive efficiency of the local areas is lower than that of highly urbanized regions, with that of Okinawa being the lowest at 0.358. This result likely occurs because in local areas, the decentralized population weakens regional agglomeration economies. However, when calculating growth over the observation period, the region with the highest growth in productive efficiency is Hokuriku, at 1.94 times, followed by Kyusyu, at 1.74 times, which shows that growth is high in the local areas. In contrast, the productive efficiency of the Greater Tokyo Area is mostly flat, with a growth of just 1.02 times. This is likely due to the effect of unbalanced allocations of SOC investment in the local areas during the observation period, as well as the decreased production share of manufacturing in the large metropolitan areas and the increased production share of the service industry.

Table 4.4 Levels of productive efficiency in Japan's regions

	1980	1990	2000	2010	Period average	2010/1980
Hokkaido	0.706	0.843	0.914	0.917	0.846	1.30
Tohoku	0.422	0.556	0.655	0.715	0.587	1.69
North Kanto	0.541	0.738	0.828	0.891	0.755	1.65
Greater Tokyo Area	0.960	0.981	0.983	0.983	0.979	1.02
Chubu	0.705	0.868	0.931	0.961	0.876	1.36
Hokuriku	0.403	0.603	0.707	0.782	0.628	1.94
Kansai	0.685	0.819	0.879	0.893	0.829	1.30
Chugoku	0.532	0.677	0.735	0.764	0.683	1.44
Shikoku	0.401	0.525	0.595	0.648	0.543	1.62
Kyushu	0.417	0.530	0.619	0.724	0.568	1.74
Okinawa	0.266	0.341	0.409	0.386	0.358	1.45
National average	0.552	0.685	0.757	0.804	0.703	1.46

Notes: (1) The values in the table were calculated using Eq. (4.5)
(2) The values in the table are means of prefectures within each region
(3) See Fig. 1.2 in Chap. 1 for the regional classification

Finally, we seek to identify which determinants contribute to productive efficiency improvements and determine the degree to which these contributions influence TFP growth. Table 4.5 shows the results of decomposition for each region using Eq. (4.7).

Hokuriku region has the highest TFP growth, at 1.111%, followed by North Kanto and Chubu regions. The region with the lowest TFP growth is Okinawa, which registers minimal growth. Comparing the contributions of productivity and productive efficiency effects vis-à-vis TFP growth by region reveals that the contribution of the productivity effect is more significant. Specifically, the productivity effect of SOC makes the most significant contribution, especially in regions other than the Greater Tokyo Area (around 0.8%), explaining more than half of TFP growth. By contrast, only a small contribution is made by regional agglomeration because the change in population density is minimal throughout the observation period. Thus, regional agglomeration impacts TFP growth only minimally. However, the contribution of regional agglomeration is more substantial in the Greater Tokyo Area than in other regions.

Another notable characteristic is that the contribution of productive efficiency to TFP growth is small in the Greater Tokyo Area but substantial in local areas. Chubu saw the highest contribution from productive efficiency at 0.816%, followed by the Kyushu, North Kanto, and Tohoku regions. In Chubu and Kyushu, the productive efficiency improvement factors are increases in SOC and improvements in the manufacturing industry ratio, the sizes of which explain more than half of the contribution from productive efficiencies. However, the contribution of regional agglomeration is small. Thus, it can be said that the most significant contributions to improvement in productive efficiency in each region are the unbalanced allocation of SOC investment and a shift to the manufacturing industry, that is, industrial

Table 4.5 Analysis of the contribution levels of TFP growth (%, annual average)

	TFP growth	Social overhead capital	Population density	Productive efficiency					Other
				(Total of productive efficiency)	Social overhead capital	Population density	Manufacturing industry ratio	Service industry ratio	
	(Total) = a + b + c + h	(a)	(b)	(c) = d + e + f + g	(d)	(e)	(f)	(g)	(h)
Hokkaido	0.612	0.847	−0.049	0.308	0.589	−0.017	−0.269	0.005	−0.495
Tohoku	0.669	0.846	−0.070	0.681	0.588	−0.024	0.152	−0.035	−0.788
North Kanto	0.966	0.878	0.055	0.746	0.610	0.019	0.170	−0.054	−0.713
Greater Tokyo Area	0.789	0.693	0.189	0.165	0.482	0.065	−0.342	−0.040	−0.258
Chubu	0.924	0.826	0.040	0.816	0.574	0.014	0.185	0.043	−0.758
Hokuriku	1.111	0.899	0.004	0.781	0.625	0.002	0.142	0.013	−0.574
Kansai	0.855	0.856	0.049	0.402	0.595	0.017	−0.137	−0.073	−0.452
Chugoku	0.712	0.847	−0.034	0.553	0.589	−0.012	−0.018	−0.006	−0.654
Shikoku	0.879	0.901	−0.032	0.459	0.626	−0.011	−0.100	−0.057	−0.449
Kyushu	0.665	0.878	0.008	0.815	0.610	0.003	0.192	0.010	−1.036
Okinawa	0.025	1.301	0.071	0.229	0.905	0.024	−0.520	−0.180	−1.577
National average	0.746	0.888	0.021	0.541	0.618	0.007	−0.050	−0.034	−0.705

Notes: (1) The values in the table are calculated by applying the estimation results of Model B (Table 4.3) to Eq. (4.7)
(2) See Fig. 1.2 in Chap. 1 for the regional classification

structural changes. The contribution of SOC was positive in all regions, and no substantial differences were observed apart from Okinawa. Regional agglomeration hinders regions already experiencing population declines, such as Hokkaido, Tohoku, Chugoku, and Shikoku. Conversely, the Greater Tokyo Area is characterized by an increasing population concentration, which contributes to productive efficiency, being the primary beneficiary of agglomeration economies. Thus, the Greater Tokyo Area grows by leveraging the economic power of significant agglomeration.

4.4 Conclusions

In this chapter, we measured the TFP index of 47 Japanese prefectures and analyzed their growth determinants. Specifically, by decomposing the effect of external economies on a region's TFP growth into productivity and productive efficiency effects, we conducted empirical analyses on how SOC and regional agglomeration affect TFP growth. The results show that SOC contributes to TFP growth, and the productive efficiency effect is identified in addition to the productivity effect. SOC provides the most significant contribution to improvements in TFP. Moreover, productive efficiency is high in manufacturing-intensive regions, which suggests that the concentration of the competitive manufacturing industry in a region improves the productive efficiency of that region's economy. By contrast, the effect of regional aggregation is active only in large metropolitan areas, and the Greater Tokyo Area benefits from considerable agglomeration economies. The empirical results confirm that external economies, via regional agglomeration, shift production frontiers upward in the Greater Tokyo Area.

The findings of this chapter suggest that SOC investment improves productivity as well as productive efficiency, as previously recognized. High-quality SOC not only brings regions closer to a production frontier but also shifts the production frontier itself, realizing sustainable growth for the region's economy. The results suggest that Japan's government should promote the development of SOC with a cost-effective strategy. Providing high-quality public infrastructure and enhancing regional productivity are essential strategies for achieving regional sustainability.

To reinforce this conclusion, it is necessary to extend this study by considering the geographical aspects of SOC. Notably, the development of SOC has spillover effects. This study could be extended by modifying our SFA to include spatial dimensions. Since the 2010s, numerous studies on stochastic frontier models have considered spatial dependence. In recent studies, Tsukamoto (2019) and De Graaff (2020) show how to combine a spatial dependence structure with a stochastic frontier model. Another possible extension would be to consider spillover effects by using an index of the geographical structure (i.e., inter-regional networks). Part II considers inter-regional network economies to explore the policy options available to Japan's government and their implications for regional sustainability.

References

Ashauer DA (1989) Is public expenditure productive? J Monetary Econ 23:177–200

Aw BY, Chen X, Roberts MJ (2001) Firm-level evidence on productivity differentials and turnover in Taiwanese manufacturing. J Dev Econ 66(1):51–86

Carlino G, Kerr WR (2015) Agglomeration and innovation. In: Duranton G, Henderson JV, Strange W (eds) Handbook of regional and urban economics, vol 5A. Elsevier, Amsterdam, pp 349–404

Ciccone A (2002) Agglomeration effects in Europe. Eur Econ Rev 46(2):213–227

Ciccone A, Hall R (1996) Productivity and the density of economic activity. Am Econ Rev 86 (1):54–70

Coelli TJ (1996) A guide to FRONTIER version 4.1: a computer program for stochastic frontier production and cost function estimation. CEPA working papers no. 96/07. University of new England, NSW, Australia

Combes PP, Gobillon L (2015) The empirics of agglomeration economies. In: Duranton G, Henderson JV, Strange W (eds) Handbook of regional and urban economics, vol 5A. Elsevier, Amsterdam, pp 247–348

De Graaff T (2020) On the estimation of spatial stochastic frontier models: an alternative skew-normal approach. Ann Reg Sci 64:267–285

Duranton G, Puga D (2000) Diversity and specialization in cities: why, where and when does it matter? Urban Stud 37:533–555

Eberts RW, McMillen DP (1999) Agglomeration economies and urban public infrastructure. In: Cheshire P, Mills ES (eds) Handbook of urban and regional economics, vol 3. North-Holland, New York, pp 1455–1495

Fritsch M, Slavtchev V (2011) Determinants of the efficiency of regional innovation systems. Reg Stud 45(7):905–918

Fujita M, Thisse J (2002) The economics of agglomeration: cities, industrial location and regional growth. Cambridge University Press, Cambridge

Good DH, Nadiri MI, Sickles RC (1997) Index number and factor demand approaches to the estimation of productivity. Handbook Appl Econ Microecon 2:14–80

Graham DJ (2009) Identifying urbanization and localization externalities in manufacturing and service industries. Pap Reg Sci 88(1):63–84

Graham DJ, Melo PS, Jiwattamalilpaisarn P, Noland PB (2010) Testing for causality between productivity and agglomeration economies. J Reg Sci 50(5):935–951

Hayashi M (2003) The simultaneity problems in the estimation of effect of public capital: a review of the Japanese studies. Econ Anal 169:88–104. (in Japanese)

Henderson JV (2003) Marshall's scale economies. J Urban Econ 53(1):1–28

Hirschman AO (1958) The strategy of economic development. Yale University Press, New Haven

Hitomi K, Hamagata S (2008) Development of social overhead capital data by prefecture in Japan: 1980–2004. CRIEPI report Y08006. (in Japanese)

Kanemoto Y, Ohkawara T, Suzuki T (1996) Agglomeration economies and a test for optimal city sizes in Japan. J Jpn Int Econ 10(4):379–398

Kataoka M (2005) Effect of public investment on the regional economies in postwar Japan. Rev Urban Reg Dev Stud 17:115–139

Ke S, Yu Y (2014) The pathways from industrial agglomeration to TFP growth: the experience of Chinese cities for 2001–2010. J Asia Pac Econ 19(2):310–332

Marshall A (1890) Principles of economics. Macmillan, London

Mera K (1973) Regional production functions and social overhead capital: an analysis of the Japanese case. Reg Urban Econ 3(2):157–186

Merriman D (1990) Public capital and regional output: another look at some Japanese and 18 American data. Reg Sci Urban Econ 20(4):437–458

Mizutani F, Tanaka T (2010) Productivity effects and determinants of public infrastructure investment. Ann Reg Sci 44:493–521

Otsuka A (2017) Regional determinants of total factor productivity in Japan: stochastic frontier analysis. Ann Reg Sci 58(3):579–596

Otsuka A, Goto M (2015a) Regional policy and the productive efficiency of Japanese industries. Reg Stud 49(4):518–531

Otsuka A, Goto M (2015b) Agglomeration economies in Japanese industries: the Solow residual approach. Ann Reg Sci 54(2):401–416

Otsuka A, Goto M, Sueyoshi T (2010) Industrial agglomeration effects in Japan: productive efficiency, market access, and public fiscal transfer. Pap Reg Sci 89(4):819–840

Rosenthal S, Strange W (2004) Evidence on the nature and sources of agglomeration economies. In: Henderson JV, Thisse JF (eds) Handbook of regional and urban economics, vol 4. Elsevier, Amsterdam, pp 2119–2171

Shioji E (2001) Public capital and economic growth: a convergence approach. J Econ Growth 6 (3):205–227

Tsekeris T, Papaioannou S (2017) Regional determinants of technical efficiency: evidence from the Greek economy. Reg Stud 52(10):1398–1409

Tsukamoto T (2019) A spatial autoregressive stochastic frontier model for panel data incorporating a model of technical inefficiency. Jpn World Econ 50:66–77

Yamano N, Ohkawara T (2000) The regional allocation of public investment: efficiency or equity? J Reg Sci 40:205–229

Part II
Inter-regional Network Economies

Chapter 5
Inter-regional Networks and Productivity Dynamics

Abstract For the society of population decline, improving productivity is crucial for achieving regional sustainability. This chapter presents the concept of inter-regional network economies as a new paradigm for agglomeration economies and clarifies the effect of high-speed transportation networks on total factor productivity (TFP) by using Japan's regional data. The results show that inter-regional networks contribute more to TFP growth in many regions than regional agglomeration does. The development of high-quality transportation networks has promoted the inter-regional flow of economic agents. By increasing opportunities for interaction, these inter-regional flows increase knowledge spillovers between regions. That is, connecting cities through high-quality transportation networks and strengthening their connections with each other will lead to significant spillover from agglomeration economies, previously restricted to cities, to other regions. The results of this chapter confirm that high-quality transportation networks spread the economic benefits of agglomeration across a broader area through the effect of borrowed size. It can be concluded that measures for the development of high-quality transportation networks are essential for regional sustainability in the sense of expanding geographical externalities.

Keywords Agglomeration economies · Borrowed size · Inter-regional network · Partial adjustment model · Total factor productivity (TFP)

5.1 Introduction

Regional agglomeration is well known to improve productivity significantly. External economies, referred to as "economies of agglomeration," have been discussed by scholars for many decades (Marshall 1890). The economies of agglomeration, as described by Marshall (1890), are defined by reduced costs and improved

This chapter is based on Otsuka (2018).

A. Otsuka, *A New Driver of Regional Sustainability in Japan*, New Frontiers in Regional Science: Asian Perspectives 54,
https://doi.org/10.1007/978-981-16-3709-4_5

productivity achieved through spatial clustering among economic agents. Many empirical studies have shown that agglomeration plays a role in improving regional productivity and increasing global competitiveness (Rosenthal and Strange 2004; Combes and Gobillon 2015). In the stream of related studies, many studies have focused on region or city size to explain the improvements in productivity that accompany agglomeration. Recently, however, along with an increased emphasis on the significance of knowledge spillover for economic growth, many studies have focused on the spatial spread of agglomeration economies (Carlino and Kerr 2015).

In the agglomeration area, economic agents with diverse ideas, knowledge, and skills actively interact with each other. According to Jacobs (1969), agglomeration serves as a melting pot, in which heterogeneous groups come into contact and fuse. Agglomeration spreads knowledge by creating an environment in which a heterogeneous group of economic agents can interact. Furthermore, in instances where firms are concentrated in a specific location, agglomeration facilitates social interactions between employees from different firms. Familiarity is bred through face-to-face communication occurring at industry-wide meetings, encounters during lunch breaks, socialization during sports activities, and other opportunities for informal social interaction (McCann 2001).

We know that the importance of these interactions lies in the sharing of tacit knowledge between participants (Hippel 1994). This tacit knowledge includes information related to new products, personnel, technology, and market trends. This knowledge is spread through face-to-face communication and the transfer of highly skilled workers. Knowledge spillover frequently occurs in an environment where highly educated and skilled workers can quickly transfer from one firm to another, such as in Silicon Valley, where many small high-tech firms are concentrated. The accumulation of tacit knowledge enables firms in the agglomeration area to benefit from more significant knowledge transfers and reduced transaction costs (Polanyi 1966; Granovetter 1985; Porter 1998).

Therefore, geographic proximity allows firms to connect through the exchange of ideas, information, and knowledge in ways that facilitate research, development, and innovation (Glaeser et al. 1992; Fujita and Thisse 2002). The benefits of agglomeration include an increase in and improvement of available knowledge for all market participants through geographic proximity. Mutual exchanges of knowledge allow market participants to make more accurate and relevant predictions about the market environment, thus increasing market competitiveness. The knowledge accumulated by a firm is transmitted to other firms in a variety of forms. Through this knowledge spillover, new products and technologies are developed, and the productivity of the overall region increases.

The formation of high-quality inter-regional networks, such as high-speed transportation networks, expands the area affected by the knowledge spillover that occurs in an agglomerated area. For example, upgrading high-speed rail and airports decreases travel costs, thereby increasing opportunities for interaction. Such networks not only directly increase the productivity of the firms that use them but also increase the productivity of surrounding firms by increasing the rate at which information is exchanged. For example, if the travel time to a highly agglomerated area can be decreased, then firms located in remote areas will be able to attend meetings or business conferences there. This, in turn, makes the collection and application of knowledge related to new products and technologies easier for such firms. These actions increase productivity not only in the agglomerated area but also in the surrounding regions. Thus, improved access to agglomeration economies increases remote firm productivity. Knowledge spillover beyond a region's boundaries through face-to-face communication represents an expansion of the geographical range of agglomeration economies. This chapter investigates the impact of inter-regional network economies as a new effect of geographical (spatial) externalities.

This chapter makes a threefold contribution to the literature. First, it is the first study to analyze the impact of inter-regional networks on TFP from the perspective of passenger transport. Although much research is being conducted on how the establishment of public infrastructure enhances agglomeration economies, previous studies have focused on the significance of highways and the inter-regional flow of goods (Lall et al. 2004; Rice et al. 2006; Graham 2007; Montolio and Solé-Ollé 2009; Holl 2012; Otsuka and Goto 2015; Stelder 2016; Melo et al. 2017). The increase in interactions between economic agents that come with passenger transport networks, such as airports and railways, both expand the scope of agglomeration economies and affect the TFP of other regions. However, to the best of our knowledge, such effects have not been fully elucidated.

Second, most of the literature that has focused on the relationship between agglomeration economies and TFP uses a static panel data model (Beeson 1987, 1990; Dekle 2002; Henderson 2003; Combes and Gobillon 2015). Panel data offer an advantage over cross-sectional data in that they include the dimension of time. This increases the number of observed values and permits changes both in the cross section and in time. However, even with panel data, dynamic effects cannot be fully captured by a static panel model. Using a dynamic panel model makes it possible to measure both short- and long-term effects (i.e., short- and long-run elasticity) on the TFP of inter-regional networks. Identifying the long-term effects allows us to evaluate the dynamic impact of inter-regional networks on TFP growth.

Third, the endogeneity problem and omitted-variable bias can be dealt with using the fixed effect instrumental variable (FE-IV) method and the dynamic panel GMM method. Most studies on agglomeration economies have adopted an analytical approach using a production function (Rosenthal and Strange 2004; Combes and Gobillon 2015). However, endogeneity and omitted variable bias are generated in such cases (Graham 2009; Graham et al. 2010). Analysis using the FE-IV and dynamic panel GMM methods can reduce the estimation bias produced due to endogeneity and omitted variables.

The structure of this chapter is as follows. Section 5.2 provides a new concept on the geographical range of agglomeration economies, particularly the relevance between the range of agglomeration economies and inter-regional networks. In Sect. 5.3, the methods and data used in the analysis are discussed, including measuring the TFP index and the determinants model of the TFP index. In Sect.

5.4, the estimation results of the model are presented and interpreted. Section 5.5 presents the conclusions and discusses the policy implications.

5.2 The Concept of Inter-regional Network Economies

In this section, we define the concept of inter-regional network economies. Relatively few studies have examined the geographical range of agglomeration economies (Parr 2002; Johansson and Quigley 2003; Phelps and Ozawa 2003; Camagni et al. 2015). The most crucial point is that there are both immobile and mobile elements in geographical externalities that are the source of agglomeration economies (Burger and Meijers 2016). The former elements, such as urban facilities, are spatially concentrated, and the externalities decrease with distance. On the other hand, the latter elements, such as human travel, are not spatially constrained and depend on the strength of the connections between cities (i.e., urban networks; Van Meeteren et al. 2016). Alonso (1973) introduced the concept of "borrowed size" to explain the dynamics of mobile elements. This concept suggests that urban growth will be realized by a small urban area that "borrows" the benefits of more significant neighborhood agglomeration. The phenomenon of borrowed size requires a view of the overall network because the availability of inter-regional networks for small cities is a prerequisite for borrowed size to occur. The traditional concept of borrowed size mixes up populations, functions, and critical mass effects of demand and supply in order to posit that in small cities, "while they retain many advantages of smaller size, such as lower levels of congestion, they enjoy advantages of larger size through their easy access to other centers. Their people can use the shopping and entertainment facilities of other cities to complement their own, their businessmen can share such facilities as warehousing and business services, and their labor markets enjoy a wider and more flexible range of demand and supply" (Alonso 1973, p. 200).

Meijes and Burger (2017) summarize the concept of borrowed size as defined by Alonso in five features. First, borrowed size is an observable and analytic concept. Second, it is a one-way process in which a small city borrows size from a neighboring large city but not the other way around. Third, not all small cities can borrow size. Alonso emphasizes the need for geographic proximity and functional interconnectedness. In order to borrow the size of a large city, a small city must be located in close proximity to the large city and form part of the same functional entity. In other words, a small city must belong to a city-region or mega-region. Fourth, small cities in mega-regions perform better than isolated small cities because they have a better balance between the benefits and costs of agglomeration. Fifth, access to the benefits of urbanization in large cities gives smaller cities an advantage. Accessibility and network connectivity are necessary for borrowed size to occur.

According to Camagni et al. (2016), the concept of borrowed size is also linked to demographic potential. Demographic potential refers to the three advantages gained by the entire regional system. The first is the advantage gained from a pooled and

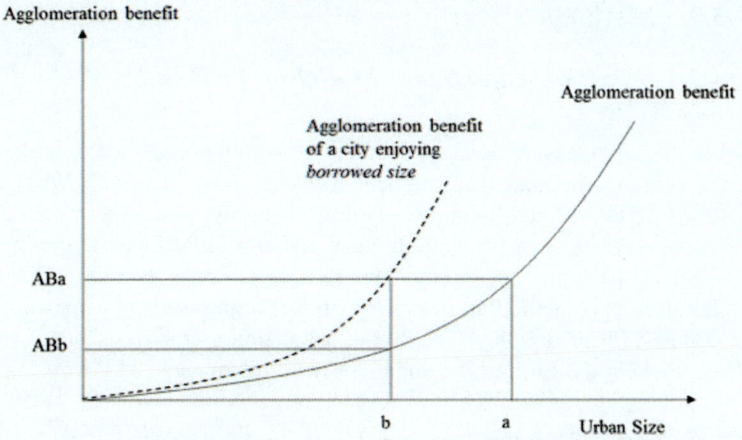

Fig. 5.1 Agglomeration economies and borrowed size. Note: The original explanation for this figure is in Camagni et al. (2016)

diversified labor supply, the second is the advantage gained from large markets for final goods and services, and the third is gaining population spillover from large cities.

Figure 5.1 shows the benefits of agglomeration for different levels of urban size. A city enjoying borrowed size obtains average benefits (*ABa*) from its size (*b*), which are typical of those of a larger city (*a*). This means that size and proximity generate spatial externalities that boost the productivity of small cities to the level of larger ones. This approach indirectly explains urban growth, and the introduction of geographical space explains small city growth (geographic proximity, and not solely the size of the urban production complex) as a source of externalities and, indirectly, of growth itself.

The formation of high-quality transportation networks connecting cities affects agglomeration and networks from two sides. The first is to strengthen the centripetal forces of the agglomeration through the reduction of transport costs. The spatial economics show that if the transport cost is reduced via transportation infrastructure improvement, the centripetal forces will be strengthened toward the threshold value (Fujita and Thisse 2002). Second, improvements in high-quality transportation networks facilitate inter-regional mobility, which strengthens urban network externalities. In other words, improvements in the transportation infrastructure expand borrowed size. These effects will enhance the productivity of urban and surrounding areas and contribute to the sustainable development of the overall regional economy. The issue requiring empirical analysis is how regional agglomeration and inter-regional networks are practically interrelated or disentangled despite their interrelatedness in theoretical frameworks. We seek to identify both factors by using an index representing the strength of inter-regional networks.

5.3 Methods

5.3.1 Partial Adjustment Model of TFP Index

For the TFP measurement, we used the measurement method described in Chap. 3—the non-parametrical measurement method of Good et al. (1997) and Aw et al. (2001). This method assumes a typical economy with an average output and input size at a certain point in time. It calculates the TFP of each economy as a disparity relative to a typical economy. The TFP of a typical economy changes over time; therefore, this method allows us to conduct a time-series comparison of TFP.

The TFP of region j ($j = 1, \cdots, N$) at time t ($t = 1, \cdots, P$) is measured using Eq. (5.1) in the form of a comparison with the average TFP level

$$\begin{aligned} ln\,TFP_{jt} &= \left(ln\,Y_{jt} - \overline{ln\,Y_t} \right) + \sum\nolimits_{s=1}^{t} \left(\overline{ln\,Y_s} - \overline{ln\,Y_{s-1}} \right) \\ &\quad - \left[\sum\nolimits_{i=1}^{n} \frac{1}{2} \left(S_{ijt} + \overline{S_{it}} \right) \left(ln\,X_{ijt} - \overline{ln\,X_{it}} \right) \right. \\ &\quad \left. + \sum\nolimits_{s=1}^{t} \sum\nolimits_{i=1}^{n} \frac{1}{2} \left(\overline{S_{is}} + \overline{S_{is-1}} \right) \left(\overline{ln\,X_{is}} - \overline{ln\,X_{is-1}} \right) \right], \end{aligned} \tag{5.1}$$

where Y_{jt} represents the output of region j at time t, X_{ijt} is the input factor i ($i = 1, \cdots, n$) for region j at time t, and S_{ijt} is the cost share of input factor i in region j at time t. The overline above each symbol expresses the inter-regional average value of each variable. Equation (5.1) shows that in addition to the comparable TFP level at a given point in time and a given region, it is possible to measure the regional TFP level by considering the TFP level change in a time series.

The underlying determinants model of the TFP index has the following logarithmic linear form:

$$\begin{aligned} ln\,TFP_{jt} &= \beta_1\, ln\,D_{jt} + \beta_2\, ln\,ACC_{jt} + \beta_3\, ln\,G_{jt} + \beta_4\, ln\,MR_{jt} + \beta_5\, ln\,SR_{jt} + \alpha_j \\ &\quad + u_{jt}. \end{aligned} \tag{5.2}$$

Note that all the variables in Eq. (5.2) are expressed logarithmically. D is population density, ACC is the index of inter-regional networks, G is social overhead capital, MR is the manufacturing industry ratio, SR is the service industry ratio, and u is an error term. This model is an extension of the model used in Chap. 4.

Both α and β are the estimated coefficients. Because panel data are used, α represents the individual effect, which controls for the regional characteristics that cannot be expressed by explanatory variables. The increase in population density improves TFP; thus, β_1 is expected to have a positive sign. The improvement of inter-regional networks and social overhead capital enhances TFP; thus, β_2 and β_3 are also expected to have a positive sign. Japan's manufacturing industry has high productivity, while the service industry has low productivity.[1] Therefore, the sign of β_4 will be positive, whereas the sign of $\boldsymbol{\beta}_5$ will be negative.

Two essential identification issues must be considered in the estimation of Eq. (5.2): the potential endogeneity problem for agglomeration and the reverse causality between agglomeration and productivity.[2] These concerns can be addressed using a fixed-effects (FE) model and an instrumental variable (IV) method. The IV method has often been used in previous studies (Ciccone and Hall 1996; Ciccone 2002; Rice et al. 2006; Rosenthal and Strange 2008; Glaeser and Gottlieb 2009; Combes and Gobillon 2015). Furthermore, these concerns can be mitigated using the TFP index approach (Otsuka and Goto 2015). Therefore, we estimate a regular fixed-effects model as well as a TFP determinant model using an instrumental variable and verify the estimation results of the model.

One controversial issue with Eq. (5.2) is the assumption that TFP immediately reflects changes in socioeconomic variables. It seems plausible that the effects of inter-regional networks and social overhead capital development appear with a time delay due to the time lag for firms' location decisions and relocation costs. That is, a more realistic setting is that TFP is affected by changes in socioeconomic variables, such as inter-regional networks and social overhead capital, with a specific time lag. Therefore, this study considers the determinants of TFP with a time lag by using a partial adjustment model as the second model.

Let y^*_{jt} represent the desirable TFP level in region j at time t. We assume that this desirable level of TFP is a function of an independent variable represented by the vector $\boldsymbol{x}_{jt}$. The following equation expresses this relationship:

$$y^*_{jt} = \boldsymbol{\beta}' \boldsymbol{X}_{jt} + \varepsilon_{it}, \tag{5.3}$$

where the error term $\boldsymbol{\varepsilon}_{jt} = \boldsymbol{\alpha}_j + \boldsymbol{u}_{jt}$ includes the region's individual effect $\boldsymbol{\alpha}$. The adjustment process follows a partial adjustment model that relates the actual TFP $\boldsymbol{y}_{jt}$ to the desired level of TFP y^*_{jt}:

$$y_{jt} - y_{jt-1} = (1 - \boldsymbol{\lambda})\left(y^*_{jt} - y_{jt-1}\right), \tag{5.4}$$

where λ is a measurement of the adjustment from the actual level of TFP to the desirable level of TFP.

The following equation is obtained by combining Eqs. (5.3) and (5.4):

[1] See Table 2.7 in Chap. 2 for the relationship between industry ratio and regional economic performance.

[2] See Sect. 3.3 in Chap. 7 for further discussions on the estimation concerns of agglomeration economies.

$$y_{jt} = \widehat{\boldsymbol{\beta}}' \boldsymbol{X}_{jt} + \lambda y_{jt-1} + \widehat{\varepsilon}_{jt}, \tag{5.5}$$

where $\widehat{\boldsymbol{\beta}} = (1 - \lambda)\boldsymbol{\beta}$ is the effect (short-run elasticity) that a short-run change in x has on y, and $\widehat{\boldsymbol{\beta}}/(1 - \lambda)$ is the effect (long-run elasticity) that a long-run change in x has on y. The error term is $\widehat{\boldsymbol{\varepsilon}} = (1 - \lambda)\boldsymbol{\varepsilon}$.

The partial adjustment model in Eq. (5.5) contains a lagged dependent variable in the regressors. The presence of such a variable is endogenous to the fixed effects in the error term, which creates dynamic panel bias (Cameron and Trivedi 2009). Dynamic panel bias reduces the reliability of long-run elasticities as it makes the coefficient of a lagged dependent variable biased. To address this concern, Arellano and Bond (1991) proposed a generalized method of moments for dynamic panel estimates that are consistent under these conditions. Therefore, we used this dynamic panel estimation method to estimate the parameters of Eq. (5.5) as the second model.

5.3.2 Data

This study uses panel data pooled from 47 prefectures covering 1980 to 2010. In the measurement of the TFP index, the dataset on output and input was used in Chap. 3. Population density (D), the index of inter-regional networks (ACC), social overhead capital (G), the manufacturing industry ratio (MR), and the services industry ratio (SR) are used as determinants of the TFP index.

Population density (D) is the ratio of the population to the residential area. Population density is a proxy variable used to evaluate the size of agglomeration economies within the regions.[3] The population data were obtained from the *Basic Resident Registers* (Ministry of Internal Affairs and Communications). The residential area data were taken from the *System of Social and Demographic Statistics* (Ministry of Internal Affairs and Communications).

In the ACC index, the following general form is defined following Hansen (1959) and Camagni et al. (2016):

$$ACC_{jt} \equiv \sum\nolimits_{k \neq j} \frac{D_{kt}}{d_{jkt}},$$

where d_{jkt} represents the distance resistance (travel time) between regions j and k in period t. The travel time is obtained by calculating the weighted average of the share of the time required for air, rail, and automobile travel for all combinations of departure places and destinations. For each combination, the shortest amount of time required to reach a destination when traveling by air, rail, or automobile is

[3] See Sect. 2.2 in Chap. 4 for discussions on the relationships between population density and agglomeration economies.

included in the calculation.[4] The characteristic of the *ACC* index is that its degree is determined by the borrowed size via agglomerations, which is combined with the travel cost (travel time) needed to access the agglomeration economies that other regions enjoy. If the agglomeration size of the other regions (D_{kt}) increases, the corresponding variable increases. Furthermore, when the travel time from one region to another region (d_{jkt}) decreases, the value of *ACC* increases. That is, the borrowed size is considered to increase with the improvement in inter-regional networks.

Social overhead capital (G) is used to identify the effect of public infrastructure on regional productivity. The data on social overhead capital comes from the estimates of the Central Research Institute of the Electric Power Industry.[5] The manufacturing and services industry ratios (*MR* and *SR*) were introduced to control for the regional industrial structure. Ratios for the manufacturing and service industries are obtained by dividing their respective production values by the total prefectural production value. In both cases, data from the *Annual Report on Prefectural Accounts* (Cabinet Office) were used.

Figures 5.2, 5.3, and 5.4 illustrate the relationship between TFP (vertical axis) and population density, the *ACC* index, and social overhead capital (horizontal axes). Each figure shows the values for each prefecture in 2010. As indicated by the upward-sloping scatterplots from bottom left to top right, population density, the *ACC* index, and social overhead capital have positive correlations with TFP. In other words, the higher a region's population density, the higher its TFP, and the higher a region's inter-regional networks, the higher its TFP. Furthermore, the higher a region's public infrastructure, the higher its TFP. These positive relationships appear to be stable.

5.4 Results and Discussion

Table 5.1 shows the estimation results of Eq. (5.2). Models A and B show the estimation results of the regular fixed-effects (FE) model, whereas Models C and D show the estimation results of the fixed-effects model estimated using the FE-IV method. Based on the results of an F-test conducted to verify the existence or nonexistence of individual effects, a null hypothesis stating that individual effects did not exist is rejected at a significance level of 1%. In a Hausman test on a null hypothesis stating that the individual effects were random, the null hypothesis was rejected at a significance level of 1%. Accordingly, the estimation results shown in Table 5.1 are from the fixed-effects model.

The results in Table 5.1 show that agglomeration economies, expressed by population density, generate high TFP values. As the explanatory and dependent variables are both logarithmic values, the parameters express elasticity. The

[4]See MLIT (2017) for further details.

[5]See Chap. 4 for detail on social overhead capital data.

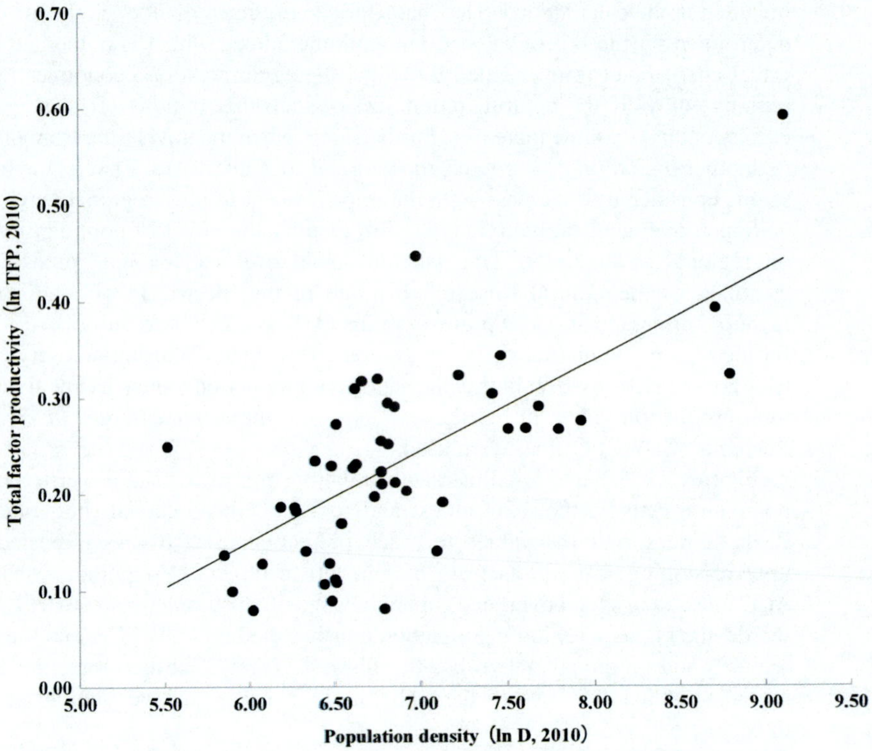

Fig. 5.2 Static relationship between TFP and population density in 2010

estimated values of the parameters (elasticity) signify the magnitude of the effect of the explanatory variable on the dependent variable. The table indicates that the effect of population density is more substantial than those of other variables. A 1% increase in population density leads to a 0.3% increase in TFP, while the effects of social overhead capital and inter-regional networks are minor. Regarding industrial structure, the results show that TFP increases along with the concentration of the manufacturing industry and decreases along with the concentration of the service industry.

To ensure that the estimation is credible and robust, endogeneity concerns about the variables of external economies must be addressed. Therefore, we refer to the results estimated by the IV method using Models C and D. We can confirm that the estimated parameters are almost the same as those in the fixed-effects model. Therefore, even if endogeneity is produced, the estimation bias is likely to be small.

Next, we consider the estimation results of Eq. (5.5), which considers dynamic changes in TFP. Table 5.2 shows the results of the dynamic panel GMM estimates performed using Eq. (5.5). In the dynamic panel GMM estimates, a variable (G) on social overhead capital is excluded from the explanatory variables because changes in social overhead capital are mutually correlated with changes in inter-regional

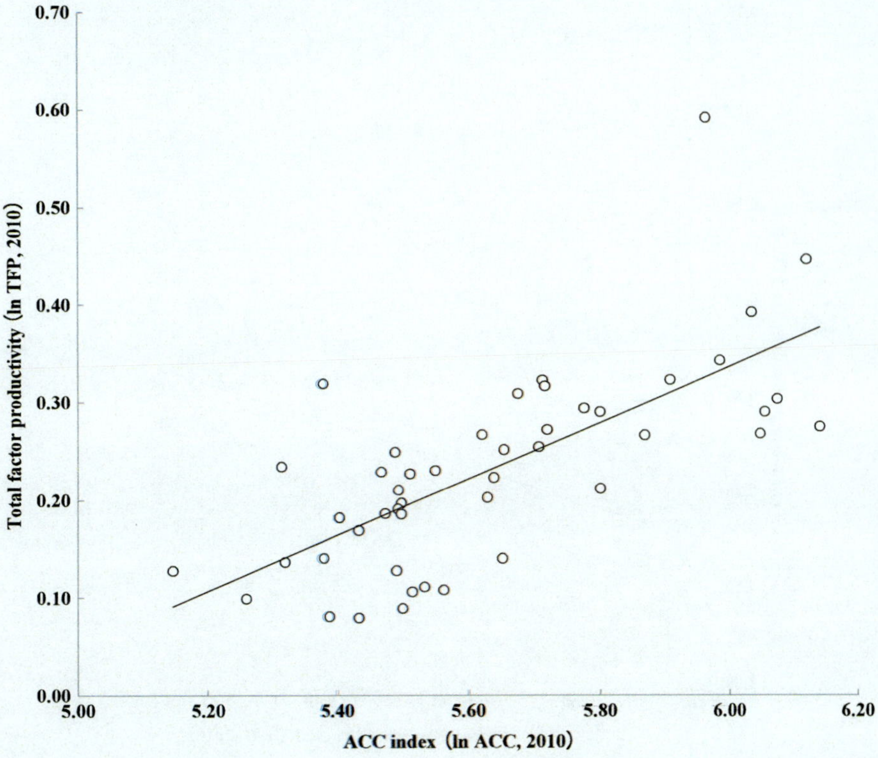

Fig. 5.3 Static relationship between TFP and ACC index in 2010

networks. Social overhead capital includes transportation infrastructure, such as harbors, airports, and railways. When investments are made in transportation infrastructure, an increase in both social overhead capital and ACC is observed because ACC increases because of the reduced time distance between regions (the correlation coefficient between ΔG and ΔACC is 0.5). Therefore, to avoid multiple collinearities, the variables for social overhead capital were excluded from the estimation model below.

Dynamic panel GMM estimation is performed by using instrumental variables, which are both the available lags of the dependent variable from the second period and the independent variables. Since the dynamic panel GMM estimation is applied, we employ the Sargan-Hansen test to check for overidentifying restrictions (Hayashi 2000). Under the null hypothesis that all instruments are valid, it can be shown that the test statistics have an asymptotic chi-squared distribution with degrees of freedom equal to the number of overidentifying restrictions. The null hypothesis is not rejected in all models, so the models are valid.

The second step of the dynamic panel GMM estimation is to test whether the error terms are serially correlated. The GMM estimator requires that the null of no serial

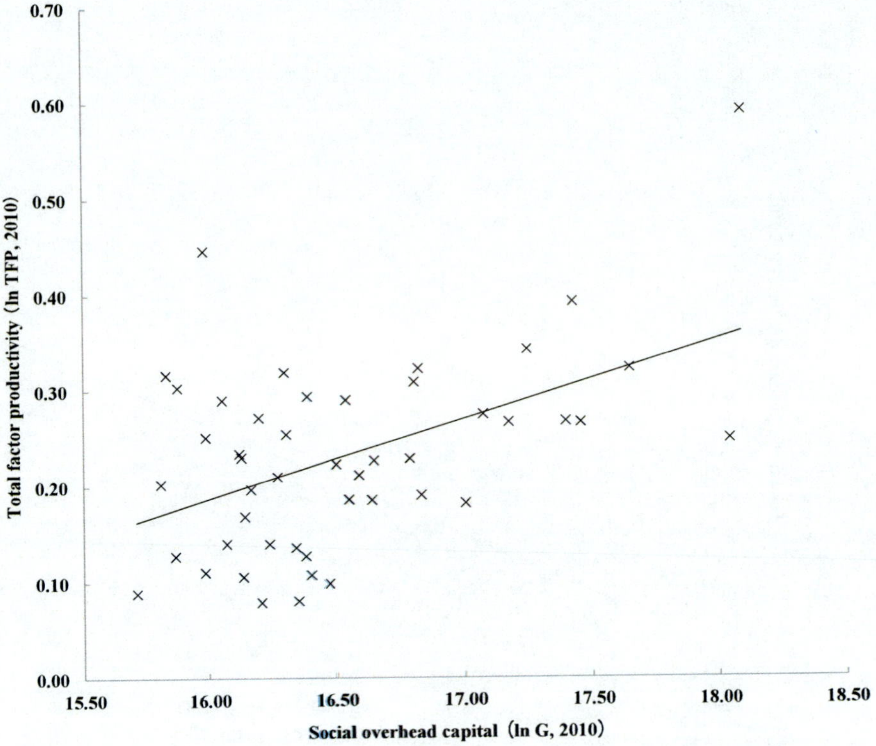

Fig. 5.4 Static relationship between TFP and social overhead capital in 2010

correlation for the first-order serial correlation be rejected but not the null hypothesis for the second-order serial correlation (Baltagi 2013). The m-statistics in Table 5.2 test the first- and second-order serial correlations.[6] All the models in Table 5.2 are appropriate because the null hypothesis is rejected for the first-order serial correlation and cannot be rejected for the second-order correlation.

On the estimated parameters, it is clear that population density has a significant effect on TFP growth. The *ACC* index also showed a significant effect. The short- and long-run elasticities can be calculated from these estimated parameters. While

[6]For models estimated by GMM, we can compute the first- and second-order serial correlation statistics proposed by Arellano and Bond (1991) as one method of testing for serial correlation. The test actually returns two separate statistics: one for the first-order correlation and one for the second-order correlation. If the innovations are independently and identically distributed (i.i.d.), we expect the first-order statistic to be significant (with a negative autocorrelation coefficient) and the second-order statistic to be insignificant. The m-statistics are calculated as

$m_j = \frac{\rho_j}{\sqrt{VAR(\rho_j)}}, \rho_j = \frac{1}{T-3-j}\sum_{t=4+j}^{T} \rho_{jt}$, and $\rho_{jt} = E(\Delta\varepsilon_{i,t}, \Delta\varepsilon_{i,t-j})$,where ρ_j is the average j^{th} order auto-covariance.

Table 5.1 Panel estimation results

Regressors	FE Model A		FE Model B		FE-IV Model C		FE-IV Model D	
Constant	−5.683	**	−1.917	**	−5.771	**	−1.776	**
	(0.260)		(0.459)		(0.293)		(0.490)	
ln *D*	0.342	**	0.306	**	0.336	**	0.273	**
	(0.036)		(0.036)		(0.040)		(0.040)	
ln *ACC*	0.222	**	0.092	**	0.222	**	0.099	**
	(0.021)		(0.023)		(0.022)		(0.024)	
ln *G*	0.196	**	0.030		0.203	**	0.026	
	(0.007)		(0.020)		(0.007)		(0.021)	
ln *MR*	0.036	**	0.040	**	0.029	*	0.041	**
	(0.009)		(0.009)		(0.011)		(0.011)	
ln *SR*	−0.332	**	−0.369	**	−0.318	**	−0.336	**
	(0.020)		(0.024)		(0.023)		(0.027)	
Number of observations	1457		1457		1410		1410	
Adjusted R-squared	0.920		0.931		0.925		0.935	
F-statistic	331.24	**	244.17	**	315.88	**	230.88	**
Hausman test	263.48	**	65.28	**	221.30	**	36.13	**
Time effect	Excluded		Included		Excluded		Included	

Notes: (1) FE = fixed-effects model; FE-IV = fixed-effects model using the instrumental variable method
(2) ** and * indicate significance at the 1% and 5% levels, respectively
(3) The values in parentheses indicate standard errors
(4) One-period lag of the explanatory variable is used as the instrumental variable

changes in population density have a 0.1–0.2% effect on TFP growth in the short term, this effect becomes more prominent, at 0.7–0.9%, in the long term. Similarly, although the *ACC* index has an effect of only 0.1% in the short term, this effect increases to between 0.5% and 0.6% in the long term. Hence, the effects of inter-regional interactions facilitated by the construction of high-quality transportation networks are more significant in the long term than in the short term.

In summary, the results indicate that regional agglomeration and inter-regional networks have significant effects. In a combined model that relies on both static and dynamic models, no significant differences were observed in the signs of estimated parameters related to population density and inter-regional networks. These results suggest that the enhancement of regional agglomeration and the formation of high-quality transportation networks are drivers of increased TFP.

Finally, we clarify the extent to which the TFP determinants contribute to improvements in regional TFP. Under long-run equilibrium, the actual TFP y_{jt} equals the desirable TFP y^*_{jt}. In other words, $y^*_{jt} = y_{jt} = y_{jt-1}$. This relationship can be used to express Eq. (5.5) as the difference formula:

Table 5.2 Dynamic panel estimation results

Regressors	Dynamic panel GMM			
	Model E		Model F	
Δ ln *TFP* (*t* − 1)	0.784	**	0.726	**
	(0.023)		(0.020)	
Δ ln *D*	0.151	**	0.244	**
	(0.025)		(0.045)	
Δ ln *ACC*	0.133	**	0.131	**
	(0.020)		0.027	
Δ ln *MR*	0.040	**	0.062	**
	(0.007)		(0.009)	
Δ ln *SR*	−0.162	**	−0.112	**
	(0.018)		(0.019)	
Number of observations	1363		1363	
J-statistic	44.451		41.886	
Probability (J-statistic)	0.369		0.476	
m-statistic (AR(1))	−2.909	**	−1.808	*
m-statistic (AR(2))	1.166		1.657	
Instrumental variable	*EI (t-2)*		*EI (t-2)* *D (t-1)*	

Notes: (1) Estimates are a two-step dynamic generalized method of moments estimates
(2) ** and * indicate significance at the 1% and 5% levels, respectively
(3) The values in parentheses indicate standard errors
(4) The J-statistic is the Sargan-Hansen test (a test of exogeneity) for the instrumental variable
(5) The m-statistics are the Arellano-Bond test for first- and second-order serial correlation

$$\Delta y_{jt} = \frac{\widetilde{\boldsymbol{\beta}}}{1-\lambda}\Delta \boldsymbol{X}_{jt} + \Delta\varepsilon_{jt}. \tag{5.6}$$

We applied the estimated coefficients to Eq. (5.5) from model E in Table 5.2. to Eq. (5.6), from which we calculate each explanatory variable's contribution (annual average percentage) to changes in regional TFP.

The results are presented in Table 5.3. The region with the highest TFP growth is Hokuriku, followed by North Kanto and Chubu. The region with the lowest TFP growth is Okinawa, which shows hardly any growth. The contribution of inter-regional networks to TFP growth is more significant than the contribution of population density in every region. It is most significant in regions such as Hokkaido, Shikoku, Kyushu, and North Kanto, where it explains most of the TFP growth, at approximately 0.5–0.7%. The upgrading of high-quality transportation infrastructure in local areas facilitates access from one region to another, thus enhancing TFP growth in the local area. Conversely, the contribution of regional agglomeration within regions is small in every region. However, agglomeration

Table 5.3 Contributions of each factor to changes in TFP (1980–2010; annual average; %)

Rate of change of TFP (Δ ln *TFP* = a + b + c + d + e)						
	Δ ln *TFP*	Population density	*ACC* index	Manufacturing industry ratio	Services industry ratio	Other
	(Total)	(a)	(b)	(c)	(d)	(e)
Hokkaido	0.612	−0.127	0.635	−0.244	0.014	0.334
Tohoku	0.669	−0.180	0.465	0.138	−0.101	0.347
North Kanto	0.966	0.142	0.475	0.155	−0.156	0.349
Greater Tokyo Area	0.789	0.491	0.359	−0.311	−0.117	0.367
Chubu	0.924	0.104	0.418	0.168	0.123	0.111
Hokuriku	1.111	0.012	0.291	0.129	0.037	0.642
Kansai	0.855	0.126	0.414	−0.124	−0.210	0.649
Chugoku	0.712	−0.088	0.374	−0.016	−0.017	0.461
Shikoku	0.879	−0.082	0.698	−0.091	−0.165	0.518
Kyushu	0.665	0.021	0.529	0.175	0.029	−0.089
Okinawa	0.025	0.184	0.339	−0.473	−0.523	0.497
National average	0.746	0.055	0.454	−0.045	−0.099	0.381

Notes: (1) The values in the table are calculated by applying the estimation results of Model E (Table 5.2) to Eq. (5.6)
(2) See Fig. 1.2 in Chap. 1 for the regional classification

economies are considerably more significant in the Greater Tokyo Area than in any other region. This is due to the migration from more local areas to the Greater Tokyo Area, which led to a high population concentration there and, in turn, to more substantial agglomeration externalities.

The impact of each determinant on TFP growth can be evaluated from the respective sizes of the contribution values on population density and the *ACC* index. In other words, while the effect on TFP growth caused by regional agglomeration itself is significant for the Greater Tokyo Area, it is small for the other regions. This implies that the centripetal forces outside of the Greater Tokyo Area are weak. On the other hand, the significant effect of inter-regional networks indicates that being able to access the agglomerated areas of other regions has a significant effect on TFP growth. This reflects the inter-regional spillover effect of agglomeration. It is thus concluded that high-quality transportation networks expand the geographical scope of economic activities and that spatial externalities mutually interact across regional boundaries.

5.5 Conclusions

This chapter evaluated inter-regional network economies in 47 Japanese prefectures using a TFP index. The analysis focuses on how inter-regional networks, regional agglomeration, social overhead capital, and industry structure affect TFP as external economies. The results show that developing high-quality inter-regional networks is an essential policy measure for increasing regional TFP. The results also highlight the significance of regional agglomeration and spatial concentration in the manufacturing industry.

Our quantitative comparison shows that inter-regional networks contribute more to TFP growth in many regions than regional agglomeration does. The development of high-quality transportation networks has promoted the inter-regional flow of economic agents. By increasing opportunities for interaction, these inter-regional flows increase knowledge spillovers between regions. Meanwhile, the regional agglomeration has a more significant effect than inter-regional networks only in the Greater Tokyo Area. The economic performance of the Greater Tokyo Area was significantly affected by agglomeration. Therefore, it is concluded that economic growth in the Greater Tokyo Area is compatible with population inflow.

As mentioned in Chap. 1, Japanese government policy aims to spur innovation and achieve sustainability. This can be accomplished by increasing the number of opportunities for face-to-face communication and by reducing the travel time between regions, thus expanding the geographical area of interaction of economic agents. In other words, connecting cities through high-quality transportation networks and strengthening their connections with each other will lead to significant spillover from agglomeration economies, previously restricted to cities, to other regions. The results of this chapter confirm that high-quality transportation networks spread the economic benefits of agglomeration across a broader area through the effect of borrowed size. The development of high-quality transportation networks fosters economic growth by increasing regional productivity. Such measures are essential for regional sustainability.

Regional disparities in Japan have been decreasing over the long term. Chap. 2 shows that public infrastructure (i.e., inter-regional networks) is one potential factor that can affect regional disparities. Therefore, our subsequent research agenda is to clarify the impact of inter-regional networks on regional disparities and provide more precise guidance for regional policies. Chap. 6 focuses on the relationship between inter-regional networks and regional disparities.

References

Alonso W (1973) Urban zero population growth. Daedalus 102(4):191–206

Arellano M, Bond SR (1991) Some tests of specification for panel data: Monte Carlo evidence and an application to employment equations. Rev Econ Stud 58(2):277–297

Aw BY, Chen X, Roberts MJ (2001) Firm-level evidence on productivity differentials and turnover in Taiwanese manufacturing. J Dev Econ 66(1):51–86

Baltagi BH (2013) Econometric analysis of panel data, 4th edn. John Wiley and Sons Ltd, Chichester

Beeson PE (1987) Total factor productivity growth and agglomeration economies in manufacturing, 1959–73. J Reg Sci 27(2):183–199

Beeson PE (1990) Sources of the decline of manufacturing in large metropolitan areas. J Urban Econ 28(1):71–86

Burger MJ, Meijers EJ (2016) Agglomerations and the rise of urban network externalities. Pap Reg Sci 95(1):5–15

Camagni R, Capello R, Caragliu A (2015) The rise of second-rank cities: what role for agglomeration economies? Eur Plan Stud 23(6):1069–1089

Camagni R, Capello R, Caragliu A (2016) Static vs. dynamic agglomeration economies. Spatial context and structural evolution behind urban growth. Pap Reg Sci 95(1):133–158

Cameron CA, Trivedi PK (2009) Microeconometrics using Stata. Stata Press, College Station, Texas

Carlino G, Kerr WR (2015) Agglomeration and innovation. In: Duranton G, Henderson JV, Strange W (eds) Handbook of regional and urban economics, vol 5A. Elsevier, Amsterdam, pp 349–404

Ciccone A (2002) Agglomeration effects in Europe. Eur Econ Rev 46(2):213–227

Ciccone A, Hall R (1996) Productivity and the density of economic activity. Am Econ Rev 86 (1):54–70

Combes PP, Gobillon L (2015) The empirics of agglomeration economies. In: Duranton G, Henderson JV, Strange W (eds) Handbook of regional and urban economics, vol 5A. Elsevier, Amsterdam, pp 247–348

Dekle R (2002) Industrial concentration and regional growth: evidence from the prefectures. Rev Econ Statistics 84(2):310–315

Fujita M, Thisse J (2002) The economics of agglomeration: cities, industrial location and regional growth. Cambridge University Press, Cambridge

Glaeser EL, Gottlieb JD (2009) The wealth of cities: agglomeration economies and spatial equilibrium in the United States. J Econ Lit 47(4):983–1028

Glaeser EL, Kallal HD, Scheinkman JA, Shleifer A (1992) Growth in cities. J Polit Econ 100 (6):1126–1152

Good DH, Nadiri MI, Sickles RC (1997) Index number and factor demand approaches to the estimation of productivity. In: Pesaran MH, Schmidt P (eds) Handbook of applied econometrics: microeconometrics, Wiley-Blackwell, vol II. Malden, MA, pp 14–80

Graham DJ (2007) Variable returns to urbanization and the effect of road traffic congestion. J Urban Econ 62(1):103–120

Graham DJ (2009) Identifying urbanization and localization externalities in manufacturing and service industries. Pap Reg Sci 88(1):63–84

Graham DJ, Melo PS, Jiwattamalilpaisarn P, Noland PB (2010) Testing for causality between productivity and agglomeration economies. J Reg Sci 50(5):935–951

Granovetter MS (1985) Economic action and social structure: the problem of embeddedness. Am J Sociol 91(3):481–510

Hansen WG (1959) How accessibility shapes land use. J Am Inst Plan 25:73–76

Hayashi F (2000) Econometrics. Princeton University Press, Princeton

Henderson JV (2003) Marshall's scale economies. J Urban Econ 53(1):1–28

Hippel EV (1994) Sticky information and the locus of problem solving: implications for innovation. Manag Sci 40(4):429–548

Holl A (2012) Market potential and firm-level productivity in Spain. J Econ Geogr 12 (6):1191–1215

Jacobs J (1969) The economy of cities. Vintage Books, New York

Johansson B, Quigley JM (2003) Agglomeration and networks in spatial economies. Pap Reg Sci 83(1):165–176

Lall SV, Shalizi Z, Deichmann U (2004) Agglomeration economies and productivity in Indian industry. J Dev Econ 73(2):643–673

Marshall A (1890) Principles of economics. Macmillan, London

McCann P (2001) Urban and regional economics. Oxford University Press, Gosport, Hampshire

Meijes EJ, Burger MJ (2017) Stretching the concept of 'borrowed size. Urban Stud 54(1):269–291

Melo PS, Graham DJ, Levinson D, Aarabi S (2017) Agglomeration, inter-regional networks and productivity: evidence for large metropolitan areas in the US. Urban Stud 54(1):179–195

MLIT (2017) The development of land policy simulation model, FY2017 edn. Ministry of Land, Infrastructure, Transport and Tourism, Tokyo. http://www.mlit.go.jp/kokudoseisaku/kokudoseisaku_tk3_000085.html. Accessed January 2021

Montolio D, Solé-Ollé A (2009) Road investment and regional productivity growth: the effects of vehicle intensity and congestion. Pap Reg Sci 88(1):99–118

Otsuka A (2018) Dynamics of agglomeration, accessibility, and total factor productivity: evidence from Japanese regions. Econ Innov New Technol 27(7):611–627

Otsuka A, Goto M (2015) Agglomeration economies in Japanese industries: the Solow residual approach. Ann Reg Sci 54(2):401–416

Parr JB (2002) Agglomeration economies: ambiguities and confusions. Environ Plann A 34 (4):717–732

Phelps NA, Ozawa T (2003) Contrasts in agglomeration: proto-industrial, industrial and post-industrial forms compared. Prog Hum Geog 27(5):583–604

Polanyi M (1966) The tacit dimension. Garden City, New York

Porter ME (1998) On competition. Harvard Business School Press, Boston

Rice P, Venables AJ, Patacchini E (2006) Spatial determinants of productivity: analysis for the regions of Great Britain. Reg Sci Urban Econ 36(6):727–752

Rosenthal S, Strange W (2004) Evidence on the nature and sources of agglomeration economies. In: Henderson JV, Thisse JF (eds) Handbook of regional and urban economics, vol 4. Elsevier, Amsterdam, pp 2119–2171

Rosenthal S, Strange W (2008) The attenuation of human capital spillovers. J Urban Econ 64 (2):373–389

Stelder D (2016) Regional inter-regional networks trends in Europe: road infrastructure, 1957–2012. Reg Stud 50(6):983–995

Van Meeteren M, Neal Z, Derudder B (2016) Disentangling agglomeration and network externalities: a conceptual typology. Pap Reg Sci 95(1):61–81

Chapter 6
Inter-regional Networks and Regional Disparities

Abstract This chapter analyzes the relationship between inter-regional network economies and regional disparities using stochastic frontier analysis. The current dynamics in Japan's regional economic systems reveal a monocentric concentration in the Greater Tokyo Area. When the lock-in effect of agglomeration occurs, economic disparities between large metropolitan areas and local areas should expand. However, in Japan, regional disparities have not increased. Instead, economic performance in local areas has improved, and economic disparities between large metropolitan areas and local areas are narrowing. Therefore, Japan's situation requires an explanation that goes beyond conventional agglomeration theory. This chapter shows that inter-regional networks enhance the effectiveness of borrowed size and repair the lost links between regional economic systems and agglomeration theory. The chapter reveals that the borrowed size effect has significantly improved production efficiency in local areas in Japan. The impact of the borrowed size effect is greater than the agglomeration benefit derived from the local size. The results also show that the development of high-quality transportation networks has enabled local areas to catch up to large metropolitan areas and reduce regional disparities. This suggests that the establishment of high-quality inter-regional networks is a significant policy measure to help reduce regional disparities in Japan's economy.

Keywords Agglomeration economies · Borrowed size · Inter-regional network · Productive efficiency · Regional disparities · Stochastic frontier analysis (SFA)

6.1 Introduction

Agglomeration, the spatial concentration of economic agents, enhances economic performance and contributes to cumulative economic growth. The economies of agglomeration have been explained in terms of three elements: sharing, matching,

This chapter is based on Otsuka (2020).

A. Otsuka, *A New Driver of Regional Sustainability in Japan*, New Frontiers in Regional Science: Asian Perspectives 54,
https://doi.org/10.1007/978-981-16-3709-4_6

and learning (Fujita and Thisse 2002). Theories on agglomeration predict cumulative, endogenous, and largely selective growth at the expense of local (peripheral) areas. When the lock-in effect of agglomeration occurs, economic disparities between large metropolitan areas and local areas should expand. In Japan, however, regional disparities have not increased even though the monocentric concentration in the Greater Tokyo Area has accelerated since the mid-1990s.[1] Instead, economic performance in local areas has improved, and economic disparities between large metropolitan areas and local areas are narrowing. Conventional theory cannot satisfactorily explain these realities.

One potential explanation is the geographical scope of the agglomeration economies. High-quality and high-speed transportation networks have been developed nationwide in Japan, with Tokyo serving as the network hub. The formation of high-quality inter-regional networks through investments in transportation infrastructure has expanded the geographical scope of innovation and knowledge spillovers. The development of high-speed railways and airports reduces travel time costs and increases opportunities for face-to-face contact. Advances in transportation infrastructure improve productivity not only for firms located in agglomeration areas but also for remote firms by increasing the frequency of information exchange. Remote firms can improve their production ability by quickly accessing massive agglomerations. The knowledge spillover that occurs beyond the region suggests that the geographical scope of agglomeration economies is expanding. These phenomena of the expanding geographic coverage of agglomeration have been identified in many countries (Lall et al. 2004; Rice et al. 2006; Graham 2007; Montolio and Solé-Ollé 2009; Holl 2012; Stelder 2016; Melo et al. 2017). However, research on Japan is lacking.

This chapter analyzes the impact of inter-regional networks on productive efficiency in Japan and examines the impact of inter-regional networks on regional disparities. As described in Chap. 2, large metropolitan areas in Japan strengthen centripetal forces and enjoy agglomeration economies. In contrast, in many local areas outside large metropolitan areas, the population is declining, and centripetal forces are weakening. However, local areas have succeeded in shortening the travel time to large metropolitan areas through high-quality transportation networks and have achieved economic growth by "borrowing" agglomeration economies (see Chap. 5). This chapter contributes to the literature by providing new findings on whether regional disparities have narrowed due to the ability of local areas to borrow the agglomeration economies of large metropolitan areas.

In this chapter, we focus on the differences in inter-regional network externalities between industries. In regional economies, the manufacturing industry has traditionally been regarded as the basic (export) industry, and the non-manufacturing industry has been regarded as a nonbasic industry (McCann 2001). A relatively large number of transactions occur outside the region in the manufacturing industry (which is the export industry); product planning, development, procurement, and

[1]See Chap. 2 for detailed discussions on Japan's regional economic structure.

delivery cycles are likely to occur across regions. However, since the non-manufacturing industry is centered on the local service sector, economic activity across regions may be less frequent than it is in the manufacturing industry. We clarify whether the inter-regional network externalities in the manufacturing industry outweigh those in the non-manufacturing industry.

Furthermore, the analysis in this chapter has important policy implications for Japan. Japan's national land plan aims to make cities more compact and to strengthen inter-regional networks in order to counter the economic shrinkage caused by population decline.[2] The Japanese government aims to achieve sustainable growth by forming a "super-mega-region" in which several large metropolitan areas integrate into a single economic zone and by using the significant agglomeration externalities generated there. However, there is no empirical evidence supporting this government policy. Therefore, we provide valuable insights into the validity of government policies on inter-regional networking.

The remainder of this chapter is structured as follows. In Sect. 6.2, we revisit the concept of borrowed size as an extension of Chap. 5. Section 6.3 describes the study's framework for empirical analysis. Section 6.4 presents and discusses empirical evidence. Finally, Section 6.5 concludes the chapter.

6.2 Theoretical Background: A Revisiting

The current theory on agglomeration posits that diversity, economies of scale, and transport costs are the primary factors shaping urban functions and spatial organizations (Fujita and Thisse 2002). The urban scale is characterized by high efficiency, and higher efficiency is considered to lead to higher growth. However, the conventional theory on agglomeration cannot explain the reality that the growth of local areas exceeds that of large metropolitan areas and that they are catching up in terms of economic performance. The city network theory solves this contradiction by proposing that cities can borrow the functions of other cities, not only because of their physical proximity to them but also because of their horizontal and nonhierarchical relationships, known as "urban network externalities" (Camagni 1993; Capello 2000; Camagni and Capello 2004; Boix and Trullen 2007). This concept has been demonstrated in many studies (Camagni 1993; Hall and Pain 2006; Boix and Trullen 2007).

The starting point for this concept is a theory developed based on Alonso's concept of "borrowed size" (Burger et al. 2015; Meijers et al. 2016). As described in Chap. 5, the concept of borrowed size mixes demographics, functionality, and critical mass effects for demand and supply. In small cities, "people can use the shopping and entertainment facilities of other cities to complement their own, businessmen can share such facilities as warehousing and business services, and

[2]See Appendix in Chap. 1 for Japan's national land plan.

labor markets enjoy a wider and more flexible range of demand and supply" (Alonso 1973, p. 200). The theory posits that small cities can borrow some of the benefits of agglomeration while avoiding congestion. This approach underscores the fact that the agglomeration economies of cities are not necessarily limited to their physical boundaries but may spread to surrounding areas. This can explain why local areas are more efficient than larger cities and why efficient urban structures appear in local areas. The concepts of "externality fields" (Phelps et al. 2001) and "regional externalities" (Parr 2002) have been proposed to highlight the spatial scope of the urban advantage that extends far beyond city boundaries.

The expansion of the spatial scope of urban externalities means that agglomeration economies, which have been limited to urban spaces, have expanded widely beyond the boundaries of cities. In other words, the concept of "borrowed size" may be one way to explain the development of the entire regional economy beyond cities. The theory on borrowed size overcomes one limitation of traditional geographic approaches, which assume that only cities adjacent to large cities accrue efficiency gains. The concept of borrowed size also overcomes another limitation of geographic approaches that assume that size is the only determinant of economic performance in urban and regional areas. Incorporating long-distance cooperation agreements across regional networks can improve a region's productive efficiency, even if it is a small local area.

The degree of borrowed size is usually measured by an indicator (Camagni et al. 2015, 2016),[3] which is calculated as the population of neighboring cities discounted by distance:

$$\text{borrowed size}_{\mathrm{c}} = \sum_{j=1}^{n} \frac{pop_j}{w_{c,j}}, \forall \mathrm{c} \neq \mathrm{j}, \tag{6.1}$$

where c and j are different cities, w is a distance matrix representing the spatial interdependence between all cities, and POP is the urban population. The borrowed size of cities is a function of the population and distance of neighboring cities. In other words, the more neighboring populations increase, the larger the borrowed size becomes, and the shorter the distance to large cities, the greater the borrowed size.

The borrowed size index (1) emphasizes positive urbanization economies through connectivity in networks. However, it should also be noted that network connectivity can have adverse economic effects because of competitive processes. This negative economic impact is captured by the notion of "agglomeration shadows," which is described by the new economic geography (NEG) theory. NEG models predict the shadow effects of surrounding agglomerations (Dobkins and Ioannides 2001; Fujita et al. 2018). In other words, there are positive and negative effects on the inter-regional network economies. When the positive effects outweigh the negative effects

[3]See Batty (2009) for detailed reviews on this indicator.

for a region, that region enjoys inter-regional network externalities. In this study, we evaluated the net impact of inter-regional network externalities.

6.3 Methods

6.3.1 Stochastic Frontier Analysis

We undertake a stochastic frontier analysis (SFA) to estimate the effects of regional agglomeration and inter-regional networks on productive efficiency.[4] The SFA employed in this study conforms to the stochastic frontier function conditions proposed by Aigner et al. (1977). Furthermore, we utilize the one-step approach of Battese and Coelli (1995), which simultaneously estimates the production frontier function and the productive inefficiency term's determinant. A two-step estimation method is traditionally used, in which inefficiency is first obtained by estimating the stochastic frontier function, and the value of inefficiency is subsequently regressed to the determinant. In this case, however, there is a discrepancy between the hypothesis regarding the distribution of the stochastic frontier function's inefficiency term and the hypothesis regarding the regression equation that analyzes the inefficiency determinant. Thus, consistent estimation results cannot be guaranteed using a two-step approach (Coelli 1995). The one-step approach allows us to avoid this problem. This SFA model approximates the productive efficiency level based on a non-negative error term on one side.

As a production frontier function, the translog production function is formulated as follows:

$$\begin{aligned} ln\, Y_{jt} = {} & \alpha_L\, ln\, L_{jt} + \alpha_K\, ln\, K_{jt} + \alpha_T T + \frac{1}{2}\alpha_{LL}\left(ln\, L_{jt}\right)^2 + \frac{1}{2}\alpha_{KK}\left(ln\, K_{jt}\right)^2 \\ & + \frac{1}{2}\alpha_{TT}T^2 + \alpha_{LK}\, ln\, L_{jt}\, ln\, K_{jt} + \alpha_{LT}\, ln\, L_{jt}T + \alpha_{KT}\, ln\, K_{jt}T + \alpha_j + v_{jt} \\ & - u_{jt}, \end{aligned} \tag{6.2}$$

where j is a region, t is time, Y is output, L is labor input, K is capital input, and T is the time trend variable representing technological progress. α is an estimation parameter. Fixed effects α_j are used to control for regional characteristics that cannot be captured by explanatory variables.

The error term $(v_{jt} - u_{jt})$ consists of two parts: a random error term v_{jt} and an error term on productive efficiency u_{jt}. v_{jt} follows a normal distribution $N(0, \sigma^2)$ and is assumed to be independent of u_{jt} and all explanatory variables. It is assumed that u_{jt} is a non-negative stochastic variable and follows a normal distribution, $N\left(\mu, \sigma_u^2\right)$.

[4]By using SFA, many previous studies have identified the relationship between regional agglomeration and productive efficiency for many countries (see Appendix).

Under the specifications of Eq. (6.2), the score of productive efficiency TEF_{jt} is defined as the ratio of the observed output Y_{jt} to the output y_{jt} on the production frontier as follows:

$$TEF_{jt} = Y_{jt}/y_{jt} = e^{-u_{jt}}.$$

Furthermore, the following equation explains the average μ of productive inefficiency:

$$\mu_{jt} = \delta_0 - \delta_{DEN}\, ln\, DEN_{jt} - \delta_{ACC}\, ln\, ACC_{jt}, \tag{6.3}$$

where δ is an estimation parameter. *DEN* is population density, which is defined as the population per habitable land area and represents the size of intra-regional agglomeration. The *ACC* measures the strength of inter-regional networks. These variables are used as a measure of regional agglomeration and market potential (Fritsch and Slavtchev 2011; Otsuka et al. 2010; Tsekeris and Papaioannou 2017).

Note that if the determinants improve productive efficiency, δ_{DEN} and δ_{ACC} become positive[5]; that is, the determinants work to reduce the average inefficiency μ. When the population density increases, this can have a positive effect on productive efficiency due to agglomeration economies. Strengthening inter-regional networks by investing in transportation infrastructure also increases productive efficiency. However, if an agglomeration shadow occurs, the growth of inter-regional networks may reduce productive efficiency. Therefore, the impact of inter-regional networks on productive efficiency yields both positive and negative effects.

The *ACC* index measuring the strength of the inter-regional network was calculated as follows:

$$ACC_{jt} = \sum\nolimits_{k \neq j} \left(\frac{POP_{kt} / \sum_{k \neq j} POP_{kt}}{T_{jkt}} \right), \tag{6.4}$$

where POP_{kt} is the population in region k over period t and denotes the market size. T_{jkt} is the distance resistance (travel time) to travel from region j to region k over period t. Conventional studies evaluate T based on physical distance (Hansen 1959; Camagni et al. 2016), whereas index (6.4) evaluates T by travel time for the distance.

[5]In previous studies (Otsuka et al. 2010; Fritsch and Slavtchev 2011; Tsekeris and Papaioannou 2017), the signs for population density and the *ACC* index are shown as negative because each variable reduces inefficiency. In this study, both variables are originally defined as negative for ease of understanding. Therefore, we expect the signs of δ_{DEN} and δ_{ACC} to be positive. In other words, if the signs of δ_{DEN} and δ_{ACC} are positive, as expected, the impact of each variable on productive inefficiency will be negative, and, in that sense, our setting does not contradict that of previous studies.

The travel time is obtained by calculating the weighted average of the share of the time required for air, rail, and automobile travel for all combinations of departure places and destinations. For each combination, the shortest amount of time required to reach a destination when traveling by air, rail, or automobile is included in the calculation.[6]

The distinguishing feature of the index (6.4) is that its consideration of inter-regional networks is not limited to the relative market scale of the other regions but also considers the travel time needed to access other regions. That is, this index increases as the travel time for a distance between regions decreases. If the travel time to large market regions decreases, this index increases significantly. This would mean that the market potential of this region would increase with the improvement of inter-regional networks.

Based on the model structure above, the estimated level of productive efficiency TEF_{jt} becomes a non-negative value with an upper limit of 1:

$$TEF_{jt} = E(exp(-u_{jt}) \mid v_{jt} - u_{jt}),\ 0 < TEF_{jt} \leq 1.$$

Given this relationship, the rate of change in productive efficiency is expressed by the following equation:

$$T\dot{E}F_{jt} = \delta_{DEN} D\dot{E}N_{jt} + \delta_{ACC} A\dot{C}C_{jt}, \tag{6.5}$$

where the dot over each variable represents the percentage change in that variable. Changes in productive efficiency can be decomposed into (a) changes in population density and (b) changes in inter-regional networks.

6.3.2 Convergence of Productive Efficiency

The presence or absence of convergence in productive efficiency can be verified by regressing the change rate of productive efficiency at its initial level. This can be determined by observing the regression coefficient known as the "convergence coefficient."[7] This is expressed by the following equation:

$$T\dot{E}F_{jt} = \alpha + \beta \cdot TEF_{j0} + \varepsilon_j. \tag{6.6}$$

The left side of Eq. (6.6) is the annual average rate of change in productive efficiency from the initial point at time 0 until period t. When the regression coefficient β is negative, it means that the regional disparities have been reduced; conversely, if β is positive, it means that regional disparities have increased. The size of the regression coefficient β represents the speed of convergence or divergence.

---

[6]See MLIT (2017) for further details.

[7]Fukao and Yue (2000) and Otsuka (2017) discuss the convergence coefficient in the context of regional disparities of labor productivity.

When *TEF* is represented as *e*, the regression coefficient β is represented by the regression equation, as follows:

$$\beta = \frac{\sum_j \left(e_{j0} - \bar{e_0}\right) \cdot \left(\dot{e}_j - \bar{\dot{e}}\right)}{\sum_j \left(e_{j0} - \bar{e_0}\right)^2}.$$

Because the annual average rate of change in productive efficiency is expressed by Eq. (6.5), we conveniently replace each term on the right-hand side of Eq. (6.5), using the following equation:

$$\dot{e}_j = \dot{e}_j(DEN) + \dot{e}_j(ACC). \tag{6.7}$$

Based on Eq. (6.7), when calculating the covariance between the average rate of change in productive efficiency and initial productive efficiency, we obtain the following equation:

$$cov\left(e_{j0}, \dot{e}_j\right) = \frac{\sum_j \left(e_{j0} - \bar{e_0}\right)\left(\dot{e}_j - \bar{\dot{e}}\right)}{n} = cov\left(e_{j0}, \dot{e}_j(DEN)\right) + cov\left(e_{j0}, \dot{e}_j(ACC)\right).$$

If we divide both sides by the variation in productive efficiency at the initial time, we obtain the following formula:

$$\frac{\sum_j \left(e_{j0} - \bar{e_0}\right)\left(\dot{e}_j - \bar{\dot{e}}\right)}{\sum_j \left(e_{j0} - \bar{e_0}\right)^2} = \frac{\sum_j \left(e_{j0} - \bar{e_0}\right)\left(\dot{e}_j(DEN) - \dot{e}(\bar{DEN})\right)}{\sum_j \left(e_{j0} - \bar{e_0}\right)^2} + \frac{\sum_j \left(e_{j0} - \bar{e_0}\right)\left(\dot{e}_j(ACC) - \dot{e}(\bar{ACC})\right)}{\sum_j \left(e_{j0} - \bar{e_0}\right)^2}.$$

Because the value on the left side is the regression coefficient β, replacing the variables for each term on the right side again yields the decomposition formula of the convergence coefficient, as follows:

$$\beta = \beta_{DEN} + \beta_{ACC}. \tag{6.8}$$

Each term on the right side is a coefficient that regresses each growth contribution to the level of its initial productive efficiency. If the convergence contribution coefficient β_i ($i = DEN, ACC$) is positive, it means that the element's change has increased the regional disparities in productive efficiency. By contrast, if the convergence contribution coefficient β_i is negative, it means that the element's change has reduced the regional disparities in productive efficiency. Moreover, if $\beta_{DEN} + \beta_{ACC} < 0$ is realized even for $\beta_{DEN} > 0$ and $\beta_{ACC} < 0$, this can be interpreted as a reduction in regional disparities for all of the elements of productive efficiency.

6.3.3 Data

The data used in this study are panel data for 47 prefectures in Japan covering 1980 to 2014. We compiled a dataset for both manufacturing and non-manufacturing industries.

The output data by industry are taken from the *Annual Report on Prefectural Accounts* (Cabinet Office). They are deflated by the GDP deflator reported in the *System of National Accounts* (SNA). The labor input by industry is calculated by multiplying the number of employees by the number of hours worked. The data on the number of employees are taken mainly from the *Annual Report on Prefectural Accounts* (Cabinet Office). Working hour data were taken from the *Monthly Labor Survey* (Ministry of Health, Labour and Welfare). The capital input by industry is the private capital stock multiplied by the capital utilization ratio. Private capital stock data are estimates from the Central Research Institute of Electric Power Industry. The capital utilization ratio of the manufacturing industry is taken from indices of industrial production published by the Ministry of Economy, Trade, and Industry. For the capital utilization ratio of the non-manufacturing industry, we use estimates because no official statistics are available.[8]

Population density is the ratio of the population to a residential area. The population data were obtained from the *Basic Resident Registers* (Ministry of Internal Affairs and Communications). The residential area data were taken from the *System of Social and Demographic Statistics* (Ministry of Internal Affairs and Communications). In calculating the *ACC* index, the data for the time-distance matrix between regions were taken from the *National Integrated Transport Analysis System* (Ministry of Land, Infrastructure, Transport and Tourism).

Descriptive statistics by industry are presented in Table 6.1. The output increased during the observation period in the manufacturing and non-manufacturing industries. After rising from the 1980s to the 1990s, the pace of increase in the 2000s was moderate. Labor input steadily decreased from 1990, while capital input increased throughout the observation period. Population density rose moderately between 1980 and 2010 and then declined slightly in 2014 owing to a nationwide decline in population. The *ACC* index increased sharply from 1990, suggesting that interregional networks were strengthened by the opening of many bullet trains (Yamagata Shinkansen, Akita Shinkansen, Nagano Shinkansen, and Kyushu Shinkansen).

Table 6.2 shows the mean values of population density and the *ACC* index over time by region. Population density is high in Japan's three major metropolitan areas—the Greater Tokyo Area, Kansai, and Chubu—while Hokkaido has the lowest population density. The *ACC* index is also higher than average in the Greater Tokyo Area, Kansai, and Chubu. This means that the transportation network is mainly constituted of large cities. In particular, Japan has a high-speed transportation network with Tokyo as its hub. Therefore, the *ACC* index tends to be higher in

[8]See footnote 2 in Chap. 3 for the estimate procedure on the capital utilization ratio.

Table 6.1 Descriptive statistics

		Value-added (million yen)			Labor input (person-hour)			Capital input (million yen)				
		All industries	Manufacturing industry	Non-manufacturing industry	All industries	Manufacturing industry	Non-manufacturing industry	All industries	Manufacturing industry	Non-manufacturing industry	Population density	ACC index
1980	Mean	7,730,508	1,372,122	6,284,633	1,364,909	295,799	1,067,572	8,496,714	3,335,672	5,248,584	1276	22.25
	Standard deviation	10,233,479	1,821,621	8,442,672	1,399,606	335,341	1,084,151	9,115,215	3,624,570	6,210,252	1506	6.00
	Maximum	62,919,057	9,063,891	53,336,575	8,410,740	1679,754	6,729,076	45,566,369	14,405,245	36,582,428	8372	36.14
	Minimum	1,659,582	94,180	1,458,760	373,549	31,930	311,600	1,155,407	252,337	762,589	262	13.34
1990	Mean	10,837,508	2,037,251	8,675,979	1,470,828	324,310	1,138,736	15,529,807	5,886,160	9,907,896	1336	22.35
	Standard deviation	15,406,048	2,390,362	13,204,132	1,614,268	346,780	1,281,201	17,910,196	6,215,941	13,483,438	1574	6.16
	Maximum	96,483,934	9,839,002	85,211,889	9,669,281	1,670,266	7,929,467	99,568,959	28,157,387	84,514,309	8456	35.91
	Minimum	2,123,197	148,651	1,773,178	362,099	32,312	289,755	2,681,166	482,733	1,951,542	259	12.93
2000	Mean	10,765,104	2,011,027	8,770,252	1,372,705	254,102	1,102,140	20,111,686	7,117,994	13,695,435	1350	25.25
	Standard deviation	14,822,163	2,032,771	13,348,402	1,478,683	254,968	1,217,629	23,431,277	7,104,309	18,975,392	1585	6.01
	Maximum	93,658,397	9,050,237	86,801,664	8,715,110	1,155,040	7,370,153	131,564,767	34,653,218	117,445,951	8413	38.51
	Minimum	2,127,374	184,599	1,759,982	328,361	27,728	270,074	3,606,780	658,160	2,705,984	260	17.18
2010	Mean	11,158,051	2,280,320	8,839,387	1,233,226	190,603	970,214	27,177,667	7,422,947	18,874,986	1360	26.01
	Standard deviation	15,275,105	2,204,401	13,654,808	1,355,706	183,762	1,067,624	32,341,314	7,345,204	27,271,084	1679	6.11
	Maximum	96,217,403	10,735,264	88,808,855	7,949,085	853,089	6,373,482	182,997,919	39,024,137	169,716,749	9066	39.65
	Minimum	1,857,687	191,663	1,591,060	279,522	25,422	227,706	4,724,266	692,392	3,654,294	249	15.86
2014	Mean	11,662,718	2,436,275	9,150,756	1,207,253	190,814	952,281	31,586,469	7,828,993	22,145,309	1353	26.60
	Standard deviation	16,115,681	2,603,710	14,321,806	1,322,034	182,418	1,053,709	38,003,200	7,665,752	32,478,660	1694	6.00
	Maximum	101,186,156	14,521,490	93,367,789	7,733,538	890,263	6,308,599	216,663,687	41,205,418	202,599,244	9185	39.65
	Minimum	1,867,750	198,327	1,630,076	271,509	26,047	226,042	5,387,930	736,874	4,229,472	245	17.56
1980–2014	Mean	10,341,909	1,964,520	8,355,152	1,364,108	262,363	1,078,642	18,940,610	6,133,024	12,795,671	1343	24.16
	Standard deviation	14,229,589	2,174,343	12,550,135	1,458,832	280,623	1,172,863	24,227,938	6,464,148	19,722,313	1587	6.24
	Maximum	101,828,797	14,572,817	93,616,142	9,669,281	1,707,001	7,929,467	216,663,687	43,011,704	202,599,244	9185	40.03
	Minimum	1,659,582	94,180	1,458,760	271,509	23,323	226,042	1,155,407	252,337	762,589	245	12.90

Table 6.2 Regional average of population density and ACC index

	Population density	ACC index
Hokkaido	257	17.88
Tohoku	493	19.25
North Kanto	798	25.64
Greater Tokyo Area	4619	35.93
Chubu	1246	25.82
Hokuriku	738	20.64
Kansai	2407	32.13
Chugoku	864	20.33
Shikoku	864	21.08
Kyushu	846	20.34
Okinawa	1158	24.46
National average	1343	24.16

Notes: (1) The values in the table are the values of the observation period (1980–2014)

(2) The values in the table are means of prefectures within each region

(3) See Fig. 1.2 in Chap. 1 for the regional classification

regions with shorter travel times from Tokyo. The *ACC* index in Okinawa is higher because of the greater number of flights to Tokyo than to other local areas.

6.4 Results and Discussion

Table 6.3 presents the results of the maximum likelihood estimation using Eq. (6.2) and Eq. (6.3). The equation for the determinants of productive efficiency is estimated simultaneously with the production frontier function: The two models are estimated from the perspective of introducing time effects in terms of population density and the *ACC* index. In Models A, C, and E, no time effects are introduced, while time effects are introduced in Models B, D, and F.

To determine whether the deviations from the estimated frontier were due to the effects of inefficiency, the null hypothesis $\gamma = 0$ is tested against the alternative hypothesis $\gamma > 0$. The null hypothesis is rejected at the 1% significance level, and γ is statistically distinct from zero. This result suggests that there is an efficiency effect, and we can thus confirm the estimates of the variables on the determinants of efficiency. There is no significant difference in the estimation results according to whether the time effect is considered. Models B, D, and F are selected from the log-likelihood values, and the results are evaluated as follows.

The coefficient sign of population density and the *ACC* index, which are variables explaining productive efficiency, are positive and statistically significant. This result indicates that regional agglomeration and inter-regional networks positively influence productive efficiency. The *ACC* index parameters exceed the population density parameters in both the manufacturing and non-manufacturing industries. In

Table 6.3 Estimation results

	All industries				Manufacturing industry				Non-manufacturing industry			
	Model A		Model B		Model C		Model D		Model E		Model F	
Frontier function												
Constant (α_0)	−0.134	**	−0.064	**	−0.157	**	0.177	**	0.155	**	0.501	**
	(0.063)		(0.031)		(0.067)		(0.036)		(0.036)		(0.039)	
α_L	0.656	**	0.712	**	0.409	**	0.407	**	0.368	**	0.419	**
	(0.032)		(0.053)		(0.113)		(0.034)		(0.057)		(0.049)	
α_{LL}	0.244	**	0.227	**	0.329	**	0.255	**	0.430	**	0.444	**
	(0.116)		(0.056)		(0.094)		(0.038)		(0.058)		(0.050)	
α_K	0.299	**	0.195	**	0.526	**	0.495	**	0.669	**	0.602	**
	(0.044)		(0.062)		(0.140)		(0.039)		(0.069)		(0.059)	
α_{KK}	0.156		0.100		0.205		0.157	**	0.522	**	0.540	**
	(0.132)		(0.070)		(0.147)		(0.052)		(0.075)		(0.065)	
α_T	0.019	**	0.016	**	0.005		−0.010	**	−0.011	**	−0.041	**
	(0.000)		(0.003)		(0.008)		(0.003)		(0.004)		(0.004)	
α_{TT}	−0.001	**	−0.001	**	0.000		0.001	**	0.001	**	0.002	**
	(0.000)		(0.000)		(0.000)		(0.000)		(0.000)		(0.000)	
α_{LK}	−0.181		−0.153	**	−0.276	**	−0.232	**	−0.449	**	−0.462	**
	(0.150)		(0.062)		(0.116)		(0.043)		(0.065)		(0.056)	
α_{LT}	−0.002		−0.004		−0.001		−0.002		0.022	**	0.021	**
	(0.005)		(0.003)		(0.006)		(0.002)		(0.003)		(0.003)	
α_{KT}	0.004	**	0.007	**	0.003		0.005	**	−0.026	**	−0.025	**
	(0.001)		(0.003)		(0.008)		(0.002)		(0.004)		(0.003)	
Efficiency model												
Constant (δ_0)	0.019	**	0.075	**	0.002		0.097	**	0.101	**	0.090	**
	(0.004)		(0.005)		(0.004)		(0.011)		(0.006)		(0.005)	
δ_{DEN}	0.028	**	0.031	**	0.045	**	0.036	**	0.033	**	0.021	**

	(0.002)		(0.001)		(0.003)		(0.005)		(0.005)		(0.001)	
δ_{ACC}	0.065	**	0.048	**	0.076	**	0.083	**	0.053	**	0.063	**
	(0.002)		(0.002)		(0.012)		(0.006)		(0.002)		(0.002)	
Time effect	Excluded		Included		Excluded		Included		Excluded		Included	
σ^2	0.006	**	0.004	**	0.020	**	0.014	**	0.006	**	0.005	**
	(0.000)		(0.000)		(0.001)		(0.000)		(0.000)		(0.000)	
γ	0.090	**	0.021	**	0.064	**	0.036	**	0.016	**	0.016	**
	(0.007)		(0.003)		(0.014)		(0.005)		(0.008)		(0.003)	
Log-likelihood	2018.39		2229.87		1017.41		1182.76		1815.21		2035.75	
Observations	1645		1645		1645		1645		1645		1645	
Mean efficiency scores	0.951		0.898		0.948		0.847		0.900		0.839	

Notes: (1) ** and * indicate 1% and 5% significance levels, respectively
(2) The values in parentheses indicate standard errors
(3) The software used for the estimation is Frontier 4.1 (Coelli 1996)

Table 6.4 Average efficiency score

	All industries	Manufacturing industry	Non-manufacturing industry
Hokkaido	0.809	0.729	0.755
Tohoku	0.842	0.770	0.782
North Kanto	0.911	0.872	0.854
Greater Tokyo Area	0.989	0.971	0.938
Chubu	0.923	0.882	0.863
Hokuriku	0.871	0.806	0.808
Kansai	0.969	0.944	0.916
Chugoku	0.873	0.808	0.807
Shikoku	0.879	0.819	0.815
Kyushu	0.869	0.806	0.805
Okinawa	0.918	0.870	0.853
National average	0.898	0.847	0.839

Notes: (1) The values in the table are the mean values of the observation period (1980–2014)
(2) See Fig. 1.2 in Chap. 1 for the regional classification

particular, *ACC* index parameters are more significant in the manufacturing industry. This indicates that the borrowed size impact of inter-regional networking is higher in the manufacturing industry than in the non-manufacturing industry. In other words, the effects of inter-regional networks on passenger travel are extensive in the manufacturing industry. This result reflects the fact that the geographical scope of production activities in the manufacturing industry extends beyond the region and that the manufacturing industry is the basic (export) industry of the regional economy.

Table 6.4 shows the productive efficiency scores for 11 regions in Japan. The productive efficiency scores for each region are the average of the prefectures within each region. The region with the highest production efficiency is the Greater Tokyo Area, with an efficiency of 0.989 (close to 1) for all industries. Productive efficiency tends to be higher in large metropolitan areas, such as the Greater Tokyo Area, Kansai (0.969), and Chubu (0.923). In contrast, Hokkaido exhibits the lowest level of production efficiency at 0.809, probably due to the increasing dispersion of the population and the challenge of enjoying the benefits of inter-regional networks in regions that are not part of Japan's mainland.

The manufacturing industry has a higher level of productive efficiency than the non-manufacturing industry does. This suggests that the manufacturing industry's supply chain extends to various regions in Japan and that it is easy to enjoy the benefits of shortened domestic travel time. Non-manufacturing businesses are based on personal contact in the intra-regional market, which means that the non-manufacturing industry is centered on nonbasic industries that support the lives of workers within the region. This suggests that human contact across regions is less frequent than in the manufacturing industry. That is, travel time between regions is less relevant for some non-manufacturing businesses than for manufacturing businesses.

Table 6.5 shows the size of the contributions of regional agglomeration and inter-regional networks to improving productive efficiency based on Eq. (6.5). In Hokkaido, Shikoku, and Kyushu, productive efficiency increased significantly during the observation period, exceeding the national average. In these regions, improving access to other markets had a significant impact on improving production efficiency. For example, Hokkaido's access to the mainland of Japan has improved dramatically through an increase in available flights. In Shikoku, the Honshu Shikoku Bridge was constructed, which improved access to the mainland. In Kyushu, the Kyushu Shinkansen (bullet train) opened in 2004 and 2011. Tohoku, North Kanto, and Chubu have also been profoundly affected by improved access to other markets. In all areas, the development of high-quality transportation infrastructure has significantly improved access to other areas. On the other hand, the regional agglomeration has improved productive efficiency in some areas, but this effect is negligible. For example, an effect can be observed in North Kanto, the Greater Tokyo Area, Chubu, Kansai, and Okinawa, but the effects are minimal compared to the effects of inter-regional networks. This indicates that in Japan, the impact of inter-regional networks on improving production efficiency is more significant than the effect of spatial concentration of the populations.

Figure 6.1 plots the relationships between the improvement rate of the ACC index and the improvement rate of productive efficiency for all industries. There is a clear upward-sloping relationship, which indicates a clear correlation between improved access to other markets and improved productive efficiency. For example, Nagano and Tokushima are located in the upper right. The Nagano Shinkansen (bullet train) has improved access to markets and increased productive efficiency in Nagano. Meanwhile, in Tokushima, the opening of the Akashi Kaikyo Bridge has improved access to the mainland, indicating that productive efficiency has increased. It can thus be concluded that the development of high-quality transportation networks helped strengthen regional economic networks and significantly increased productive efficiency. This conclusion is also valid for the manufacturing and non-manufacturing industries (Fig. 6.2).

Finally, we check for the presence or absence of convergence in productive efficiency. Table 6.6 shows the convergence coefficient based on Eqs. (6.6) and (6.8). The sign of the convergence coefficient β is negative for both the manufacturing and non-manufacturing industries. This indicates a reduction in regional disparities in productive efficiency during the observation period. However, the sign of the population density coefficient is positive in both industries. This means that population agglomeration served to expand regional disparities in productive efficiency. In contrast, the sign of the coefficient of inter-regional networks is negative, and the magnitude of the coefficient dramatically exceeds the population density. While population agglomeration serves to increase regional disparities in productive efficiency, inter-regional networks serve to reduce regional disparities in productive efficiency. As the latter effect exceeds the former, it can be concluded that regional disparities in productive efficiency have diminished overall. In other words, areas with low productive efficiency caught up to areas with high productive efficiency. Productive efficiency in Nagano and Tokushima improved significantly, while that

Table 6.5 Growth rate of productive efficiency and factor contribution to productive efficiency

	All industries			Manufacturing industry			Non-manufacturing industry		
	Growth rate of efficiency score	*DEN*	*ACC*	Growth rate of efficiency score	*DEN*	*ACC*	Growth rate of efficiency score	*DEN*	*ACC*
	(a) + (b)	(a)	(b)	(a) + (b)	(a)	(b)	(a) + (b)	(a)	(b)
Hokkaido	0.187	−0.008	0.194	0.239	−0.010	0.249	0.182	−0.006	0.187
Tohoku	0.152	−0.012	0.163	0.194	−0.015	0.210	0.149	−0.009	0.158
North Kanto	0.148	0.005	0.142	0.190	0.007	0.183	0.142	0.004	0.138
Greater Tokyo Area	0.122	0.024	0.098	0.157	0.031	0.125	0.113	0.018	0.094
Chubu	0.152	0.004	0.148	0.195	0.005	0.189	0.146	0.003	0.143
Hokuriku	0.073	−0.001	0.074	0.094	−0.001	0.096	0.071	−0.001	0.072
Kansai	0.113	0.005	0.108	0.145	0.007	0.138	0.108	0.004	0.104
Chugoku	0.107	−0.006	0.113	0.137	−0.008	0.145	0.105	−0.005	0.109
Shikoku	0.192	−0.006	0.198	0.246	−0.008	0.254	0.186	−0.005	0.191
Kyushu	0.169	−0.001	0.170	0.217	−0.001	0.218	0.164	−0.001	0.164
Okinawa	0.098	0.011	0.087	0.126	0.014	0.112	0.093	0.008	0.084
National average	0.138	0.001	0.136	0.176	0.002	0.174	0.132	0.001	0.131

Notes: (1) Each growth contribution in the table is the value calculated using Eq. (6.5)
(2) See Fig. 1.2 in Chap. 1 for the regional classification

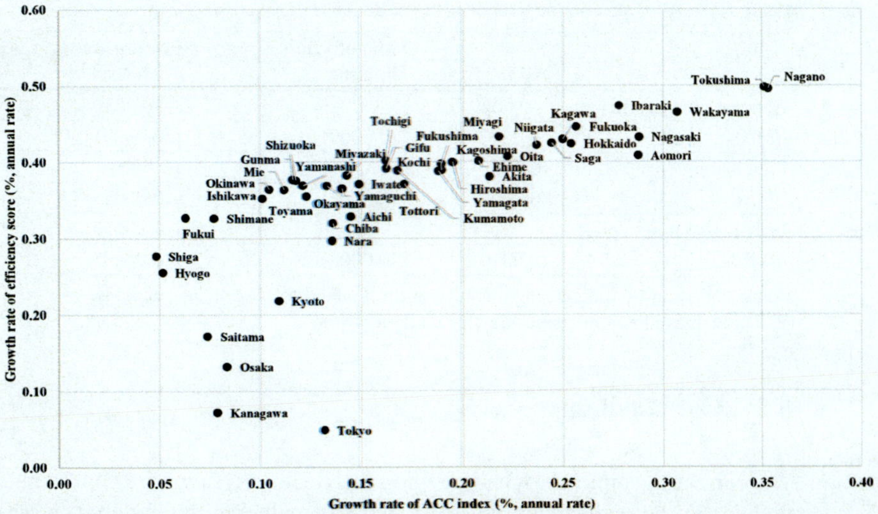

Fig. 6.1 Dynamic relationship between efficiency score and ACC index in all industries

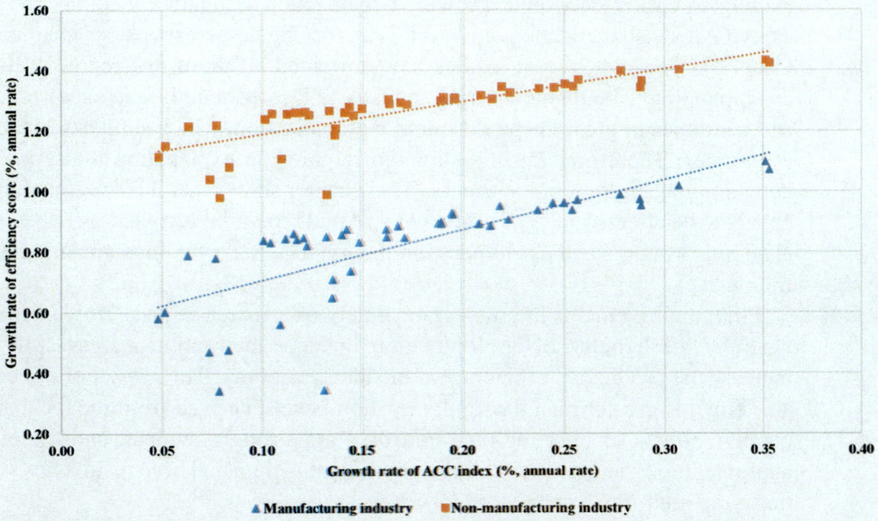

Fig. 6.2 Dynamic relationship between efficiency score and ACC index by industries

in Tokyo, Osaka, Kanagawa, and Saitama showed slight improvement. These results suggest that investment in high-quality transportation infrastructure by the Japanese government has strengthened local areas' economic power and helped reduce economic disparities between large metropolitan areas and local areas.

Table 6.6 Decomposition results of beta coefficient (1980–2014)

	All industries		Manufacturing industry		Non-manufacturing industry	
Convergence coefficient	−0.0029	**	−0.0025	**	−0.0030	**
(β)	(0.0010)		(0.0009)		(0.0009)	
Population density	0.0012	**	0.0011	**	0.0009	**
(β_{DEN})	(0.0002)		(0.0001)		(0.0001)	
Inter-regional networks	−0.0042	**	−0.0036	**	−0.0039	**
(β_{ACC})	(0.0010)		(0.0008)		(0.0009)	

Notes: (1) ** and * indicate significance at the 1% and 5% levels, respectively
(2) The values in parentheses indicate standard errors

6.5 Conclusions

The current dynamics in Japan's regional economic systems are consistent with the findings in the mainstream literature, which emphasize the importance of agglomeration economies for economic growth. Population agglomeration is progressing in three large metropolitan areas—the Greater Tokyo Area, Kansai, and Chubu—leading to strong economic growth. Urbanization is relatively stable; the Greater Tokyo Area's share of the population is increasing at the expense of local areas (see Chap. 2). However, recent studies have provided no proof that regional disparities are expanding. The manufacturing industry is located mainly outside of urban areas and continues to grow despite economic globalization, which supports Japan's local economies. Therefore, Japan's situation requires an explanation that goes beyond conventional agglomeration theory. This chapter shows that inter-regional networks enhance the effectiveness of borrowed size and repair the lost links between regional economic systems and agglomeration theory. The main findings are summarized as follows:

First, improvements in inter-regional networks increase the borrowed size effect, whereby the benefits of agglomeration in large metropolitan areas spill over to increase the productive efficiency of the local economy. The impact of the borrowed size effect is greater than the agglomeration benefit derived from the local size. The positive effects of inter-regional networks are strongly evident, and the effects of agglomeration shadows are thus not dominant in Japan. These results are similar to those reported in Chap. 5.

Second, the impact of the increase in productive efficiency due to improved inter-regional networks is more significant for the manufacturing industry than for the non-manufacturing industry. The manufacturing industry plays a role in the basic export industry in regional economies. Therefore, a network with an outside area is essential for production activities in the manufacturing industry.

Third, the economic benefits according to region size are significant in large metropolitan areas, such as the Greater Tokyo Area and Kansai. This means that large metropolitan areas enjoy high agglomeration economies driven by population agglomeration. If a positive lock-in effect operates in agglomeration, sustainable growth in large metropolitan areas is guaranteed.

Fourth, in local areas other than large metropolitan areas, the borrowed size from agglomeration is highly effective in enhancing productive efficiency. The shortened travel times to large metropolitan areas due to high-quality transportation networks generated by investments in transportation infrastructure significantly contributed to the growth of the local economy.

Fifth, the strengthening of inter-regional transportation networks contributed to the convergence of regional disparities in productive efficiency. The development of high-quality transportation networks has enabled local areas to achieve economic catch-up in large metropolitan areas through borrowed size effects.

These findings have substantial theoretical and policy implications. Theoretically, the observation that the borrowed size effect occurs in regional networks calls for the geographic base of agglomeration theory to be rebuilt. If the spatial externalities can be shared not only within the agglomeration itself but also across regional networks, it may be necessary to reconsider the appropriateness of the term "agglomeration economies." Ignoring the role of inter-regional networks is likely to cause regional development policies to be directed toward narrowly defined spatial scales. The existence of inter-regional network externalities affirms broader regional development and suggests that it can be an effective means of putting underdeveloped areas on a growth track.

This chapter provides insights into the foundations of Japan's national land policies and enables predictions concerning regional disparities. Specifically, this chapter clarifies that the development of high-quality transportation networks helps reduce regional disparities; this effect is particularly significant for the manufacturing industry. Japan aims to build a giant economic zone, a "super-mega-region," through the formation of inter-regional networks in order to create a national land structure that achieves regional sustainability. The essence of this policy is the shortening of the travel time between regions through the laying of a magnetic levitation train, namely, the *Linear-Chuo Shinkansen*. Chap. 7 evaluates the economic impact of the installation of the *Linear-Chuo Shinkansen* quantitatively using the concept of the Solow residual.

Appendix: Brief Review of Studies on Regional Agglomeration and Productive Efficiency

There is extensive literature on the relationship between regional agglomeration and productive efficiency using stochastic frontier analysis (SFA) in many countries. Most studies focus on specific economic activities (mainly manufacturing) rather than addressing all sectors of the national economy (e.g., Fritsch and Slavtchev 2011).

As an early analysis, Beeson and Husted (1989) show that urban agglomeration is associated with improved productive efficiency in the manufacturing industry in the United States. For Canada, McCoy and Moomaw (1995) show that urban agglomeration has a positive impact on productive efficiency in the manufacturing industry. In the United Kingdom, Driffield and Munday (2001) investigated the impact of spatial agglomeration on productive efficiency in UK industries.

Two studies have been conducted on the aquaculture industry. Tveteras and Battese (2006) examined the influence of industrial agglomeration on the productive efficiency of the Norwegian salmon aquaculture industry. Rahman et al. (2019) investigated the effects of industrial agglomeration on productive efficiency in Bangladesh and discussed the desirable aquaculture industry policy from the viewpoint of productive efficiency.

In India, Mitra (1999, 2000) assessed the importance of urban agglomeration and industrial spread on productive efficiency in the manufacturing industry. In China, Ke and Yu (2014) investigated whether urban agglomeration positively affects productive efficiency. In Greece, Tsekeris and Papaioannou (2017) analyzed the determinants of productive efficiency and demonstrated that inter-regional networks, specialization, and human capital are critical factors in increasing productive efficiency.

Among some studies in Japan, Mitra and Sato (2007) clarify the relationship between productive efficiency and agglomeration economies in the manufacturing industry. Otsuka et al. (2010) and Otsuka and Goto (2015) show that industrial agglomeration and improved market access have positive impacts on the productive efficiency of the manufacturing and non-manufacturing industries, respectively. They emphasize the role of inter-regional networks in regional productivity growth.

As mentioned in Chap. 4, there have been a growing number of studies on stochastic frontier models that consider spatial dependence. In the context of agglomeration economies, Kutlu and Nair-Reichert (2019) proposed a method of combining a spatial dependence structure of agglomeration with a stochastic frontier model.

References

Aigner DJ, Lovell CAK, Schmidt P (1977) Formulation and estimation of stochastic frontier production function model. J Econ 6:21–37

Alonso W (1973) Urban zero population growth. Daedalus 102(4):191–206

Battese GE, Coelli TJ (1995) A model for technical inefficiency effects in a stochastic frontier production function for panel data. Empir Econ 20(2):325–332

Batty PWJ (2009) Accessibility: in search of a unified theory. Environ Plann B 36:191–194

Beeson PE, Husted S (1989) Patterns and determinants of productive efficiency in the state manufacturing. J Reg Sci 29(1):15–28

Boix R, Trullen J (2007) Knowledge, networks of cities and growth in regional urban systems. Pap Reg Sci 86(4):551–574

Burger MJ, Meijers EJ, Hoogerbrugge MM, Tresserra JM (2015) Borrowed size, agglomeration shadows and cultural amenities in North-West Europe. Eur Plan Stud 23(6):1090–1109

Camagni R (1993) From city hierarchy to city networks: reflections about an emerging paradigm. In: Lakshmanan LTR, Nijkamp P (eds) Structure and change in the space economy: festschrift in honour of Martin Beckmann. Springer Verlag, Berlin, pp 66–87

Camagni R, Capello R (2004) The city network paradigm: theory and empirical evidence. In: Capello R, Nijkamp P (eds) Urban dynamics and growth. Elsevier, Amsterdam, pp 495–529

Camagni R, Capello R, Caragliu A (2015) The rise of second-rank cities: what role for agglomeration economies? Eur Plan Stud 23(6):1069–1089

Camagni R, Capello R, Caragliu A (2016) Static vs. dynamic agglomeration economies. Spatial context and structural evolution behind urban growth. Pap Reg Sci 95(1):133–158

Capello R (2000) The city network paradigm: measuring urban network externalities. Urban Stud 37(11):1925–1945

Coelli TJ (1995) Recent development in frontier modelling and efficiency measurement. Aust J Agr Econ 39(3):219–245

Coelli TJ (1996) A guide to FRONTIER version 4.1: a computer program for stochastic frontier production and cost function estimation. CEPA Working Papers No. 96/07. University of New England, NSW, Armidale

Dobkins LH, Ioannides YM (2001) Spatial interactions among US cities: 1900–1990. Reg Sci Urban Econ 31(6):701–731

Driffield N, Munday M (2001) Foreign manufacturing, regional agglomeration and technical efficiency in UK industries: a stochastic production frontier approach. Reg Stud 35(5):391–399

Fritsch M, Slavtchev V (2011) Determinants of the efficiency of regional innovation systems. Reg Stud 45(7):905–918

Fujita M, Hamaguchi N, Kameyama Y (2018) Spatial economics in the age of declining populations. Nikkei Publishing, Tokyo. (in Japanese)

Fujita M, Thisse J (2002) The economics of agglomeration: cities, industrial location and regional growth. Cambridge University Press, Cambridge

Fukao K, Yue X (2000) Regional factor inputs and convergence in Japan: how much can we apply closed economy neoclassical growth models? Econ Rev (Keizai Kenkyu) 51(2):136–151. (in Japanese)

Graham DJ (2007) Variable returns to urbanization and the effect of road traffic congestion. J Urban Econ 62(1):103–120

Hall P, Pain K (2006) The polycentric metropolis: learning from mega-city regions in Europe. Earthscan, London

Hansen WG (1959) How accessibility shapes land use. J Am Inst Plann 25:73–76

Holl A (2012) Market potential and firm-level productivity in Spain. J Econ Geog 12(6):1191–1215

Ke S, Yu Y (2014) The pathways from industrial agglomeration to TFP growth: the experience of Chinese cities for 2001–2010. J Asia Pac Econ 19(2):310–332

Kutlu L, Nair-Reichert U (2019) Agglomeration effects and spatial spillovers in efficiency analysis: a distribution-free methodology. Reg Stud 53(11):1565–1574

Lall SV, Shalizi Z, Deichmann U (2004) Agglomeration economies and productivity in Indian industry. J Dev Econ 73(2):643–673

McCann P (2001) Urban and regional economics. Oxford University Press, Gosport, Hampshire

McCoy K, Moomaw RL (1995) Determinants of manufacturing efficiency in Canadian cities: a stochastic frontier approach. Rev Reg Stud 25(3):317–330

Meijers E, Burger MJ, Hoogerbrugge MM (2016) Borrowing size in networks of cities: City size, network connectivity and metropolitan functions in Europe. Pap Reg Sci 95(1):181–198

Melo PS, Graham DJ, Levinson D, Aarabi S (2017) Agglomeration, accessibility and productivity: evidence for large metropolitan areas in the US. Urban Stud 54(1):179–195

Mitra A (1999) Agglomeration economies as manifested in technical efficiency at the firm level. J Urban Econ 45(3):490–500

Mitra A (2000) Total factor productivity growth and urbanization economies: a case of Indian industries. Rev Urban Reg Dev Stud 12(2):97–108

Mitra A, Sato H (2007) Agglomeration economies in Japan: technical efficiency, growth and unemployment. Rev Urban Reg Dev Stud 19(3):197–209

MLIT (2017) The development of land policy simulation model, FY2017 edn. Ministry of Land, Infrastructure, Transport and Tourism, Tokyo. http://www.mlit.go.jp/kokudoseisaku/kokudoseisaku_tk3_000085.html. Accessed January 2021

Montolio D, Solé-Ollé A (2009) Road investment and regional productivity growth: the effects of vehicle intensity and congestion. Pap Reg Sci 88(1):99–118

Otsuka A (2017) A new perspective on agglomeration economies in Japan. Springer, Singapore

Otsuka A (2020) Inter-regional networks and productive efficiency in Japan. Pap Reg Sci 99 (1):115–133

Otsuka A, Goto M (2015) Regional policy and the productive efficiency of Japanese industries. Reg Stud 49(4):518–531

Otsuka A, Goto M, Sueyoshi T (2010) Industrial agglomeration effects in Japan: productive efficiency, market access, and public fiscal transfer. Pap Reg Sci 89(4):819–839

Parr JB (2002) Agglomeration economies: ambiguities and confusions. Environ Plann A 34:717–731

Phelps N, Fallon R, Williams C (2001) Small firms, borrowed size and the urban-rural shift. Reg Stud 35(7):613–624

Rahman MT, Nielsen R, Khan MA (2019) Agglomeration externalities and technical efficiency: an empirical application to the pond aquaculture of Pangas and Tilapia in Bangladesh. Aquac Econ Manag 23(2):158–187

Rice P, Venables AJ, Patacchini E (2006) Spatial determinants of productivity: analysis for the regions of Great Britain. Reg Sci Urban Econ 36(6):727–752

Stelder D (2016) Regional accessibility trends in Europe: road infrastructure, 1957–2012. Reg Stud 50(6):983–995

Tsekeris T, Papaioannou S (2017) Regional determinants of technical efficiency: evidence from the Greek economy. Reg Stud 52(10):1398–1409

Tveteras R, Battese GE (2006) Agglomeration externalities, productivity, and technical inefficiency. J Reg Sci 46(4):605–625

Chapter 7
Solow Residual Approach to Inter-regional Network Economies

Abstract This chapter reevaluates inter-regional network economies in Japan based on cost-based Solow residuals, a novel analytical approach. In most studies, inter-regional network economies have been measured as elements of technological progress in production functions. However, the conventional approach based on perfect competition raises concerns that measurements of geographical externalities depend on the behavior of economic agents. One way to mitigate this concern is to construct a model based on imperfect competition. The cost-share Solow residual approach provides reliable evidence of the geographical externalities uncovered by the conventional approach. That is, by applying this approach to geographical analysis, we can precisely identify inter-regional network economies under imperfect economies. Furthermore, by using this approach, we perform a sensitivity analysis on the installation of the *Linear-Chuo Shinkansen* (magnetic levitation train) to measure the economic impact of high-quality transportation infrastructure. The results show that the *Linear-Chuo Shinkansen* provides a significant time-saving effect not only in the region of origin but also in local regions other than those along the railway lines. That is, the results reveal that the formation of inter-regional networks can increase productivity not only in large metropolitan areas but also in local areas. The results of this chapter suggest that inter-regional networks via high-quality transportation infrastructure significantly enhance regional economic performance. This chapter provides empirical evidence for the national land plan in Japan.

Keywords Agglomeration economies · Inter-regional network · Magnetic levitation train · Solow residual · Transportation infrastructure

This chapter is based on Otsuka (2021).

A. Otsuka, *A New Driver of Regional Sustainability in Japan*, New Frontiers in Regional Science: Asian Perspectives 54,
https://doi.org/10.1007/978-981-16-3709-4_7

7.1 Introduction

The significance of inter-regional networks in regional sustainability has recently been focused on from the perspective of agglomeration economies (Burger and Meijers 2016; Meijers et al. 2016). Improvements in inter-regional networks expand the geographical scope of agglomeration economies. The development of high-speed railways and airports has reduced travel times and increased opportunities for human interaction. This increases the productivity of not only one region but also other regions by increasing the frequency of inter-regional knowledge exchange. Due to knowledge spillovers beyond the region, spatial externalities with urban agglomerations—thus far limited to urban spaces—will expand across urban boundaries.

The geographical widening of agglomeration economies was initially explained as the effect of borrowed size (Alonso 1973). As described in Chaps. 5 and 6, the concept of borrowed size can serve as a basis for explaining the development of the entire regional economy across cities. Incorporating long-distance cooperation agreements across an entire city network along with advanced functions improves the productivity of a city despite its size limitations. This phenomenon, known as "urban network externalities," has been demonstrated through many geographic approaches (Hall and Pain 2006; Boix and Trullén 2007; Camagni et al. 2016). Such inter-regional network economies have also been explained as a "wider economic impact" in the context of transport economics (Laird and Venables 2017; Graham and Gibbons 2019).

In most studies, inter-regional network economies have been measured as elements of technological progress in production functions. However, the conventional approach based on perfect competition raises concerns that measurements of geographical externalities depend on the behavior of economic agents.[1] Specifically, if we face an economy of imperfect competition, the conventional approach leads to overestimating technological progress depending on agents' behaviors and the degree of returns to scale. One way to mitigate this concern is to construct a model based on imperfect competition. It is well known that this can be achieved using the cost-share Solow residual approach (Hall 1990). This approach provides reliable evidence of the geographical externalities uncovered by the conventional approach. That is, by applying this approach to geographical analysis, we can precisely identify inter-regional network economies under imperfect economies. This is the first contribution of this study.

Furthermore, studies on inter-regional network economies have significant policy implications for Japan. The Japanese government aims to create a "super-mega-region" that combines several metropolitan areas into one economic zone and to leverage the geographical externalities via regional agglomeration to overcome the

[1]See Otsuka (2017) for detailed discussions on the measurement of technological progress.

negative effects of a shrinking economy and enhance regional sustainability.[2] A significant measure for enhancing the effectiveness of the super-mega-region is the installation of *Linear-Chuo Shinkansen* (magnetic levitation train), which is key to realizing the borrowed size effect (or wider economic impact). However, the effect of the borrowed size on this new high-speed railway has not been sufficiently examined. Therefore, by performing a sensitivity analysis, this chapter simulates the marginal effects of the *Linear-Chuo Shinkansen* on productivity. This simulation represents the second contribution of this study.

In Sect. 7.2, we describe the concerns associated with the conventional Solow residuals approach and provide solutions to these concerns. Section 7.3 describes the framework of empirical analysis. Section 7.4 presents and discusses the empirical results. Finally, Sect. 7.5 concludes the chapter.

7.2 Cost-Based Solow Residual Approach

This section reviews cost-based Solow residuals to identify technological progress and economies of scale under imperfect competition. First, we define a production function using the following formula:

$$V = A \cdot F(K, L), \tag{7.1}$$

where V is the value-added output; K and L are the capital and labor inputs, respectively; and A represents the production technology. Technological progress is captured through shifts in production functions.

By conducting a logarithmic total differential in Eq. (7.1) and dividing both sides by V yields the following equation:

$$\frac{dV}{V} = \frac{dA}{A} + A\frac{\partial F}{\partial K} \cdot \frac{K}{V} \cdot \frac{dK}{K} + A\frac{\partial F}{\partial L} \cdot \frac{L}{V} \cdot \frac{dL}{L}. \tag{7.2}$$

Here, when $x = logX$ for arbitrary variable X, Eq. (7.2) can be rewritten as

$$dv = da + A\frac{\partial F}{\partial K} \cdot \frac{K}{V} dk + A\frac{\partial F}{\partial L} \cdot \frac{L}{V} dl. \tag{7.3}$$

We assume that the firm has monopolistic power in the output market. At this time, the first-order condition for firm profit maximization is as follows:

[2]See Appendix in Chap. 1 for Japan's national land plan.

$$A\frac{\partial F}{\partial K}=\frac{P_K}{P}\mu,\ A\frac{\partial F}{\partial L}=\frac{P_L}{P}\mu, \tag{7.4}$$

where μ is the price markup, defined as the ratio of price P to marginal cost MC. Thus,

$$\mu\equiv\frac{P}{MC}=\frac{\eta-1}{\eta},$$

where η is the price elasticity of demand.

Furthermore, assuming increasing returns to scale, the following equation holds from the Euler equations:

$$A\frac{\partial F}{\partial K}\cdot\frac{K}{V}+A\frac{\partial F}{\partial L}\cdot\frac{L}{V}=\gamma, \tag{7.5}$$

where γ is the parameter indicating homogeneity.

Based on the relationship between Eqs. (7.4) and (7.5), the formula becomes

$$PV=\frac{\mu}{\gamma}[P_K K+P_L L]. \tag{7.6}$$

Exhaustion of the total product does not hold unless $\mu=\gamma$ is established. Rewriting Eq. (7.3) from Eqs. (7.4) and (7.5) yields

$$dv=da+(\gamma-\mu s_L)dk+\mu s_L dl, \tag{7.7}$$

where $s_L\equiv\frac{P_L L}{PV}$.

Now, the conventional Solow residual is derived as

$$SR\equiv dv-[(1-s_L)dk+s_L dl]=da+s_L(\mu-1)(dl-dk)+(\gamma-1)dk.$$

Because μ exceeds one under imperfect competition, the Solow residuals do not coincide with technological progress, and measurement biases arise depending on the degree of imperfect competition. In other words, the Solow residual approach overestimates technological progress owing to the presence of imperfect competition. Cost-based Solow residuals overcame this concern.

First, we define c_J as the cost share of the input factor J for total production costs:

$$c_J\equiv\frac{P_J J}{\sum_J P_J J}.$$

In this case, Eq. (7.6) can be rewritten as

$$\gamma c_L = \mu s_L. \tag{7.8}$$

From Eq. (7.8), Eq. (7.7) can be rewritten as

$$dv = da + \gamma[(1 - c_L)dk + c_L dl]. \tag{7.9}$$

Computing the cost-based Solow residuals based on Eq. (7.9) yields the following equation:

$$SR^C \equiv dv - dx = da + (\gamma - 1)dx, \tag{7.10}$$

where $dx = (1 - c_L)dk + c_L dl$. Equation (7.10) shows that technological progress and economies of scale can be accurately distinguished by defining cost-based Solow residuals under imperfect competition. Thus, by using (7.10), we can address concerns regarding the conventional Solow residuals approach.

7.3 Methods

7.3.1 Framework of Analysis

In the conventional research framework, externalities enjoyed by economic agents are internalized in the process of aggregation and form the increasing returns to scale at the aggregated level (Chipman 1970). Therefore, spatial externalities that occur within the region are described as economies of scale at the regional level.[3] On the other hand, inter-regional network economies are defined as external economies for the region because the economic agents within the region cannot control the strength and range of the inter-regional network. The region can grow by "borrowing" spatial externalities in other regions via the transportation infrastructure formed between the regions. Huge market-accessible regions can receive considerable benefits from knowledge spillovers. Furthermore, these regions enable the easy procurement of intermediate goods and can produce goods at lower costs. Therefore, productivity increases in regions with well-formed inter-regional networks because of the borrowed size effect. Recent studies in Japan have shown that regions with well-developed inter-regional networks can achieve high economic performance (Wetwitoo and Kato 2017; Otsuka 2018, 2020).

We estimate the following model for the determinants of Solow residuals:

[3] Otsuka (2017) describes that the agglomeration economies emerging within a region can be captured as economies of scale.

$$SR_{jt}^{C} = \alpha_j + \theta dx_{jt} + \beta_1 \ln ACC_{jt} + \beta_2 \ln MR_{jt} + \varepsilon_{jt}, \qquad (7.11)$$

where j and t represent the region and time, respectively; ε represents the error term; α, β, and θ are the estimated parameters; and θ represents the degree of the internalized agglomeration economies for the region and is equal to $\gamma - 1$. If $\theta = 0$, then $\gamma = 1$, indicating constant returns to scale in regional production. If θ is positive, then $\gamma > 1$, signifying increasing returns to scale in regional production, which indicates that the region enjoys the economic benefits of agglomeration. The existence of economies of scale can be verified by the rejection of the null hypothesis H_0 ($H_0 : \theta = 0$).

The *ACC* is an index representing the strength of inter-regional networks, as external economies for the region. If inter-regional network economies exist, a strengthened inter-regional network should increase productivity. However, we must note the negative impact of agglomeration, known as "agglomeration shadows," as described in Chap. 6.[4] That is, β_1 can have both positive and negative signs.

MR, the manufacturing industry ratio, is a control variable in the evaluation of inter-regional network economies. It is well established that Japan's manufacturing industry is more productive than its non-manufacturing industry.[5] That is, regional productivity should be higher in the region where the manufacturing industry is agglomerated.[6] Therefore, we assume that β_2 is positive.

The advantage of using the Solow residual approach is that we can identify the determinants of internalized agglomeration economies. We focus on the role of population density as a determinant of internalized agglomeration economies.[7] Here, we must note that a negative impact occurs in the agglomeration process, wherein excessive population density leads to high land prices, congestion, and fierce inter-firm competition, reducing the productivity of producers. Therefore, we consider the nonlinearity of the effect of population density and assume the following formula for economies of scale (γ):

$$\gamma = \delta_1 \ln D_{jt} + \delta_2 \ln D_{jt}^2,$$

where D is population density. Internalized agglomeration economies are expected to increase until the population density reaches a threshold. Thus, it is assumed that δ_1 is positive, and δ_2 is negative.

Substituting this relationship into Eq. (7.11) yields a second model:

[4]This negative impact reduces the number of agglomeration economies that can be realized within the region and intensifies monocentric concentration (Fujita and Thisse 2002).

[5]See Table 2.7 in Chap. 2 for the relationship between industry ratio and regional economic performance.

[6]See Fig. 2.9 in Chap. 2 for details.

[7]See Sect. 2.2 in Chap. 4 for discussions on the relationships between population density and agglomeration economies.

$$SR^C_{jt} = \alpha_j + \theta' dx_{jt} + \beta_1 \, ln \, ACC_{jt} + \beta_2 \, ln \, MR_{jt} + \varepsilon_{jt}, \quad (7.12)$$
$$\theta' = \gamma - 1 = \delta_1 \, ln \, D_{jt} + \delta_2 \, ln \, D^2_{jt} - 1.$$

Estimating Eqs. (7.11) and (7.12) enables us to evaluate the internalized agglomeration economies and inter-regional network economies.

7.3.2 Data

This study uses panel data on Japanese prefectures from 1980 to 2014. The output and input variables were as follows:

First, the output of each prefecture is its gross regional product, according to the *Annual Report on Prefectural Accounts* (Cabinet Office). Labor input is the number of employees multiplied by the number of hours worked. The number of employees and hours worked are obtained from the *Annual Report on Prefectural Accounts* (Cabinet Office) and the *Monthly Labor Survey* data (Ministry of Health, Labor, and Welfare), respectively. Capital input is the private capital stock multiplied by the capital utilization ratio. Private capital stock data are estimated from the Central Research Institute of Electric Power Industry. For the capital utilization ratio, we use estimates because no official statistics are available.[8]

To calculate the cost share of each input factor, we first define the total cost as the total value of capital and labor costs. The cost shares (c_K, c_L) of the capital and labor inputs are subsequently established by dividing the cost of each input factor by the total cost.

Capital cost is the variable obtained by multiplying the private capital stock by the capital service price. The capital service price is calculated using the following equation:

$$\text{Capital services price} = \frac{p_K(r + d)}{(1 - \tau)},$$

where p_K is the capital goods price, which is a deflator for private fixed capital investment derived from the *Annual Report on Prefectural Accounts* (Cabinet Office); r represents the average contract interest rate on loans and discounts published by the Bank of Japan; d represents the depreciation rate, calculated by dividing the depreciation cost by capital stock; and τ is the corporate tax rate (withholding portion). For labor cost, we adopt employee compensation from the *Annual Report on Prefectural Accounts* (Cabinet Office).

[8]See footnote 2 in Chap. 3 for the estimate procedure on the capital utilization ratio.

To measure the Solow residuals, the logarithm derivative was approximated using a discrete type. The following equations calculate the output growth (dv) and input growth (dx):

$$dv \cong ln\,V_t - ln\,V_{t-1} \text{ and}$$

$$dx \cong (1 - c_L) \cdot ln \frac{K_t}{K_{t-1}} + c_L \cdot ln \frac{L_t}{L_{t-1}}.$$

The *ACC* index is the index as that defined in Chap. 6:

$$ACC_{jt} = \sum\nolimits_{k \neq j} \left(\frac{POP_{kt} / \sum_{k \neq j} POP_{kt}}{T_{jkt}} \right),$$

where POP_{kt} is the population in region k in period t and denotes the market size. The population was obtained from the *Basic Resident Registers* (Ministry of Internal Affairs and Communications). T_{jkt} is the distance resistance (travel time) to travel from region j to region k over period t and is calculated based on the *National Integrated Transport Analysis System* (Ministry of Land, Infrastructure, Transport and Tourism).[9]

Population density is the ratio of the population to a residential area. The population data were obtained from the *Basic Resident Registers* (Ministry of Internal Affairs and Communications). The residential area data were taken from the *System of Social and Demographic Statistics* (Ministry of Internal Affairs and Communications).

Manufacturing industry ratios are introduced to control for the effect of regional industrial structure on productivity. Ratios for manufacturing industries are obtained by dividing the production values by the total prefectural production value. Data from the *Annual Report on Prefectural Accounts* (Cabinet Office) were used.

7.3.3 Estimation Concerns

Estimations of production functions are known to have potential endogeneity concerns (Graham 2009); these concerns apply equally to measuring Solow residuals. A common assumption in estimating external economies is that the error terms of the equations are distributed independently of the regression coefficients. This assumption does not hold in the presence of the endogenous regression coefficients. The factors responsible for external economies are linked to productivity and may be endogenous variables. Managers aiming for business success seek the most

[9] See Chaps. 5 and 6 for the calculation procedure on travel time.

productive regions. Hence, it is expected that highly productive areas will become dense agglomeration areas in terms of population and business. If this hypothesis is correct, high productivity creates a high spatial concentration. Although the theories that define the directions of this causality are underdeveloped, spatial externalities are likely to be determined in conjunction with productivity.

This concern has been discussed in many studies over an extended period (Ciccone and Hall 1996; Ciccone 2002; Henderson 2003; Rosenthal and Strange 2004; Combes and Gobillon 2015). Previous studies deal with this concern by using the two-stage least squares regression method with instrumental variables and generalized method of moments (GMM) estimation. However, they also reported that the estimation is unlikely to be biased, even if spatial externalities have an endogenous component. Ciccone (2002) and Ciccone and Hall (1996) show that estimations of external economies using instrumental variables vary only slightly from least squares estimates. Henderson (2003) and Rosenthal and Strange (2004) also conclude that the effects of endogenous regression coefficients are minor. However, Combes and Gobillon (2015) note that this issue should be addressed effectively, despite the lack of solid evidence of biases arising from endogeneity. Therefore, this study addresses this concern by using a fixed-effect model and panel GMM estimation.

7.4 Results and Discussion

7.4.1 Measurement of Cost-Based Solow Residual

First, we evaluated the measurement results of the cost-based Solow residual. Table 7.1 presents the average cost-based Solow residuals for each decade.

Table 7.1 Cost-based Solow residuals by region

	1980s	1990s	2000s	Total
Hokkaido	−0.023	−0.222	0.339	0.067
Tohoku	−0.063	−0.009	0.064	0.005
North Kanto	0.956	−0.633	0.594	0.340
Greater Tokyo Area	1.198	−0.772	0.221	0.216
Chubu	0.531	−0.205	0.322	0.228
Hokuriku	0.735	0.088	−0.069	0.214
Kansai	0.690	−0.625	0.141	0.077
Chugoku	0.110	−0.199	0.221	0.065
Shikoku	0.079	0.164	0.234	0.168
Kyushu	−0.400	−0.106	−0.049	−0.169
Okinawa	−0.420	−0.835	0.193	−0.290
National average	0.315	−0.263	0.174	0.087

Notes: (1) Values in the table represent the mean score in the respective region and decade
(2) See Fig. 1.2 in Chap. 1 for the regional classification

Firstly, we must note that the residuals of the Greater Tokyo Area, North Kanto, and Kansai fell sharply in the 1990s. Indeed, Japan's economy had been in a slump in large metropolitan areas since the collapse of the bubble economy, a period well-known as the "lost decade." It is said that "zombie firms" (firms that should have been culled but survived) became a hindrance to economic revitalization during this period and caused productivity to decline significantly (Caballero et al. 2008). The existence of zombie firms led to a significantly negative impact, especially in the Greater Tokyo Area.

Second, the economy recovered in the 2000s, and the Solow residuals rose in most regions. However, there was a regional difference in the growth of Solow residuals. As Japan's manufacturing industry became more internationally competitive, productivity grew in local areas such as North Kanto, Chubu, Chugoku, and Shikoku, which specialize in the manufacturing industry. On the other hand, the Solow residual growth in the Greater Tokyo Area and Kansai remained relatively low, perhaps due to the relatively low productivity of the non-manufacturing industries located in these areas.

Table 7.2 shows the average growth rates of the Solow residuals by prefecture. In the Greater Tokyo Area, the Solow residuals of Tokyo and Chiba were high, while those of Saitama and Kanagawa were low. The prefectures in Chubu have relatively high residuals. Meanwhile, Kansai displays overwhelmingly high residuals only in Shiga. In the local area, prefectures in the North Kanto region have higher Solow residuals than the national average in most regions. Yamaguchi and Tokushima also showed the highest residuals in Chugoku and Shikoku, respectively. All prefectures that experienced high growth rates of the Solow residuals were agglomeration areas in the manufacturing industry, except for Tokyo. That is, the results suggest that industrial structures must be controlled effectively when regional Solow residuals are evaluated.

We evaluate the significance of inter-regional networks as determinants of the Solow residuals and consider their relationship with the ACC index. Figure 7.1 plots the average growth rates of the Solow residuals versus the corresponding ACC indexes. Overall, a positive correlation is observed. In other words, regions with high ACC indexes tend to have higher Solow residuals. For example, Tokyo, Shiga, Aichi, and Chiba have strong inter-regional networks; these prefectures show remarkable technological progress and large Solow residuals. Conversely, local areas such as Aomori and Tottori have weak transportation networks and low rates of technological progress. The correlation coefficient between the two is 0.303, and no nonlinear relationships are observed. Therefore, it is reasonable to assume a linear relationship between the two variables.

7.4.2 Estimation Results

Based on the measurement results of the cost-based Solow residuals, we estimate the determinants of the Solow residuals. Table 7.3 shows the estimation results based on

Table 7.2 Cost-based Solow residuals by prefecture

Region	Prefecture	Average growth rate of SR	Region	Prefecture	Average growth rate of SR
Hokkaido	Hokkaido	0.067	Kansai	Shiga	0.457
Tohoku	Aomori	−0.452	Kansai	Kyoto	0.064
Tohoku	Iwate	0.383	Kansai	Osaka	−0.059
Tohoku	Miyagi	0.204	Kansai	Hyogo	−0.063
Tohoku	Akita	−0.137	Kansai	Nara	−0.040
Tohoku	Yamagata	−0.028	Kansai	Wakayama	0.104
Tohoku	Fukushima	0.088	Chugoku	Tottori	−0.542
Tohoku	Niigata	−0.022	Chugoku	Shimane	−0.001
North Kanto	Ibaraki	0.350	Chugoku	Okayama	0.300
North Kanto	Tochigi	0.390	Chugoku	Hiroshima	0.033
North Kanto	Gunma	0.406	Chugoku	Yamaguchi	0.533
North Kanto	Yamanashi	0.211	Shikoku	Tokushima	0.505
Greater Tokyo Area	Saitama	0.109	Shikoku	Kagawa	0.161
Greater Tokyo Area	Chiba	0.252	Shikoku	Ehime	0.162
Greater Tokyo Area	Tokyo	0.495	Shikoku	Kochi	−0.157
Greater Tokyo Area	Kanagawa	0.009	Kyushu	Fukuoka	−0.095
Hokuriku	Toyama	0.322	Kyushu	Saga	−0.401
Hokuriku	Ishikawa	0.215	Kyushu	Nagasaki	−0.325
Hokuriku	Fukui	0.105	Kyushu	Kumamoto	−0.336
Chubu	Nagano	0.259	Kyushu	Oita	−0.104
Chubu	Gifu	0.203	Kyushu	Miyazaki	0.174
Chubu	Shizuoka	0.339	Kyushu	Kagoshima	−0.096
Chubu	Aichi	0.316	Okinawa	Okinawa	−0.290
Chubu	Mie	0.023	National Average	National Average	0.087

Eq. (7.11). Models A and B show the results of the fixed-effect model and panel GMM estimation, respectively. The parameter θ represents a positive sign, thereby indicating the occurrence of increasing returns to scale within the region. The parameter β_1 on the *ACC* is positive and statistically significant, reflecting the inter-regional network's role in determining technological progress. In other words, technological progress is more pronounced in regions with more robust inter-regional networks and better access to other regional markets. Hence, areas with good access to agglomeration areas can achieve high productivity through spillover effects from the latter, that is, through the borrowed size effects. The parameter β_2 on the industrial structure is also positive and statistically significant, indicating that the greater the concentration of the manufacturing industry in the area, the greater the Solow residual. In other words, the impact of industrial structure

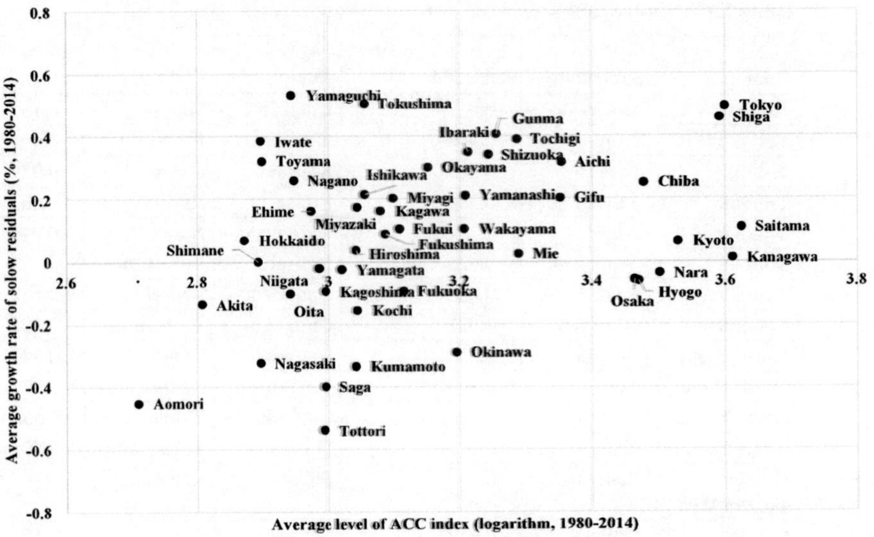

Fig. 7.1 Relationship between cost-based Solow residual and *ACC* Index

Table 7.3 Estimation results (a)

	FE		GMM	
	Model A		Model B	
Constant (α_0)	−0.171	**	−0.163	**
	(0.024)		(0.025)	
θ	0.146	**	0.172	**
	(0.033)		(0.034)	
β_1	0.024	**	0.020	**
	(0.006)		(0.006)	
β_2	0.032	**	0.034	**
	(0.004)		(0.005)	
R-squared	0.070		0.076	
J-statistic			0.821	
Observations	1598		1504	

Notes: (1) ** and * indicate significance at the 1% and 5% levels, respectively
(2) The values in parentheses indicate standard errors
(3) The J-statistic is the Sargan-Hansen test (a test of exogeneity) for the instrumental variable
(4) Two-period lag of the explanatory variable is used as the instrumental variable

on regional differences in technological progress is well controlled in our model. When comparing the results of the fixed-effect model and panel GMM estimates, we found no significant changes between the estimated parameters. This finding suggests that endogeneity is negligible.

Table 7.4 Estimation results (b)

	FE		FE		GMM		GMM	
	Model C		Model D		Model E		Model F	
Constant (α_0)	−0.144	**	−0.176	**	−0.138	**	−0.327	**
	(0.024)		(0.025)		(0.025)		(0.099)	
δ_1	0.165	**	0.345	**	0.171	**	1.316	*
	(0.005)		(0.040)		(0.005)		(0.570)	
δ_2			−0.026	**			−0.165	*
			(0.006)				(0.082)	
β_1	0.021	**	0.024	**	0.018	**	0.032	**
	(0.006)		(0.006)		(0.006)		(0.010)	
β_2	0.026	**	0.033	**	0.027	**	0.077	**
	(0.005)		(0.005)		(0.005)		(0.025)	
R-squared	0.059		0.071		0.065		0.071	
J-statistic					0.658		1.579	
Observations	1598		1598		1504		1504	

Notes: (1) ** and * indicate significance at the 1% and 5% levels, respectively
(2) The values in parentheses indicate standard errors
(3) The J-statistic is the Sargan-Hansen test (a test of exogeneity) for the instrumental variable
(4) Two-period lag of the explanatory variable is used as the instrumental variable

Next, we evaluate the nonlinear effects on internalized agglomeration economies. Table 7.4 shows the estimation results of Eq. (7.12). Models C and D are based on the fixed-effect model, while Models E and F represent the panel GMM estimates. Models C and E consider the linear relationships in population density, while Models D and F consider the nonlinear relationships in population density.

The results of Models C and E reveal that the parameter δ_1 on population density is positive and statistically significant. When densities increase by 1%, agglomeration economies increase by about 0.165%. In other words, agglomeration economies are strengthened by increasing densities: The greater the population density, the more significant the agglomeration economies. Meanwhile, the results of Models D and F reveal significantly negative sign on the parameter δ_2 for the quadratic terms of population densities. This indicates that densities are concave functions to the agglomeration economies. That is, agglomeration economies involve a threshold: They increase until they reach a particular population density threshold and decrease after that. This decrease indicates the diseconomies of agglomeration. In other words, when population density exceeds its threshold, diseconomies of agglomeration become dominant.

Based on the estimation results of Models C and D, we evaluate the level of economies of scale (see Table 7.5). The score A values on the left and the score B values on the right represent the results of linear and nonlinear relationships in population density, respectively. If nonlinear relationships are not considered, then Tokyo has the highest economies of scale, at 1.494, followed by Osaka, at 1.449; Japan's large core metropolitan area thus enjoys higher increasing returns to scale. However, the results were reversed when nonlinear relationships were considered.

Table 7.5 Scale economies score by prefecture

	Scale economies score A (average)	Scale economies score B (average)		Scale economies score A (average)	Scale economies score B (average)
Hokkaido	0.915	1.124	Shiga	1.136	1.159
Aomori	1.017	1.151	Kyoto	1.270	1.135
Iwate	0.981	1.144	Osaka	1.449	1.050
Miyagi	1.087	1.159	Hyogo	1.253	1.140
Akita	0.980	1.144	Nara	1.221	1.148
Yamagata	1.000	1.148	Wakayama	1.136	1.159
Fukushima	1.025	1.153	Tottori	1.076	1.158
Ibaraki	1.088	1.159	Shimane	1.054	1.156
Tochigi	1.073	1.158	Okayama	1.118	1.159
Gunma	1.116	1.159	Hiroshima	1.178	1.155
Saitama	1.293	1.127	Yamaguchi	1.119	1.159
Chiba	1.219	1.148	Tokushima	1.105	1.159
Tokyo	1.494	1.020	Kagawa	1.144	1.158
Kanagawa	1.423	1.066	Ehime	1.122	1.159
Niigata	1.037	1.155	Kochi	1.079	1.159
Toyama	1.056	1.157	Fukuoka	1.234	1.145
Ishikawa	1.109	1.159	Saga	1.067	1.158
Fukui	1.096	1.159	Nagasaki	1.127	1.159
Yamanashi	1.124	1.159	Kumamoto	1.075	1.158
Nagano	1.069	1.158	Oita	1.079	1.159
Gifu	1.136	1.159	Miyazaki	1.065	1.158
Shizuoka	1.189	1.153	Kagoshima	1.038	1.155
Aichi	1.277	1.133	Okinawa	1.163	1.157
Mie	1.123	1.159			

Notes: (1) Score A is based on the estimation result of Model C (Table 7.4), which considers a linear relationship
(2) Score B is based on the estimation result of Model D (Table 7.4), which considers a nonlinear relationship

The economies of scale in Tokyo and Osaka drop significantly to 1.020 and close to 1.050, respectively. Little change has been observed in many other prefectures. These results suggest that diseconomies of agglomeration occur in Tokyo and Osaka. In other words, the population densities of Tokyo and Osaka are likely to exceed the threshold. Traffic congestion, soaring land prices, air pollution, and fierce inter-firm competition have become evident in these regions. However, there is still no consensus among scholars on whether Tokyo exceeds the socially optimal city size. Kanemoto et al. (1996), an authoritative study in Japan, concluded that the size of the Tokyo metropolitan area is not too large. However, we should note that their results are based on data from the 1990s. To the best of our knowledge, no study using current data has produced robust evidence to identify the optimal city (or region) size for Tokyo.

7.4.3 Sensitivity Analysis

Finally, we examined the marginal effect of the *ACC* index using the estimation results. *Linear-Chuo Shinkansen*, a high-speed transportation system using magnetic levitation trains, is being constructed in Japan. The first part of the project will connect Shinagawa station in Tokyo to Nagoya in 2027 and will cover 286 km in 40 min (instead of 1 h and 32 min today with the current Shinkansen, accessible with the Japan Rail Pass). Subsequently, the line will be extended by 153 km to Osaka by 2045. The *Linear-Chuo Shinkansen* has the potential to increase the accessibility of inter-regional markets. The MLIT (2017) estimated the degree of time shortening achievable by the *Linear-Chuo Shinkansen*. Based on this estimation procedure, we calculate the future *ACC* index values $\widehat{ACC}_{jt}$ that should be achieved following the installation of the *Linear-Chuo Shinkansen*. The magnitude of the marginal variation of the cost-based Solow residuals on the laying of the *Linear-Chuo Shinkansen* was evaluated using the following equation:

$$\Delta\widehat{SR_{jt}^{C}} = 0.024 \times \Delta\widehat{ACC}_{jt}, \tag{7.13}$$

where $\Delta\widehat{SR_{jt}^{C}}$ represents the marginal variation in the cost-based Solow residuals according to the variation in the *ACC* index. The parameter (0.024) of the variable $\Delta\widehat{ACC}_{jt}$ in Eq. (7.13) is the estimate of model D in Table 7.4.

Table 7.6 depicts the calculation results for the magnitude of the marginal effects. Case (1) represents the connection up to Nagoya station from Shinagawa station, and case (2) represents the connection up to Shin-Osaka station from Shinagawa station.

The magnitude of the marginal effect on the Solow residuals in case (1) reveals that the largest is for Yamanashi, followed by Aichi, Gifu, Mie, Kyoto, and Tokyo. Gifu, Mie, and Kyoto are evaluated highly because of the decreased distance to Tokyo via Nagoya. Meanwhile, case (2) has more significant Solow residuals because the connection with Osaka helps expand the geographical range of the economic activities that can be completed in a short time. The Solow residuals are high not only in Yamanashi, Aichi, Gifu, Mie, Kyoto, Tokyo, and Osaka but also in Hyogo, Okayama, and Hiroshima that are not along the *Linear-Chuo Shinkansen*. Hyogo has a high value because it is adjacent to Osaka. Okayama and Hiroshima also show a sizeable marginal effect because of the decreased time distance to Tokyo via Osaka. With the current Shinkansen, Hiroshima and Okayama are located at the boundaries of areas that are accessible from Tokyo within 4 h. For this reason, a shorter aviation route is often used to travel to Hiroshima and Okayama. With the opening of the *Linear-Chuo Shinkansen*, the travel area by rail would expand,

Table 7.6 Marginal effects of *Linear-Chuo Shinkansen* installation on cost-based Solow residuals

	Marginal effects for case (1)	Marginal effects for case (2)		Marginal effects for case (1)	Marginal effects for case (2)
Hokkaido	0.004	0.005	Shiga	0.114	0.114
Aomori	0.030	0.041	Kyoto	0.168	0.168
Iwate	0.053	0.071	Osaka	0.097	0.214
Miyagi	0.056	0.070	Hyogo	0.106	0.204
Akita	0.024	0.027	Nara	0.086	0.086
Yamagata	0.045	0.059	Wakayama	0.054	0.129
Fukushima	0.077	0.096	Tottori	0.036	0.068
Ibaraki	0.071	0.094	Shimane	0.034	0.069
Tochigi	0.120	0.146	Okayama	0.114	0.221
Gunma	0.059	0.084	Hiroshima	0.099	0.194
Saitama	0.081	0.099	Yamaguchi	0.062	0.131
Chiba	0.077	0.103	Tokushima	0.018	0.048
Tokyo	0.134	0.175	Kagawa	0.069	0.137
Kanagawa	0.108	0.151	Ehime	0.044	0.087
Niigata	0.052	0.066	Kochi	0.020	0.042
Toyama	0.000	0.000	Fukuoka	0.040	0.086
Ishikawa	0.000	0.000	Saga	0.019	0.042
Fukui	0.077	0.077	Nagasaki	0.014	0.031
Yamanashi	0.375	0.408	Kumamoto	0.013	0.029
Nagano	0.000	0.024	Oita	0.015	0.033
Gifu	0.176	0.221	Miyazaki	0.017	0.029
Shizuoka	0.000	0.042	Kagoshima	0.009	0.020
Aichi	0.244	0.321	Okinawa	0.000	0.000
Mie	0.172	0.182			

Notes: (1) Case (1) is the simulation result when expanding the line up to Nagoya station
(2) Case (2) is the simulation result when expanding the line up to Shin-Osaka station

potentially shifting the travel mode between Tokyo and Hiroshima or Okayama from air to land.

7.5 Conclusions

This chapter evaluates Japan's inter-regional network economies based on cost-based Solow residuals, overcoming the issues associated with conventional analytical approaches. The empirical results can be summarized as follows. First, the cost-based Solow residuals are higher not only in large metropolitan areas, such as the Greater Tokyo Area and Kansai, but also in local areas specializing in the manufacturing industry. The dynamic changes in Solow residuals reveal a marked recovery from the economic downturn in local areas specializing in the manufacturing industry. Second, the results show that spatial externalities have a threshold, suggesting nonlinearity in internalized agglomeration economies. Third, inter-regional network formation increases productivity. In particular, this chapter simulates the marginal effects of the new high-speed railway, the *Linear-Chuo Shinkansen*, on regional productivity. The simulation results show that the raying of the *Linear-Chuo Shinkansen* is likely to increase productivity not only in the large metropolitan area comprising core areas but also in local areas.

These results suggest that inter-regional networks play a significant role in regional sustainability. Improving regional networks can enhance regional economic performance. Japan's high-quality transportation networks have made the Greater Tokyo Area a nation's transportation hub. In Japan, there is a notion that this inter-regional network has enhanced the monocentric concentration of economic agents in the Greater Tokyo Area (Fujita et al. 2018). However, the simulation results of this chapter show that the *Linear-Chuo Shinkansen* provides a significant time-saving effect not only in the region of origin but also in local regions other than those along the railway lines. That is, the concerns posed by the monocentric concentration of economic agents in the Greater Tokyo Area are likely to be overcome by the *Linear-Chuo Shinkansen*.

However, the analysis in this chapter has two main limitations. First, we do not identify the threshold levels of internalized agglomeration economies. Identifying these factors would make a significant contribution to the debate on the optimal size of regions or cities. Therefore, the left research agenda is to find the optimal population density while controlling for network economies. This requires further geographical research focusing on the inter-regional movements of economic agents.

The second limitation relates to the negative impact of inter-regional networks and agglomeration shadow. Reduced inter-regional travel times due to the improvement of transportation infrastructure allow for day trips from large cities to local areas, thereby eliminating the need to locate branch offices in local areas to trade with local firms. A rational firm would shut down branches and concentrate personnel at headquarters in large cities. As a result, local areas would suffer job losses and the outflow of human resources. The same effect applies to consumer purchasing behavior: With easier access to large cities, consumers are more likely to purchase goods from shops in large cities rather than in local areas. When more consumers can easily access national suppliers, competition in large cities intensifies, resulting in the growth of competitive firms in large cities and the decline of firms in local areas. The degree of these negative impacts must be identified when assessing the impact of the borrowed size. Future research would do well to identify this negative effect quantitatively.

References

Alonso W (1973) Urban zero population growth. Daedalus 102(4):191–206

Boix R, Trullén J (2007) Knowledge, networks of cities and growth in regional urban systems. Pap Reg Sci 86(4):551–574

Burger MJ, Meijers EJ (2016) Agglomerations and the rise of urban network externalities. Pap Reg Sci 95(1):5–15

Caballero RJ, Hoshi T, Kashyap AK (2008) Zombie lending and depressed restructuring in Japan. Am Econ Rev 98(5):1943–1977

Camagni R, Capello R, Caragliu A (2016) Static vs. dynamic agglomeration economies. Spatial context and structural evolution behind urban growth. Pap Reg Sci 95(1):133–158

Chipman JS (1970) External economies of scale and competitive equilibrium. Q J Econ 84 (3):347–385

Ciccone A (2002) Agglomeration effects in Europe. Eur Econ Rev 46(2):213–227

Ciccone A, Hall RE (1996) Productivity and the density of economic activity. Am Econ Rev 86 (1):54–70

Combes PP, Gobillon L (2015) The empirics of agglomeration economies. In: Duranton G, Henderson JV, Strange W (eds) Handbook of regional and urban economics, vol 5A. Elsevier, Amsterdam, pp 247–348

Fujita M, Hamaguchi N, Kameyama Y (2018) Spatial Economics in the Age of Declining Population. Nikkei Publishing, Tokyo. (in Japanese)

Fujita M, Thisse J-F (2002) Economics of agglomeration: cities, industrial location, and regional growth. Cambridge University Press, Cambridge

Graham DJ (2009) Identifying urbanization and localization externalities in manufacturing and service industries. Pap Reg Sci 88(1):63–84

Graham DJ, Gibbons S (2019) Quantifying wider economic impacts of agglomeration for transport appraisal: Existing evidence and future directions. Econ Transp 19. Article 100121

Hall P, Pain K (2006) The polycentric metropolis: Learning from mega-city regions in Europe. Earthscan, London

Hall RE (1990) Invariance properties of Solow's productivity residual. In: Diamond P (ed) Growth/ productivity/unemployment: Essays to celebrate Bob Solow's birthday. MIT Press, Cambridge, pp 71–112

Henderson JV (2003) Marshall's scale economies. J Urban Econ 53(1):1–28

Kanemoto Y, Ohkawara T, Suzuki T (1996) Agglomeration economies and a test for optimal city sizes in Japan. J Jpn Int Econ 10(4):379–398

Laird JJ, Venables AJ (2017) Transport investment and economic performance: A framework for project appraisal. Transp Policy 56:1–11

Meijers EJ, Burger MJ, Hoogerbrugge MM (2016) Borrowing size in networks of cities: City size, network connectivity and metropolitan functions in Europe. Pap Reg Sci 95(1):181–198

MLIT (2017) The development of land policy simulation model (FY2017 edition). Ministry of Land, Infrastructure, Transport and Tourism, Tokyo. http://www.mlit.go.jp/kokudoseisaku/kokudoseisaku_tk3_000085.html. Accessed January 2021 (in Japanese)

Otsuka A (2017) A new perspective on agglomeration economies in Japan. Springer, Singapore

Otsuka A (2018) Dynamics of agglomeration, accessibility, and total factor productivity: evidence from Japanese regions. Econ Innov New Technol 27(7):611–627

Otsuka A (2020) Inter-regional networks and productive efficiency in Japan. Pap Reg Sci 99 (1):115–133

Otsuka A (2021) A new approach to inter-regional network economies in Japan. Reg Sci Policy Pract 13(3):1051–1067

Rosenthal S, Strange W (2004) Evidence on the nature and sources of agglomeration economies. In: Henderson JV, Thisse JF (eds) Handbook of regional and urban economics, vol 4. Elsevier, Amsterdam, pp 2119–2171

Wetwitoo J, Kato H (2017) Inter-regional transportation and economic productivity: A case study of regional agglomeration economies in Japan. Ann Reg Sci 59(2):321–344

Part III
Regional Sustainability and Energy Conservation

Chapter 8
Regional Sustainability and Energy Intensity

Abstract Controlling greenhouse gas emissions by improving energy intensity and boosting regional economic growth are essential policy goals for realizing regional sustainability. Given the potential conflicts between these goals, this chapter examines whether regional agglomeration, which is considered a driving force for productivity improvement, contributes to improved energy intensity. Originally, regional agglomeration was considered to enhance productivity and competitiveness via knowledge spillover. Spillover effects, wherein advances in one firm's efficiency spread rapidly to other firms, lower the overall cost threshold for improvements in energy efficiency. In other words, the regional agglomeration has the potential to improve energy efficiency. The results of this chapter demonstrate the significant effect of regional agglomeration on energy intensity. Notably, it was confirmed that regional agglomeration affects not only regional disparities in energy intensity but also temporal dynamic changes. This finding suggests that differences in regional agglomeration affect energy demand patterns via energy intensity. Furthermore, this chapter clarifies the regional disparities in the agglomeration effect on energy intensity. The local area specialized in the manufacturing industry has a more significant potential to improve energy intensity than the large metropolitan area. These results highlight the importance of regional agglomeration as a primary factor in energy intensity and suggest that regional agglomeration should be encouraged in regions to improve energy intensity, which could protect the environment while fostering economic growth.

Keywords Agglomeration · Energy conservation · Energy intensity · Partial adjustment model · Sustainability

---

This chapter is based on Otsuka and Goto (2018).

A. Otsuka, *A New Driver of Regional Sustainability in Japan*, New Frontiers in Regional Science: Asian Perspectives 54,
https://doi.org/10.1007/978-981-16-3709-4_8

8.1 Introduction

Boosting regional economic growth and curbing greenhouse gas (GHG) emissions by improving energy efficiency is a crucial policy agenda for Japan because most GHG emissions are produced from energy use. The Japanese government has considered several potential policies for reducing GHGs, mainly centered on green innovation and renewable energy expansion. However, the hot-button issue of climate change has recently become too large to handle only individual technologies. Japan must pursue the United Nations Global Compact Cities initiative of urban and regional development, which is designed to reduce carbon emissions through urban and regional policies, including new system design, system changes, and regulation or deregulation.

Regional agglomeration is a new concept for improving regional energy intensity. Originally, regional agglomeration was thought to enhance productivity and competitiveness (Rosenthal and Strange 2004; Combes and Gobillon 2015). According to Porter and van der Linde (1995), enhanced productivity is compatible with an increase in energy efficiency. Efforts to improve the productivity of the entire production process under appropriate environmental regulations have resulted in a significant investment in energy conservation, which in turn leads to increased overall energy efficiency. Boyd and Pang (2000) argue that energy efficiency is essential for enhancing productivity and that productivity improves energy efficiency. Regional agglomeration generates knowledge spillovers. Spillover effects, wherein advances in one firm's efficiency spread rapidly to other firms, lower the overall cost threshold for improvements in energy efficiency. Thus, regional agglomeration—the driving force behind productivity gains—has the potential to improve energy efficiency.

From an engineering perspective, regional agglomeration induces improvements in energy efficiency. For example, the agglomeration of plants allows for the introduction of "cogeneration systems," which tend to be more energy efficient and can utilize the waste heat from those plants effectively. Therefore, the spatial concentration of plants creates a production environment with high energy efficiency. Furthermore, high energy efficiency can be achieved in commercial buildings by the electrification of buildings, such as the introduction of energy control systems, called "building and energy management systems (BEMS)." The electrification process progresses along with urbanization and regional agglomeration (Otsuka 2020a).

Furthermore, agglomeration (urbanized) areas have many multi-dwelling houses, such as apartments. Multi-dwelling houses have concrete structures with narrow rooms and few windows compared to detached houses. Therefore, their thermal insulation level is high, causing them to waste less energy than detached houses. In addition, residents in agglomeration areas have more opportunities to share electric lighting and car pool, which leads to energy conservation in the region. Moreover, energy markets in agglomeration areas feature fierce competition between power and gas, so there is a greater incentive for power companies to supply energy efficiently (Otsuka 2020b).

Several studies have shown that regional agglomeration suppresses energy intensity and contributes to energy conservation (see Appendix 1). Based on the stream of the study, this chapter analyzes energy intensity in Japan. Using Japanese regional data, we attempt to analyze the effect that regional agglomeration (the driving force behind sustainable regional economic growth) has on energy intensity in regional economies. The analysis provides valuable evidence for regional and energy policies designed to reduce GHG emissions by improving energy intensity. This chapter contributes to the literature in two ways.

First, we clarify the effect of regional agglomeration on energy intensity from both static and dynamic perspectives. Previous studies have examined the relationship between energy intensity and regional agglomeration from static perspectives based on cross-sectional or panel data (Morikawa 2012; Otsuka et al. 2014). However, regional agglomeration affects not only regional disparities in energy intensity but also temporal dynamic changes. A static model would not allow us to conduct an adequate analysis of dynamic effects. In contrast, a dynamic model enables us to analyze both the short-run effects (short-run elasticity) and long-run effects (long-run elasticity) of regional agglomeration on energy intensity.

Second, we clarify the impact of regional agglomeration on energy intensity in each region. Japan's commercial sector is clustered in large metropolitan areas with concentrated populations. The energy intensity in Japan's commercial sectors has not improved compared to the manufacturing sector (see Appendix 2). Thus, regional agglomeration in large metropolitan areas is not likely to be linked to improvements in energy intensity in the area. On the other hand, local areas are likely to be more efficient than large metropolitan areas because of the spatial concentration of manufacturing sectors. Energy intensity in the manufacturing sector has improved significantly; therefore, the impact of regional agglomeration on energy intensity might be vital in local areas. In this section, we verify the hypothesis.

The remainder of this chapter proceeds as follows. Section 8.2 defines the energy intensity and describes the methods and data used for the empirical analysis. Section 8.3 summarizes the results of our empirical analysis. Finally, Sect. 8.4 presents the conclusions and policy suggestions.

8.2 Methods

8.2.1 Definition of Energy Intensity

Intensity refers to the number of goods or hours used to produce a given amount of product. In the case of energy, energy intensity (*EI*) refers to the volume of energy consumption (*EC*) required to produce a given quantity of a product; it is defined by the International Energy Agency and the United Nations as energy uses per unit of gross value added (*GVA*):

$$EI = EC/GVA. \tag{8.1}$$

Therefore, the absolute volume of energy consumption can be obtained by the following equation using Eq. (8.1):

$$EC = EI \times GVA. \tag{8.2}$$

By logarithmically differentiating Eq. (8.2), changes in energy consumption can be broken down into changes in energy intensity and economic growth. Thus, the following equation is established:

$$\Delta EC = \Delta EI + \Delta GVA, \tag{8.3}$$

where Δ is the rate of change. Equation (8.3) shows that improvements in energy intensity lead to energy conservation. The energy intensity reflects improved energy efficiency. Therefore, the energy intensity concept is essential when setting policy objectives and evaluating the performance of climate-change measures, energy conservation, resource conservation, and environmental pollutant reduction.

However, there are many concerns regarding the assessment of energy intensity as an indicator of energy efficiency (Energy Information Administration 1995, 2013; International Energy Agency 2009). First, energy intensity is affected by changes in industrial structures. The transition from energy-intensive to energy-saving industries reduces energy intensity, regardless of the level of energy efficiency. Second, energy intensity is affected by demographic migration. Population migration from cold to warm areas reduces the energy intensity of heating in housing and increases the energy intensity of cooling. Third, energy intensity is affected by changes in household size. Increasing the number of residents in the home increases the likelihood of sharing energy use and decreasing energy intensity. Fourth, energy intensity is affected by the aging population. As the population ages, the use of heating increases, resulting in increased energy intensity. Moreover, energy intensity increases as aging residents stay at home for longer. In both cases, the efficiencies of the heating facilities remained unchanged, but the energy intensity of the housing increased. Fifth, the energy intensity is affected by the weather. When the mean air temperature rises, the energy intensity of housing and commercial buildings increases because of the increase in indoor cooling, even though the efficiency of cooling facilities remains unchanged. These concerns arise even when the energy intensity is assessed by sectors. Thus, to evaluate energy efficiency, we must control for several socioeconomic variables that can affect it.[1]

[1]Several alternative indicators on energy efficiencies are being developed to replace energy intensity. See Chap. 9 for discussions of desirable energy efficiency indicators.

8.2.2 *Determinants of Energy Intensity*

Below, we provide a framework for identifying the determinants of energy intensity, measured as energy consumption per GVA.

Our focus is on evaluating the effectiveness of regional agglomeration as a significant determinant of energy intensity. Previous studies (e.g., Morikawa 2012; Otsuka et al. 2014) on the relationship between population density and energy conservation for individual applications (e.g., the manufacturing or commercial sector) show a positive correlation between these factors. As in previous studies, we used population density (*DENS*), the total population divided by the habitable land area measured in km^2, as the index of regional agglomeration.[2] Using population density enables us to clarify whether urban and regional structures (i.e., regional agglomeration) improve a region's energy intensity.

Furthermore, several socioeconomic variables were included in our model as determinants of energy intensity. The selection of these variables, based on variables used in several previous studies (e.g., Metcalf 2008; Wu 2012; Otsuka et al. 2014; Otsuka and Goto 2015), is described below.

First, we consider the energy price (*P*). According to economic theory, energy consumption decreases when energy prices increase as long as the price elasticity of demand is not zero. Moreover, another effect is caused by an increase in energy prices: The increased production cost induces producers to improve energy conservation. Thus, if the energy market is functioning adequately, higher energy prices are expected to improve energy intensity through more efficient or reduced energy use. Because of this relationship, the coefficient of *P* for the energy intensity is expected to be negative.

Second, we consider per capita income (*Y*). This variable reflects the level of economic development in these regions. According to economic theory, rising incomes increase energy demand but also affect human behavior, such as adopting more energy-efficient residential lifestyles. Thus, rising income is expected to improve energy intensity. Therefore, the coefficient of *Y* for the energy intensity is expected to be negative.

Third, we incorporate the capital-labor ratio (*KL*) to account for the effect of capital intensity on energy intensity. Thompson and Taylor (1995) and Metcalf (2008) show that capital and energy have a substitution relationship in both the short and long run. Here, the capital-labor ratio is employed as a proxy for the level of technology involved. Thus, the *KL* variable might be negatively related to energy intensity. Thus, energy intensity is expected to improve as production technology improves.

Fourth, we consider the effect of the capital stock's vintage, which partially reflects the speed at which old machines and structures are replaced. New capital might be endowed with energy-saving technology and thus be more energy efficient.

[2]See Sect. 2.2 in Chap. 4 for discussions on the relationships between population density and agglomeration economies.

Regional industries that are quick to invest in upgrading capital stock might replace it with more energy-efficient capital, thereby improving the industry's energy intensity. In contrast, low investment in capital stock upgrading in a regional industry suggests that the industry's energy intensity may also be low. We consider the investment-capital ratio (*IK*) to measure this capital vintage effect. The coefficient of *IK* for the energy intensity is expected to be negative.

Fifth, we use temperature data to account for the effects of temperature changes on production activities. Specifically, we used cooling degree days (*COOL*) and heating degree days (*HEAT*). In energy economics analyses, these indexes are usually used as variables representing cooling and heating, respectively (Metcalf 2008). These indexes are assumed to be related to energy consumption, and studies have used them in this manner. For example, Metcalf and Hassett (1999) and Reiss and White (2008) used cooling and heating degree days to analyze energy consumption.

Finally, the time trend (*Time*) is included in the model to capture the general trend of technology change over time. This is expected to have a negative impact on energy intensity.

8.2.3 Empirical Models

Based on the determinants of energy intensity, we analyze the effect of regional agglomeration on energy intensity by using static and dynamic panel models. The first model, the static panel model, is as follows:

$$\begin{aligned} ln\left(EI_{jt}\right) = {} & \beta_1\, ln\left(P_t\right) + \beta_2\, ln\left(Y_{jt}\right) + \beta_3\, ln\left(DENS_{jt}\right) + \beta_4\, ln\left(KL_{jt}\right) \\ & + \beta_5\, ln\left(KL_{jt}\right)^2 + \beta_6\, ln\left(IK_{jt}\right) + \beta_7\, ln\left(IK_{jt}\right)^2 + \beta_8\, ln\left(COOL_{jt}\right) \\ & + \beta_9\, ln\left(HEAT_{jt}\right) + \beta_{10} Time + \alpha_j + u_{jt}. \end{aligned} \tag{8.4}$$

Note that all the variables in Eq. (8.4) are logarithmically expressed. The subscript j represents the region ($j = 1, \cdots, J$), and t represents the time ($t = 1, \cdots, T$). *EI* is energy intensity (final energy consumption per unit of GVA), *P* is the energy price, *Y* is per capita income, *DENS* is population density, *KL* is the capital-labor ratio (capital stock divided by the number of workers), *IK* is the investment-capital ratio (private sector corporate capital investment divided by capital stock), *COOL* is the cooling degree days, *HEAT* is the heating degree days, *Time* is the time trend, and u is an error term. The squared terms of several variables measure the possibility of nonlinearity.[3]

[3]We check the possible nonlinearity of *DENS* in the estimation and confirm that a coefficient of the quadratic term of *DENS* is not statistically significant at the 5% level. Therefore, we do not incorporate the quadratic term of *DENS* into our models.

Both $\boldsymbol{\alpha}$ and $\boldsymbol{\beta}$ are estimation coefficients. Because panel data are used, $\boldsymbol{\alpha}$ represents individual effects. As the energy price increases, the energy intensity β_1 is expected to have a negative sign. If increasing income improves energy intensity, β_2 is also expected to have a negative sign. If population density improves energy intensity, then the sign of β_3 will be negative, whereas if population density worsens energy intensity, its sign will be positive. Moreover, the signs of β_4 and β_5 will be negative if capital and energy have a substitution relationship, while those of β_6 and β_7 will be negative if capital upgrading improves energy intensity. Furthermore, β_{10} is expected to have a negative sign because of technological developments.

One concern with Eq. (8.4) is the assumption that the energy intensity immediately reflects changes in economic variables. A more realistic assumption is that energy intensity is affected by changes in economic variables, such as energy price, after a certain time lag.[4] Accordingly, we consider the influence of a time lag by using a partial adjustment model as the second model.[5] We construct a partial adjustment model for the energy intensity as follows:

$$y_{jt} = \boldsymbol{x}'_{jt}\widehat{\boldsymbol{\beta}} + \lambda y_{jt-1} + \widehat{\varepsilon}_{jt}, \tag{8.5}$$

where y_{jt} represents the energy intensity level in region j at time t. The vector $\boldsymbol{x}_{jt}$ represents the determinants of energy intensity. $\widehat{\varepsilon}$ is the error term, which includes the individual effect $\boldsymbol{\alpha}$. λ is a measurement of the adjustment from the actual to the desirable level of energy intensity. $\widehat{\boldsymbol{\beta}} = (1-\lambda)\boldsymbol{\beta}$ is the effect (short-run elasticity) that a short-run change in x has on y, and $\widehat{\boldsymbol{\beta}}/(1-\lambda)$ is the effect (long-run elasticity) that a long-run change in x has on y. In Eq. (8.5), the lagged form of the explained variable is included as an explanatory variable. Therefore, a correlation exists between the explanatory variable and the error term, creating an inconsistency in standard ordinary least squares estimates. To address this concern, Arellano and Bond (1991) proposed a generalized method of moments for dynamic panel estimates that are consistent under these conditions. We use this dynamic panel estimation method to estimate the parameters in Eq. (8.5).

8.2.4 Data

The data used for the analysis are based on the final energy consumption of Japan's regions, comprising 47 prefectures, from 1990 to 2010. These are, therefore, panel data by prefecture and year. Final energy refers to the amount of energy consumed in the industrial, commercial, transport, and household sectors. Energy is generally

---

[4] See Filippini et al. (2018) and Otsuka (2019) for more in-depth considerations of the dynamism in energy consumption behavior.

[5] See Nordhaus (1979) and Cuddington and Dagher (2015) for theoretical background on partial adjustment models of energy demand.

composed of primary and secondary energy. Primary energy is directly obtained from nature, such as crude oil, coal, natural gas, hydropower, nuclear power, wind power, and geothermal power. In contrast, secondary energy is converted and processed for easy use via primary energy, such as petroleum products refined at refineries, electricity generated at power plants, city gas, and coke for steelmaking. The final energy consumption is the net total of the primary and secondary energy consumed. The energy consumed during processing and conversion, such as in electricity and petroleum refining, was counted separately as part of the energy conversion sector. In other words, the final energy consumption is the total amount of energy consumed at the consumer level, such as industrial activities, transport, and households.

Most of the data were extracted from the official statistics of the Japanese government. The source of the prefectural final energy consumption data is the *Energy Consumption Statistics by Prefecture* (Agency for Natural Resources and Energy, Ministry of Economy, Trade, and Industry). The GVA, which is used as the denominator in the calculation of energy intensity, represents the gross regional product extracted from the *Annual Report on Prefectural Accounts* (Cabinet Office). Energy price data were obtained from the International Energy Agency. Income figures are obtained from the *Annual Report on Prefectural Accounts* (Cabinet Office) and converted to real figures based on the gross regional expenditure deflator. Population and habitable land area data were extracted from the *Basic Resident Registers* and the *System of Social and Demographic Statistics*, respectively (Statistics Bureau, Ministry of Internal Affairs and Communications). The data on private capital investments and private capital stock are estimates from the Central Research Institute of Electric Power Industry. The number of employees was obtained from the *Annual Report on Prefectural Accounts*. Data on cooling degree and heating degree days were obtained from the meteorological observation points. The annual number of cooling degree days is the cumulative difference of temperatures between 22 °C and the average temperature on each day in a year whose average temperature exceeds 24 °C. The annual number of heating degree days is the cumulative difference of temperatures between 14 °C and the average temperature on each day in an annual period whose average temperature is below 14 °C. All variables were standardized, making it possible to compare each estimated coefficient and interpret the magnitude of the effect of different variables measured at different scales.

Table 8.1 shows the descriptive statistics for the variables. The average energy intensity for the entire sample was 28.619 GJ per million yen. Energy intensity remained relatively constant during the 1990s and then improved significantly during the 2000s. The improvement rate of the energy intensity during the observation period was 8.7%. The average population density during the observation period was 1355 people per km^2. The population density increased from the 1990s to the 2000s. This trend indicates that regional agglomeration increased during the observation period, suggesting a high possibility that the observed energy intensity improvements were caused by enhanced regional agglomeration. Regarding socio-economic variables other than population density, energy prices declined in the

Table 8.1 Descriptive statistics

		Energy intensity	Energy price	Per capita income	Population density	Capital-labor ratio	Investment-capital ratio	Cooling degree days	Heating degree days
		(GJ per million yen)	(2010 = 100)	(million yen)	(people per km^2)	(million yen per person)		(degree days)	(degree days)
		(*EI*)	(*P*)	(*Y*)	(*DENS*)	(*KL*)	(*IK*)	(*COOL*)	(*HEAT*)
1990	Mean	29.520	94	2.518	1336	10.726	0.099	413	1048
	Standard deviation	19.796	0	0.469	1574	1.801	0.009	163	411
	Maximum	105.394	94	4.542	8456	14.701	0.118	864	2239
	Minimum	8.483	94	1.818	259	7.274	0.071	45	5
2000	Mean	29.280	85	2.750	1350	15.951	0.057	412	1140
	Standard deviation	17.638	0	0.446	1585	2.383	0.006	140	533
	Maximum	87.916	85	4.953	8413	20.896	0.078	840	2769
	Minimum	8.937	85	1.977	260	11.137	0.044	66	3
2010	Mean	26.953	100	2.879	1360	19.491	0.045	492	1267
	Standard deviation	15.745	0	0.442	1679	3.023	0.004	137	467
	Maximum	83.860	100	4.854	9066	26.189	0.055	909	2591
	Minimum	8.288	100	2.180	249	12.975	0.035	124	122
1990–2010	Mean	28.619	92	2.715	1355	15.481	0.061	367	1106
	Standard deviation	16.948	7	0.469	1592	3.506	0.016	176	471
	Maximum	105.394	111	5.478	9066	26.189	0.118	1186	2769
	Minimum	8.288	85	1.818	249	7.274	0.035	0	0

Table 8.2 Correlation matrix between independent variables

	ln(*P*)	ln(*Y*)	ln (*DENS*)	ln(*KL*)	ln(*IK*)	ln (*COOL*)	ln (*HEAT*)	*Time*
ln(*P*)	1.000	0.106	−0.008	0.280	−0.118	0.032	0.005	0.499
ln(*Y*)	0.106	1.000	0.653	0.545	−0.135	0.142	0.224	0.221
ln (*DENS*)	−0.008	0.653	1.000	0.233	0.063	0.401	−0.213	−0.006
ln(*KL*)	0.280	0.545	0.233	1.000	−0.641	0.200	0.165	0.740
ln(*IK*)	−0.118	−0.135	0.063	−0.641	1.000	−0.048	−0.079	−0.827
ln (*COOL*)	0.032	0.142	0.401	0.200	−0.048	1.000	−0.459	0.125
ln (*HEAT*)	0.005	0.224	−0.213	0.165	−0.079	−0.459	1.000	0.014
Time	0.499	0.221	−0.006	0.740	−0.827	0.125	0.014	1.000

1990s before increasing markedly in the 2000s. The average per capita income during the observation period was JPY 2.715 million. Per capita income rose steadily during the 1990s and the 2000s, and it is highly likely that higher incomes contributed to improved energy intensity. The average capital-labor ratio during the observation period was 15.481. The capital intensity increased from the 1990s through the 2000s; therefore, it is highly likely that production processes were increasingly mechanized. The average investment-capital ratio (0.061) during the observation period was low, declining from the 1990s to the 2000s. This suggests that little upgrading of production equipment occurred.

Table 8.2 shows the correlation matrix of these explanatory variables. Several variables are correlated with the time trend. For example, *KL* and the time trend are highly correlated; the correlation coefficient is positive. Moreover, *IK* and the time trend are highly correlated, while the sign of the correlation coefficient is negative. These correlations might affect the sign of the regression coefficient of the time trend. However, multicollinearity is not a significant concern because we use panel data estimation.

Figure 8.1 illustrates the static relationship between energy intensity (vertical axis) and population density (horizontal axis). The figure shows the values for each prefecture in 1990 and 2010. As indicated by the downward-sloping scatterplots from northwest to southeast, energy intensity and population density have a negative correlation. In other words, the higher a region's population density, the lower its energy intensity. This negative relationship between energy intensity and population density is stable and occurs in the other years between 1990 and 2010.

Figure 8.2 illustrates the dynamic relationship between the change in energy intensity (vertical axis) and that in population density (horizontal axis) between 1990 and 2010. Similar to the static relationship, these change variables might also be negatively correlated, indicating that the increasing population density might have

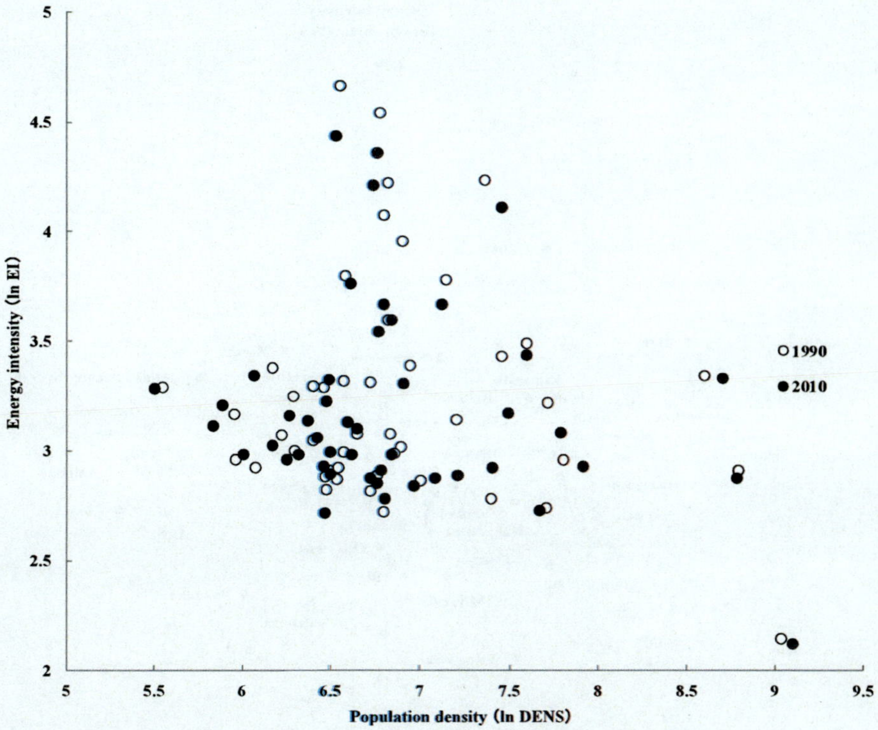

Fig. 8.1 Relationship between energy intensity and population density

contributed to improvements in energy intensity.[6] For example, population density increased in the Greater Tokyo Area (consisting of Saitama, Chiba, Tokyo, and Kanagawa), while energy intensity decreased. The following section quantitatively examines the degree to which the changes in population density affect those in energy intensity.

8.3 Results and Discussion

Table 8.3 shows the estimation results of Eq. (8.4), which is the static panel model of the energy intensity. Model A's results are for the standard fixed-effects model, while Model B's results are for the fixed-effects model estimated using the instrumental variable method. First, we perform an F-test to check for fixed effects and then reject the null hypothesis of the nonexistence of individual effects at the 1% significance

[6]The change in energy intensity had a correlation coefficient of −0.38 with the change in population density.

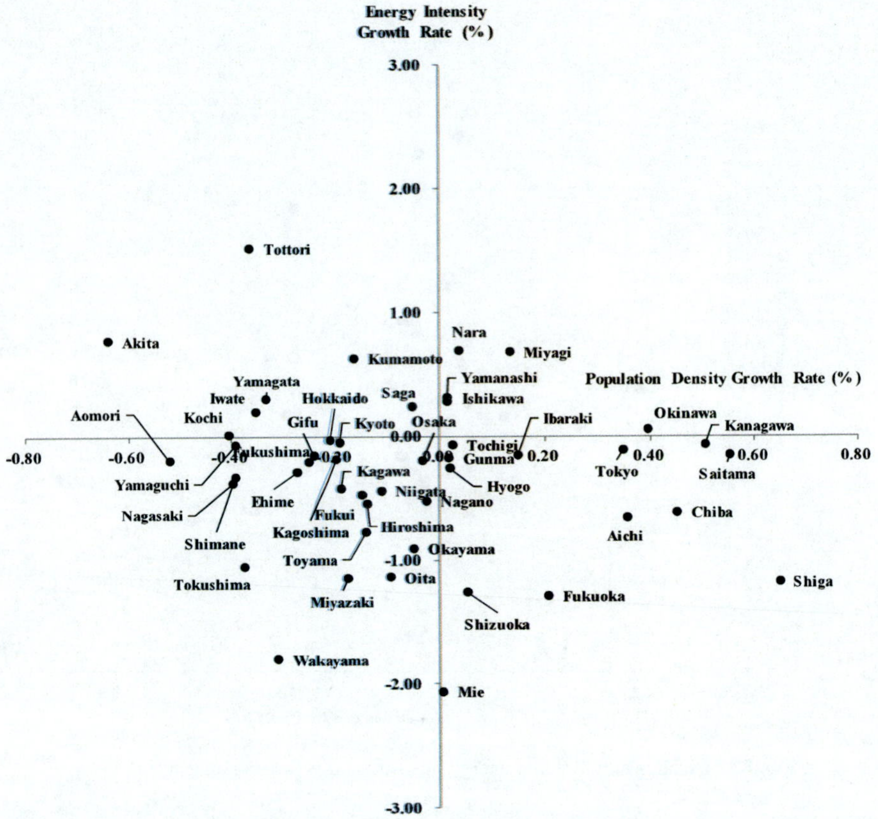

Fig. 8.2 Dynamic relationship between energy intensity and population density

level. We then perform a Hausman test on the hypothesis that the observed individual effects are random effects; we reject this null hypothesis at the 1% significance level. Therefore, the results shown in Table 8.3 are for the fixed-effects model as the static panel model (Models A and B).

Table 8.3 shows that population density is negatively associated with energy intensity. As both the explanatory and dependent variables are logarithmic values, coefficients β_1 through β_{10} represent degrees of elasticities. Accordingly, the more significant the estimated coefficients (elasticities), the stronger the effect of the corresponding explanatory variable on the dependent variable. Therefore, as shown in the table, the effects of population density significantly exceed those of the other explanatory variables. The coefficients of energy price and per capita income have negative signs; thus, the sign condition is satisfied. In other words, increases in both energy prices and incomes improve energy intensity. The sign of the coefficient on the capital-labor ratio is negative; therefore, capital and energy consumption have a substitution relationship, meaning that a higher capital-labor

Table 8.3 Estimation results for static panel models

Regressors	Coefficient	FE		FE-IV	
		Model A		Model B	
ln(*P*)	β_1	−0.019	**	−0.038	*
		(−3.09)		(−2.05)	
ln(*Y*)	β_2	−0.156	**	−0.159	**
		(−12.06)		(−6.74)	
ln(*DENS*)	β_3	−0.747	**	−0.915	**
		(−4.91)		(−3.04)	
ln(*KL*)	β_4	−0.081	**	−0.219	**
		(−2.80)		(−3.09)	
ln(*KL*)^2	β_5	−0.033	**	−0.033	**
		(−10.53)		(−4.25)	
ln(*IK*)	β_6	−0.023	*	−0.058	*
		(−2.21)		(−2.06)	
ln(*IK*)^2	β_7	−0.025	**	−0.030	**
		(−6.69)		(−3.84)	
ln(*COOL*)	β_8	0.021	**	−0.055	
		(3.48)		(−1.14)	
ln(*HEAT*)	β_9	−0.002		−0.220	
		(−0.15)		(−1.11)	
Time	β_{10}	0.002		0.018	
		(0.41)		(1.68)	
Number of observations		987		940	
F-test		1791.2	**	1732.5	**
Hausman test		39.78	**		

Notes: (1) FE = fixed-effects model; FE-IV = fixed-effects model using the instrumental variable method
(2) ** and * indicate significance at the 1% and 5% levels, respectively
(3) The values in parentheses indicate t-statistics
(4) One-period lag of the explanatory variable is used as the instrumental variable

ratio translates into lower energy intensity. Moreover, the coefficient of the investment-capital ratio is negative, indicating that upgrading capital stock improves energy intensity. Although statistically significant, the estimated parameters are much smaller than are those of income and density. Thus, the effect of the investment-capital ratio is negligible.

It is crucial to avoid an endogeneity problem to ensure that the fixed-effects model estimates are meaningful. We might need to consider the endogeneity problem between *DENS* and *EI* because of the possible influence of omitted variables in Eq. (8.4).[7] To address this concern, we use the instrumental variable method to show the results (Model B) to estimate Eq. (8.4). The coefficient of population density in

[7]Note that there are concerns about the evaluation of regional agglomeration using production functions. See Sect. 3.3 in Chap. 7 for details.

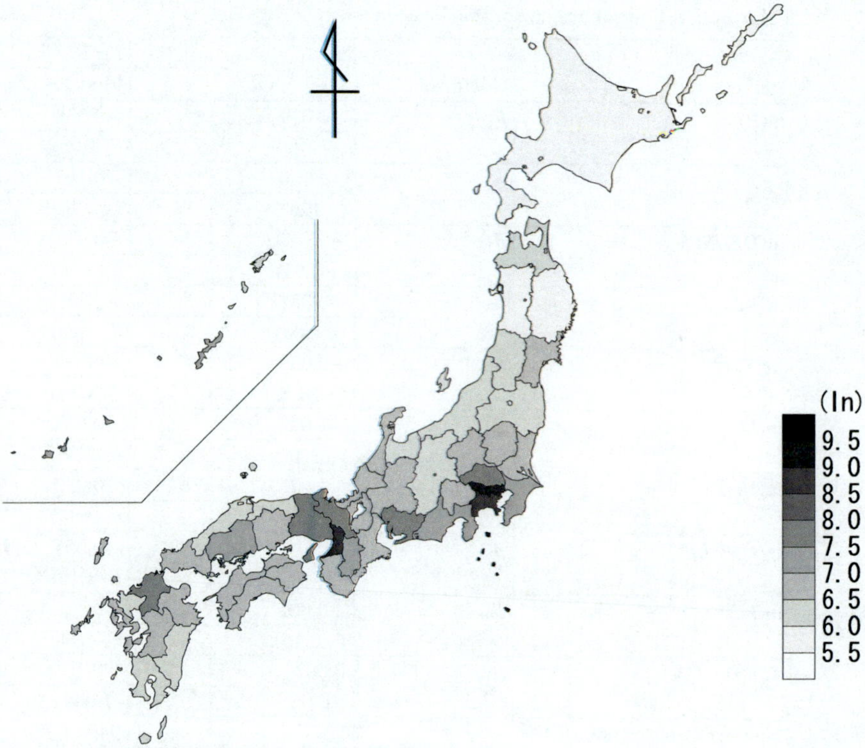

Fig. 8.3 Population density (Y2010, logarithmic value)

Model B is similar to that in Model A. Hence, it is reasonable to assume that any potential endogeneity problem in the equation would have a negligible influence.

Figure 8.3 shows the regional distribution of population density. The population is concentrated in large metropolitan areas, such as Tokyo, Osaka, and Aichi prefecture. In particular, there is a significant disparity in the changes in population density between these large metropolitan areas and local areas (see Fig. 8.4). The population concentration in large metropolitan areas has progressed over the study period. In contrast, local areas have experienced spatial dispersion of their populations. This strongly suggests that the effects of population density changes on energy intensity differ among regions.

Therefore, we evaluate inter-regional differences in the impact of population density by extending the fixed-effects model by considering a regional dummy (*dum*) for population density as follows:

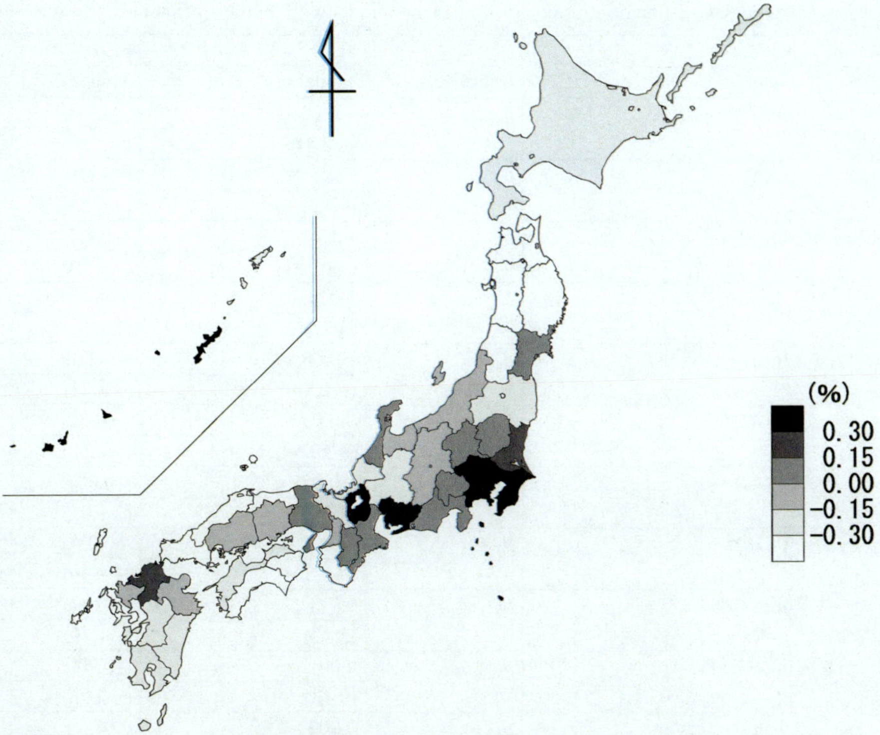

Fig. 8.4 Changes in population density (%, annual growth rate)

$$ln\left(EI_{jt}\right) = \beta_1\, ln\left(P_t\right) + \beta_2\, ln\left(Y_{jt}\right) + \left(\beta_3 + \delta dum\right) \cdot ln\left(DENS_{jt}\right) + \beta_4\, ln\left(KL_{jt}\right)$$
$$+ \beta_5\, ln\left(KL_{jt}\right)^2 + \beta_6\, ln\left(IK_{jt}\right) + \beta_7\, ln\left(IK_{jt}\right)^2 + \beta_8\, ln\left(COOL_{jt}\right)$$
$$+ \beta_9\, ln\left(HEAT_{jt}\right) + \beta_{10} Time + \boldsymbol{\alpha}_j + u_{jt}.$$

Table 8.4 shows the estimation results for the dummy variable static panel model. A regional dummy variable takes a value of 1 for large metropolitan (urban) areas and 0 for local areas; large metropolitan areas include the Greater Tokyo Area, Kansai, and Chubu, while local areas are defined as all other regions. In Model C, the regression coefficient of population density for large metropolitan areas is 0.2012 (= 1.2147 + 1.0135), and that for local areas is 1.2147. This implies that the marginal effect of population density on energy intensity is higher in local areas. This result reveals that regional agglomeration in local areas has the potential to improve energy intensity, reflecting the fact that manufacturing sectors, which have a high impact of industrial agglomeration on energy intensity, are concentrated in local areas.

Next, Table 8.5 shows the results of estimating Eq. (8.5), which considers dynamic changes in energy intensity. According to the standard for dynamic panel estimates, Eq. (8.5) is estimated using the level of the lagged explained variable

Table 8.4 Estimation results for static panel model with dummy variable

Regressors	Coefficient	FE Model C		FE-IV Model D	
ln(*P*)	β_1	−0.021	**	−0.041	*
		(−3.41)		(−2.20)	
ln(*Y*)	β_2	−0.158	**	−0.159	**
		(−12.26)		(−6.89)	
ln(*DENS*)	β_3	−1.215	**	−1.237	**
		(−6.19)		(−2.50)	
dum	δ	1.014	**	0.634	
		(3.73)		(1.11)	
ln(*KL*)	β_4	−0.083	**	−0.220	**
		(−2.87)		(−3.21)	
ln(*KL*)^2	β_5	−0.033	**	−0.032	**
		(−10.68)		(−4.11)	
ln(*IK*)	β_6	−0.022	*	−0.055	*
		(−2.15)		(−1.91)	
ln(*IK*)^2	β_7	−0.025	**	−0.031	**
		(−6.83)		(−3.90)	
ln(*COOL*)	β_8	0.021	**	−0.056	
		(3.42)		(−1.19)	
ln(*HEAT*)	β_9	0.002		−0.200	
		(0.13)		(−0.96)	
Time	β_{10}	0.001		0.018	
		(0.28)		(1.74)	
Number of observations		987		940	
F-test		1784.5	**	1711.3	**
Hausman test		49.54	**		

Notes: (1) FE = fixed-effects model; FE-IV = fixed-effects model using the instrumental variable method
(2) ** and * indicate significance at the 1% and 5% levels, respectively
(3) The values in parentheses indicate t-statistics
(4) One-period lag of the explanatory variable is used as the instrumental variable

(period $t - 2$) as the instrumental variable. When conducting the dynamic panel estimates, it is essential to avoid serial correlation with the error term because consistent estimators are obtained only when this condition is satisfied. We thus perform Arellano-Bond tests to check for serial correlation.[8] A significant first-order serial correlation is permitted in the AR (1) test, but the AR (2) test must show no statistically significant second-order serial correlation. Based on the tests, we cannot reject the null hypothesis of no second-order serial correlation in Models E and F (see Table 8.5). In other words, the error term (u_{jt}) does not exhibit second-order self-correlation in either model. We then use the result of the Sargan-Hansen test (a test of

[8]See footnote 6 in Chap. 5 for a detailed explanation of Arellano-Bond tests.

Table 8.5 Estimation results for dynamic panel model with dummy variable

Regressors	Coefficient	Model E		Model F	
ln(*EI*)(−1)	λ	0.311	**	0.327	**
		(17.69)		(14.83)	
ln(*P*)	β_1	−0.012	*	−0.013	
		(−2.01)		(−1.86)	
ln(*Y*)	β_2	−0.082	**	−0.086	**
		(−6.68)		(−6.51)	
ln(*DENS*)	β_3	−0.393	*	−0.714	**
		(−2.33)		(−4.20)	
dum	δ			0.978	
				(1.76)	
ln(*KL*)	β_4	−0.079		−0.052	
		(−1.32)		(−0.76)	
ln(*KL*)^2	β_5	−0.020	**	−0.019	**
		(−4.17)		(−4.38)	
ln(*IK*)	β_6	−0.023	*	−0.021	
		(−2.28)		(−1.79)	
ln(*IK*)^2	β_7	−0.008		−0.006	
		(−1.43)		(−1.03)	
ln(*COOL*)	β_8	0.011	**	0.017	**
		(4.06)		(5.26)	
ln(*HEAT*)	β_9	0.008		0.005	
		(1.03)		(0.64)	
Time	β_{10}	0.003		−0.001	
		(0.30)		(−0.11)	
Number of observations		893		893	
J-statistic		41.189		41.259	
Probability (J-statistic)		0.25		0.22	
m-statistic (AR(1))		−2.94	**	−5.65	**
m-statistic (AR(2))		1.75		1.93	
Instrumental variable		Energy (t − 2)		Energy (t − 2)	

Notes: (1) Estimates are a two-step dynamic generalized method of moments estimates
(2) ** and * indicate significance at the 1% and 5% levels, respectively
(3) The values in parentheses indicate t-statistics
(4) The J-statistic is the Sargan-Hansen test (a test of exogeneity) for the instrumental variable
(5) The m-statistics are the Arellano-Bond test for first- and second-order serial correlation

exogeneity for instrumental variables) to ensure that the number of variables is not excessive. The results show that the conditions for dynamic panel estimates are satisfied. As expected, a statistically significant negative coefficient is obtained for the population density variable (representing regional agglomeration). The sign condition is also satisfied for most of the other socioeconomic variables, such as energy price and per capita income, and statistically significant values are obtained.

Table 8.6 Factor elasticities relative to energy intensity

	Short run	Long run
P	−0.01	−0.02
Y	−0.08	−0.12
DENS	−0.39	−0.57
KL	−0.12	−0.17
IK	−0.04	−0.06
COOL	0.01	0.02
HEAT	NS	NS
TIME	NS	NS

Notes: (1) The values in the table are calculated based on the estimation results of Model E (Table 8.5)
(2) NS = not statistically significant

Furthermore, we estimate the dynamic panel model considering the influence of the regional dummy (*dum*) on population density. The estimation results are shown in Model F. They indicate that the regional dummy coefficients are not statistically significant. This result differs from that of the static panel model (Model C) and suggests that the hypothesis (i.e., that the marginal effect of population density on energy intensity differs between large metropolitan areas and local areas) is not supported in the dynamic panel model. Therefore, the regional difference effects of population density on energy intensity arise solely from differences in the regional data and not from differences in the estimated coefficients.

The difference in results between the static and dynamic panel models concerning the regional dummy is likely to be caused by differences in the ease of population migration over time. In general, economic agents tend to move among regions according to environmental disparities. In the short run, population migration is not high because of the relatively high moving costs, leading to a clear difference in the influence of population density between urban and local regions. In the long run, economic agents move more freely among regions due to long-term regional benefits; thus, inter-regional disparities in the influence of population density would diminish.

Table 8.6 shows the short- and long-run elasticities of each variable relative to energy intensity, which is calculated from the estimation results of Model E shown in Table 8.5. Population density has short- and long-run elasticities of −0.39 and −0.57, respectively, which are greater than the elasticities for energy price and per capita income. This finding suggests that when population density increases by 1%, energy intensity improves by approximately 0.4% and 0.6% over the short and long run, respectively. The estimated elasticities are smaller than those obtained from static panel models, but the conclusion that population density improves energy intensity still holds. Energy prices have short- and long-run elasticities of −0.01 and – 0.02, respectively, which are smaller than those for population density and per capita income. These relative elasticities suggest that changes in energy prices have a more negligible effect on energy intensity than do either income or regional agglomeration.

These findings demonstrate the significant effect of regional agglomeration on energy intensity. We obtain consistent signs for the estimated coefficients on population density regardless of whether static or dynamic panel models are used. Therefore, it is concluded that urban and regional development policies that boost regional agglomeration improve energy intensity.

Another critical research task is to clarify the extent to which population density contributes to improvements in energy intensity. Under long-run equilibrium, the actual energy intensity y_{jt} implies a desirable energy intensity y^*_{jt}. In other words, $y^*_{jt} = y_{jt} = y_{jt-1}$. This relationship can be used to express Eq. (8.5), using the following formula:

$$\Delta y_{jt} = \Delta \mathbf{x}'_{jt} \frac{\widehat{\boldsymbol{\beta}}}{1 - \lambda} + \Delta \varepsilon_{jt}. \tag{8.6}$$

Using Eq. (8.6), we can calculate each determinant's contribution (annual average, %) to changes in energy intensity. To measure this effect, we use the estimated coefficients of Model E in Table 8.5.

Table 8.7 shows the contribution levels of the determinants of energy intensity. Population density is the second most significant negative contributing factor for the Greater Tokyo Area and Okinawa, and the third largest negative contributing factor in North Kanto, Chubu, and Kansai. For example, the contribution of population density is 0.264% for the Greater Tokyo Area. These results indicate that large metropolitan areas, except for North Kanto and Okinawa, experienced advanced regional agglomeration over the study period, which, in combination with rising productivity, has improved energy intensity. In contrast, most local areas lack advanced regional agglomeration and thus do not benefit from corresponding improvements in energy intensity.

In addition to population density, per capita income and the capital-labor ratio also contribute to improving energy intensity. These factors are essential in all regions, and the capital-labor ratio, in particular, explains the most significant part of the observed changes in energy intensity. Conversely, energy price has little effect on energy intensity, as shown by the low price elasticity of energy demand. Thus, energy intensity is affected by income and capital intensity more strongly than by energy price.

8.4 Conclusions

Japan's declining population and increasingly stringent environmental restrictions make finding a way to achieve sustainability a crucial policy issue. Grounded in the notion that we can combine improvements in energy efficiency and productivity for sustainability, this chapter clarifies the effect of regional agglomeration on energy intensity. The results show, for the first time, that regional agglomeration leads to

Table 8.7 Contributions of each factor to changes in energy intensity (1990–2010, annual averages; %)

	Rate of change of energy intensity (Δ EI = a + b + c + d + e + f + g + h + i)									
	Energy intensity	Energy price	Per capita income	Population density	Capital-labor ratio	Investment-capital ratio	Cooling degree days	Heating degree days	Time	Other factors
	(Total)	(a)	(b)	(c)	(d)	(e)	(f)	(g)	(h)	(i)
Hokkaido	−0.036	−0.005	−0.065	0.120	−0.401	0.136	0.054	0.009	0.023	0.094
Tohoku	0.155	−0.005	−0.109	0.169	−0.570	0.165	0.032	0.010	0.023	0.439
North Kanto	−0.035	−0.005	−0.107	−0.030	−0.521	0.157	0.019	0.009	0.023	0.420
Greater Tokyo Area	−0.241	−0.005	−0.028	−0.264	−0.445	0.166	0.017	0.014	0.023	0.282
Chubu	−0.934	−0.005	−0.094	−0.017	−0.523	0.160	0.011	0.010	0.023	−0.501
Hokuriku	−0.318	−0.005	−0.062	0.052	−0.430	0.146	0.016	0.013	0.023	−0.071
Kansai	−0.467	−0.005	−0.044	−0.016	−0.491	0.143	0.007	0.010	0.023	−0.093
Chugoku	−0.071	−0.005	−0.058	0.153	−0.557	0.152	0.006	0.014	0.023	0.202
Shikoku	−0.440	−0.005	−0.092	0.177	−0.572	0.141	0.007	0.008	0.023	−0.127
Kyushu	−0.471	−0.005	−0.115	0.072	−0.501	0.137	−0.002	0.014	0.023	−0.093
Okinawa	0.047	−0.005	−0.107	−0.225	−0.497	0.142	0.003	0.193	0.023	0.521

Notes: (1) The values in the table are calculated by applying the estimation results of Model E (Table 8.5) to Eq. (8.6)
(2) See Fig. 1.2 in Chap. 1 for the regional classification

improvements in energy intensity in Japan. This finding suggests that differences in regional agglomeration affect energy demand patterns via energy intensity because energy demand is calculated by multiplying energy intensity by GVA. In other words, we need to pay attention to regional energy intensity when planning national energy policies. Regional energy intensity is affected by various socioeconomic factors, such as regional population and industry structure. In this sense, this chapter highlights the importance of regional agglomeration as a primary factor in energy intensity.

Here, we note that the agglomeration effect on the energy intensity varies dramatically among regions. In our analysis, the local area specialized in the manufacturing industry has a more significant potential to improve energy intensity than the large metropolitan area. However, the reality in Japan is different. In large metropolitan areas such as the Greater Tokyo Area, Kansai, and Chubu, increased population inflow has improved energy intensity, whereas in local areas other than Okinawa and North Kanto, the opposite was observed due to the decline in population density. Thus, the enhanced regional agglomeration improved energy intensity in large metropolitan areas, but this effect was not realized in local areas due to declining population density.

Therefore, the findings of this chapter suggest that growth strategies for regional development should be tailored for each region. Exploring tailored strategies using more detailed data will be a future research agenda. In particular, it is necessary to verify whether the hypothesis on regional disparities of the agglomeration effect on energy intensity applies to end-use sectors. For this task, we must consider using a more extensive dataset of sectoral energy consumption.[9] Furthermore, we must carefully consider the fact that the level of energy intensity depends on a variety of socioeconomic factors. That is, as mentioned, energy intensity may not be a suitable index for expressing energy efficiency. Chap. 9 considers the issue of desirable measurements of energy efficiency.

Appendix 1: Brief Review of Studies on Regional Agglomeration and Energy Efficiency Improvements

This appendix briefly reviews the studies on the relationship between regional agglomeration and energy efficiency improvements.

It is well known that regions with high degrees of agglomeration are more energy saving and environmentally friendly (Glaeser 2011). The impact of regional agglomeration on energy saving has been explored by many scholars as sectoral studies. Most studies on the transportation sector show that in areas with high population density, energy consumption in the transportation sector becomes efficient because public transportation substitutes for private vehicles.

[9]See Otsuka (2020b) for sectoral considerations on regional agglomeration and energy intensity.

Newman and Kenworthy (1989) focus on the role of population density, which is a measure of regional agglomeration, and find a negative relationship between population density and gasoline consumption per capita by using data on cities in the world. Bento and Cropper (2005) show that the probability of driving to work is lower as population agglomeration and rail miles increase using data from US cities. Brownstine and Golob (2009) use US data to find that population agglomeration has a direct impact on vehicle use and fuel consumption. Karathodorou et al. (2010) revealed that fuel consumption per capita is reduced in dense cities because transport distances become shorter, the probability of commuting by walking and cycling increases, and public transportation can replace private vehicle usage. Su (2011) indicates that population agglomeration has a negative impact on gasoline consumption per household, taking into account traffic congestion and high-speed road density as urban structures in the United States.

In China, there are growing studies on regional agglomeration and improvements in energy efficiency. Liu et al. (2017) identified that regional agglomeration leads to effective energy savings. Zheng and Lin (2018) show that regional agglomeration significantly improves energy efficiency in China's paper industry. Furthermore, the contribution of regional agglomeration to energy efficiency has been clarified in studies from the perspective of carbon emissions (Zeng and Zhao 2009; Han et al. 2018; Yao et al. 2018). China has faced a polycentric spatial structure after megacities have reached a certain level in the urbanization process. Xu et al. (2021) demonstrated the impact of polycentric spatial structure on energy efficiency from the perspective of regional agglomeration and clarified the role of the regional agglomeration of environmental improvement.

Of the studies done on Japan, few examine the relationships between regional agglomeration and energy intensity from a regional perspective. This lack of analysis is partly due to the unavailability of official statistics on energy use in cities and regions. However, in recent years, new official statistics on energy use have been released, reflecting the growing global environmental concerns. The Ministry of Economy, Trade, and Industry (METI) publishes the *Energy Consumption Statistics by Prefecture*, which allows easy access to energy statistics at the prefectural level. Using official statistics in Japan, several studies discuss the relationship between regional agglomeration and energy intensity for the industrial and commercial sectors (Morikawa 2012; Otsuka et al. 2014; Otsuka 2020b). Morikawa (2012) examined the effects of population agglomeration on energy intensity in the commercial sector and showed that doubling population density improves commercial energy intensity by about 12%. Otsuka et al. (2014) show the impacts of industrial agglomeration on energy intensity in the manufacturing sector, and Otsuka (2020b) finds that population agglomeration has a significant impact on improving sectoral energy intensity.

Table 8.8 Final energy consumption by Japan's end-use sectors

	Level (PJ, 2014)	Change of level (1990 = 100)	Share (%, 2014)	Change of share (% point, 1990–2014)	Contribution to total variation (%, 1990–2014)
Final energy consumption	14,135	110.8	100.0	–	–
(A) Industry	11,273	106.7	79.8	−3.05	5.52
(i) Agriculture, fishery, mining, and construction	284	58.5	2.0	−1.79	−1.58
(ii) Manufacturing	8465	101.7	59.9	−5.31	1.13
(iii) Commercial	2525	143.3	17.9	4.05	5.97
(B) Residential	2009	124.8	14.2	1.60	3.13
(C) Transportation	853	145.6	6.0	1.45	2.09

Source: Calculations based on the *Energy Consumption Statistics by Prefecture* (Ministry of Economy, Trade and Industry)
Note: The values in the table are the sum of the values of the prefectures

Appendix 2: The Current Trend of Energy Consumption in Japan's Region

This appendix briefly explains the sectoral and regional structure in Japan's energy consumption.

Table 8.8 shows the final energy consumption of Japan's end-use sector. In 2014, the final energy consumption was 14,135PJ. Of this total, the share of the manufacturing sector is 59.9% (8465PJ). Therefore, most of Japan's energy consumption is accounted for by the manufacturing sector. The share of the residential sector is 14.2% (2009PJ), and the share of the transportation sector is only 6.0% (853PJ).

Japan's energy consumption increased from 1990 to 2014, reaching 110.8 in 2014 when the 1990 level was set as 100. Mainly, the energy consumption of the commercial, residential, and transportation sectors increased. On the other hand, energy consumption in the agriculture, fishery, mining, and construction sectors has significantly decreased, where the 2014 levels were half the 1990 levels.

As the energy consumption of the commercial sector increased, the sector's share of energy consumption increased significantly. As a result, the commercial sector made the most significant contribution to the growth of total final energy consumption, at 5.97%. The residential sector's contribution was 3.13%, and the transportation sector's contribution was 2.09%. These results show that the commercial, residential, and transportation sectors significantly increased Japan's final energy consumption.

Table 8.9 shows energy intensity levels by end-use sectors. The 2014 level is high in the manufacturing sector and low in the commercial sector. However, the annual growth rate of energy intensity of the manufacturing sector is negative, which means

Table 8.9 Energy intensity by Japan's end-use sectors

	Unit	Level (2014)	Change of level (1990 = 100)	Average growth rate (%, 1990–2014)
Final energy consumption	GJ/million yen	25.79	102.9	0.12
(A) Industry	GJ/million yen	20.57	99.1	−0.04
(i) Agriculture, fishery, mining, and construction	GJ/million yen	8.27	90.9	−0.41
(ii) Manufacturing	GJ/million yen	73.92	85.1	−0.70
(iii) Commercial	GJ/million yen	6.38	128.3	1.09
(B) Residential	GJ/person	15.89	121.2	0.84
(C) Transportation	GJ/person	6.75	141.4	1.52

Source: Calculations based on the *Energy Consumption Statistics by Prefecture* (Ministry of Economy, Trade and Industry)
Note: The values in the table are the sum of the values of the prefectures

Table 8.10 Regional trends in final energy consumption

	Level (PJ, 2014)	Share (%, 2014)	Average growth rate (%, 1990–2014)	Contribution to national variation (%, 1990–2014)
Hokkaido	609	4.31	0.48	0.50
Tohoku	1024	7.24	0.51	0.89
North Kanto	1009	7.14	0.78	1.29
Greater Tokyo Area	3537	25.03	0.72	4.23
Chubu	1893	13.39	0.37	1.21
Hokuriku	259	1.83	−0.15	−0.07
Kansai	1898	13.43	0.06	0.19
Chugoku	1907	13.49	0.34	1.13
Shikoku	492	3.48	0.29	0.25
Kyushu	1434	10.15	0.42	1.04
Okinawa	72	0.51	0.68	0.08

Source: Calculations based on the *Energy Consumption Statistics by Prefecture* (Ministry of Economy, Trade and Industry)
Note: See Fig. 1.2 in Chap. 1 for the regional classification

that energy intensity is much improved. On the other hand, the energy intensity of the commercial sector is considerably worse. The residential and transportation sectors are also worsening in energy intensity. Improving the energy intensity of these sectors is one of Japan's energy conservation policy agendas (METI 2020).

Next, we explain the regional structure of energy consumption in Japan. Table 8.10 shows the level of energy consumption by Japan's regions and their

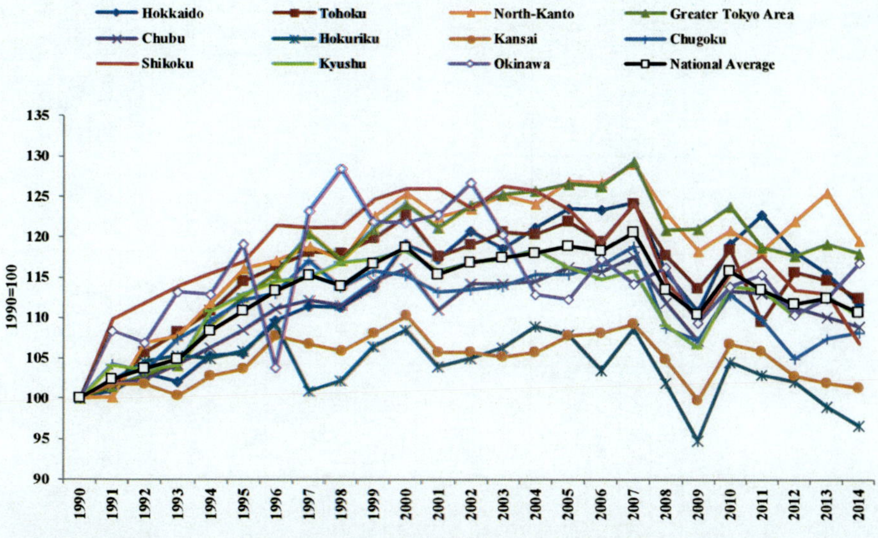

Fig. 8.5 Regional trend in final energy consumption (1990 = 100). Source: Calculations based on the *Energy Consumption Statistics by Prefecture* (Ministry of Economy, Trade and Industry). Note: See Fig. 1.2 in Chap. 1 for the regional classification

changes. The region with the highest share is the Greater Tokyo Area, with its energy consumption accounting for 25.03% of the national energy consumption. Kansai and Chubu are also large; thus, these large metropolitan areas account for the majority of the national energy consumption. In the local areas, energy consumption is significant in Chugoku and Kyushu. In the observation period, energy consumption increased in all regions except for Hokuriku, and the increasing trend of energy consumption is remarkable. The contribution degree of the Greater Tokyo Area to the overall change of energy consumption is the largest, indicating that the economic performance of this area has a significant impact on the time trend of national energy consumption.

Figure 8.5 shows the time series change of energy consumption in regions when the 1990 level is set as 100. In all regions, energy consumption increased significantly in the 1990s and then showed a downward trend in the 2000s. In particular, the increasing trend of energy consumption is remarkable in the Greater Tokyo Area and the North Kanto. On the other hand, the growth of energy consumption in Hokuriku and Kansai is weak, and it has been on a downward trend since the 2000s.

Table 8.11 shows the trend of energy consumption by end-use in regions. In the Greater Tokyo Area, the energy consumption of the commercial and the residential sector has increased significantly. In particular, the energy consumption of the commercial sector has been increasing over time, and the rate of increase is the highest among the regions. In the residential sector, energy saving progressed in the 2000s, but the degree of progress was weak. On the other hand, manufacturing energy conservation has progressed significantly. Since the scale of energy

Table 8.11 Regional trends in the final energy consumption by end-use sectors

End-use sector		Hokkaido	Tohoku	North Kanto	Greater Tokyo Area	Chubu	Hokuriku	Kansai	Chugoku	Shikoku	Kyushu	Okinawa
(A) Industry / (i) Agriculture, fishery, mining, and construction	1990	54,611	61,237	28,872	92,644	59,362	16,243	52,871	34,992	19,978	60,318	3618
	2000	41,538	58,811	24,751	69,322	50,508	15,691	49,603	30,724	18,233	50,704	3588
	2014	21,361	40,259	17,380	56,328	36,159	9045	30,155	20,381	10,843	38,899	2728
	2000 / 1990%	−2.99%	−0.45%	−1.70%	−3.17%	−1.78%	−0.38%	−0.71%	−1.43%	−1.01%	−1.91%	−0.09%
	2014 / 2000%	−4.99%	−2.87%	−2.68%	−1.58%	−2.54%	−4.15%	−3.76%	−3.11%	−3.92%	−2.02%	−2.08%
	2014 / 1990%	−4.00%	−1.81%	−2.18%	−2.14%	−2.13%	−2.51%	−2.41%	−2.32%	−2.62%	−1.89%	−1.22%
(A) Industry / (ii) Manufacturing	1990	247,787	437,971	560,884	1,915,099	1,157,762	140,390	1,184,022	1,484,254	316,669	853,617	22,514
	2000	271,303	486,415	673,834	2,313,986	1,280,330	133,024	1,213,168	1,675,875	384,073	965,038	23,313
	2014	268,770	459,180	640,370	2,028,356	1,120,424	112,005	1,042,691	1,580,031	324,813	875,791	12,224
	2000 / 1990%	1.01%	1.17%	2.06%	2.12%	1.12%	−0.60%	0.27%	1.36%	2.17%	1.37%	0.39%
	2014 / 2000%	−0.07%	−0.44%	−0.39%	−1.01%	−1.02%	−1.31%	−1.16%	−0.45%	−1.28%	−0.74%	−4.84%
	2014 / 1990%	0.35%	0.21%	0.58%	0.25%	−0.14%	−0.98%	−0.55%	0.27%	0.11%	0.11%	−2.62%
(A) Industry / (iii) Commercial	1990	89,653	166,396	103,004	486,408	214,117	43,055	304,615	109,652	55,675	173,276	16,169
	2000	115,419	219,446	141,207	643,817	284,831	58,414	371,651	139,345	75,555	230,190	22,645
	2014	110,094	204,542	142,605	793,224	324,671	56,902	416,819	133,805	68,495	244,774	28,588
	2000 / 1990%	2.85%	3.12%	3.57%	3.16%	3.22%	3.45%	2.23%	2.70%	3.45%	3.21%	3.81%
	2014 / 2000%	−0.36%	−0.54%	0.08%	1.62%	1.01%	−0.20%	0.89%	−0.31%	−0.75%	0.47%	1.81%
	2014 / 1990%	0.90%	0.90%	1.42%	2.15%	1.83%	1.22%	1.37%	0.87%	0.91%	1.51%	2.51%

(B) Residential	1990	122,934	180,918	99,839	408,728	210,477	49,582	249,219	92,100	44,595	138,752	11,655
	2000	163,103	249,895	137,142	545,373	258,633	60,029	321,581	117,098	63,292	178,743	13,572
	2014	159,062	221,104	121,835	519,548	273,718	55,104	305,859	109,210	58,127	169,505	15,445
	2000 / 1990%	3.19%	3.65%	3.59%	3.26%	2.32%	2.15%	2.87%	2.70%	3.97%	2.85%	1.71%
	2014 / 2000%	−0.19%	−0.94%	−0.91%	−0.37%	0.44%	−0.66%	−0.38%	−0.53%	−0.65%	−0.41%	1.00%
	2014 / 1990%	1.13%	0.88%	0.87%	1.05%	1.15%	0.46%	0.89%	0.74%	1.16%	0.87%	1.23%
(C) Transportation	1990	30,818	63,925	51,383	94,469	96,590	18,568	83,092	40,736	23,349	75,069	8006
	2000	58,939	101,631	82,286	148,528	142,611	23,403	108,868	66,746	38,810	113,896	12,364
	2014	50,149	98,495	86,856	139,791	137,845	25,803	102,784	63,077	29,782	105,274	13,427
	2000 / 1990%	7.47%	5.29%	5.37%	5.16%	4.42%	2.60%	3.05%	5.64%	5.81%	4.74%	4.95%
	2014 / 2000%	−1.23%	−0.24%	0.42%	−0.47%	−0.26%	0.75%	−0.44%	−0.43%	−2.02%	−0.60%	0.64%
	2014 / 1990%	2.14%	1.90%	2.31%	1.72%	1.56%	1.44%	0.93%	1.92%	1.06%	1.48%	2.27%

Source: Calculations based on the *Energy Consumption Statistics by Prefecture* (Ministry of Economy, Trade and Industry)

Note: (1) Unit on the level of energy consumption is GJ

(2) See Fig. 1.2 in Chap. 1 for the regional classification

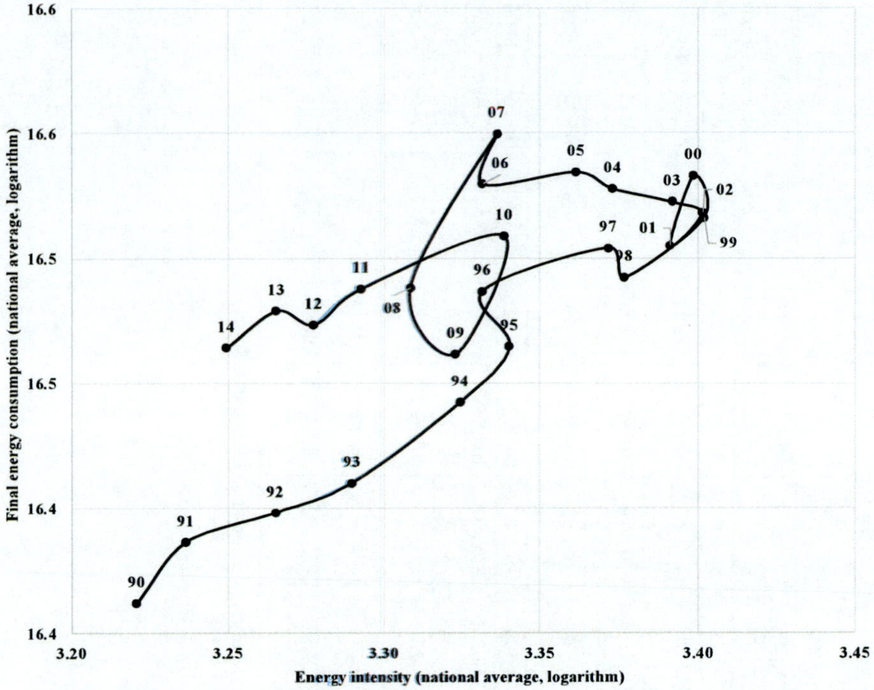

Fig. 8.6 Relationship between final energy consumption and energy intensity. Source: Calculations based on the *Energy Consumption Statistics by Prefecture* (Ministry of Economy, Trade and Industry)

consumption of the manufacturing sector is large, this energy conservation progress likely leads to a significant decline in the region's overall energy consumption.

As described in Sect. 8.2.1, there is a strong correlation between energy intensity and the volume of energy consumption. That is, improved energy intensity leads to energy conservation. Figure 8.6 shows this relationship. Energy intensity worsened from 1990 to 2000, and the volume of energy consumption increased. Since 2000, energy intensity has been improving, and energy consumption has been suppressed. This suggests that improved energy intensity is a critical driving force in achieving energy conservation.

Table 8.12 shows the level of energy intensity by end-use and its change in regions. In the Greater Tokyo Area, the deterioration of energy intensity of the commercial sector is remarkable. The energy intensity of the commercial sector has deteriorated over time, and the degree of worsening in energy intensity has been the highest in Japan. On the other hand, Hokuriku and Kansai show remarkable improvement in the energy intensity of the manufacturing sector, especially in the 2000s. This implies that the progress of energy conservation in the manufacturing sector has dramatically contributed to suppressing the energy consumption of these regions.

Table 8.12 Regional trends in the energy intensity by end-use sectors

End-use sector		Hokkaido	Tohoku	North Kanto	Greater Tokyo Area	Chubu	Hokuriku	Kansai	Chugoku	Shikoku	Kyushu	Okinawa
(A) Industry / (i) Agriculture, fishery, mining, and construction	1990	17.05	9.97	7.19	6.74	8.52	11.29	7.64	11.42	11.11	10.99	7.49
	2000	15.65	11.72	8.82	7.47	9.12	12.92	9.40	13.02	11.06	11.20	8.44
	2014	9.37	7.76	7.84	6.78	8.37	9.60	7.70	11.28	9.71	10.42	6.14
	2000 / 1990%	−0.95%	1.81%	2.30%	1.16%	0.77%	1.50%	2.33%	1.46%	−0.05%	0.21%	1.33%
	2014 / 2000%	−3.87%	−3.12%	−0.91%	−0.74%	−0.66%	−2.26%	−1.53%	−1.10%	−1.00%	−0.56%	−2.42%
	2014 / 1990%	−2.57%	−1.08%	0.38%	0.03%	−0.07%	−0.71%	0.03%	−0.06%	−0.59%	−0.23%	−0.86%
(A) Industry / (ii) Manufacturing	1990	161.19	71.38	69.93	73.71	58.83	52.72	67.61	237.76	140.90	153.00	151.46
	2000	144.87	67.33	77.51	104.40	62.75	47.85	75.43	264.02	158.10	152.35	126.29
	2014	139.00	56.46	53.63	91.07	38.97	32.95	55.97	186.15	103.72	114.85	61.64
	2000 / 1990%	−1.18%	−0.65%	1.15%	3.94%	0.72%	−1.07%	1.22%	1.17%	1.29%	−0.05%	−2.00%
	2014 / 2000%	−0.32%	−1.34%	−2.79%	−1.04%	−3.60%	−2.83%	−2.27%	−2.65%	−3.19%	−2.15%	−5.37%
	2014 / 1990%	−0.64%	−1.01%	−1.15%	0.92%	−1.77%	−2.02%	−0.82%	−1.06%	−1.32%	−1.24%	−3.83%
(A) Industry / (iii) Commercial	1990	6.08	5.98	6.04	3.93	5.29	5.22	5.03	5.80	5.95	5.61	5.90
	2000	7.72	7.25	7.93	4.91	6.45	6.67	6.21	7.27	7.51	7.11	7.81
	2014	7.31	6.83	7.46	5.45	6.93	6.64	6.70	6.63	6.63	7.10	8.08
	2000 / 1990%	2.68%	2.17%	3.07%	2.50%	2.22%	2.76%	2.36%	2.54%	2.63%	2.66%	3.17%
	2014 / 2000%	−0.42%	−0.46%	−0.47%	0.81%	0.56%	−0.04%	0.58%	−0.71%	−0.96%	−0.01%	0.27%
	2014 / 1990%	0.80%	0.58%	0.92%	1.43%	1.18%	1.05%	1.25%	0.58%	0.47%	1.03%	1.38%

(continued)

Table 8.12 (continued)

End-use sector		Hokkaido	Tohoku	North Kanto	Greater Tokyo Area	Chubu	Hokuriku	Kansai	Chugoku	Shikoku	Kyushu	Okinawa
(B) Residential	1990	21.79	14.76	13.17	13.07	12.95	15.99	12.39	11.89	10.52	10.44	9.43
	2000	28.70	20.26	17.37	16.59	15.36	19.18	15.63	15.11	15.07	13.28	10.24
	2014	29.23	19.22	15.72	14.82	16.07	18.19	14.87	14.60	14.69	12.87	10.74
	2000 / 1990%	3.11%	3.58%	3.12%	2.68%	1.92%	2.04%	2.62%	2.70%	4.08%	2.71%	0.92%
	2014 / 2000%	0.14%	−0.40%	−0.76%	−0.86%	0.35%	−0.40%	−0.38%	−0.27%	−0.20%	−0.24%	0.36%
	2014 / 1990%	1.29%	1.15%	0.77%	0.55%	0.94%	0.56%	0.80%	0.90%	1.46%	0.92%	0.56%
(C) Transportation	1990	5.46	5.21	6.78	3.02	5.94	5.99	4.13	5.26	5.51	5.65	6.48
	2000	10.37	8.24	10.42	4.52	8.47	7.48	5.29	8.61	9.24	8.46	9.33
	2014	9.22	8.56	11.20	3.99	8.09	8.52	5.00	8.43	7.52	7.99	9.33
	2000 / 1990%	7.39%	5.21%	4.89%	4.57%	4.02%	2.50%	2.79%	5.64%	5.92%	4.59%	4.14%
	2014 / 2000%	−0.90%	0.30%	0.56%	−0.96%	−0.35%	1.01%	−0.44%	−0.17%	−1.57%	−0.43%	0.00%
	2014 / 1990%	2.30%	2.18%	2.21%	1.21%	1.35%	1.55%	0.83%	2.07%	1.37%	1.52%	1.60%

Source: Calculations based on the *Energy Consumption Statistics by Prefecture* (Ministry of Economy, Trade, and Industry).

Note: (1) Energy intensity is defined as follows: (**A**) Industry: GJ/million yen; (i) agriculture, fishery, mining, and construction: GJ/million yen; (ii) manufacturing: GJ/million yen; (iii) commercial: GJ/million yen; (**B**) residential: GJ/person; (**C**) transportation: GJ/person

(2) See Fig. 1.2 in Chap. 1 for the regional classification

In Japan, energy efficiency improvement and energy conservation are progressing mainly in the manufacturing sector. While the sector has a high volume of energy consumption, the progress of energy efficiency has led to suppression in energy consumption via improving energy intensity. This situation is dominant in Hokuriku and Kansai. On the other hand, in the commercial and the residential sector, energy conservation has not progressed, and energy intensity has worsened. As a result, the energy consumption of these sectors has increased significantly. This situation is more pronounced in the Greater Tokyo Area, and it is essential to improve the energy efficiency of the commercial and the residential sector to reduce energy consumption in Japan.

References

Arellano M, Bond SR (1991) Some tests of specification for panel data: Monte Carlo evidence and an application to employment equations. Rev Econ Stud 58:277–297

Bento AM, Cropper ML (2005) The effects of urban spatial structure on travel demand in the United States. Rev Econ Stat 87(3):466–478

Boyd GA, Pang JX (2000) Estimating the linkage between energy efficiency and productivity. Energy Policy 28(5):289–296

Brownstine D, Golob TF (2009) The impact of residential density on vehicle usage and energy consumption. J Urban Econ 65(1):91–98

Combes PP, Gobillon L (2015) The empirics of agglomeration economies. In: Duranton G, Henderson JV, Strange W (eds) Handbook of regional and urban economics, vol 5A. Elsevier, Amsterdam, pp 247–348

Cuddington JT, Dagher L (2015) Estimating short and long-run demand elasticities: a primer with energy-sector applications. Energy J 36(1):185–209

Energy Information Administration (1995) Measuring energy efficiency in the United States' economy: a beginning. Energy Information Administration, DOE/EIA-0555(95)/2, Washington DC

Energy Information Administration (2013) International energy outlook 2013. U.S. Energy Information Administration, DOE/EIA-0484(2013), Washington DC

Filippini M, Hirl B, Masiero G (2018) Habits and rational behavior in residential electricity demand. Resour Energy Econ 52:137–152

Glaeser EL (2011) Triumph of the City: how our greatest invention makes us richer, smarter, greener, healthier and happier. Penguin Press, Maryland

Han F, Xie R, Fang JY (2018) Urban agglomeration economies and industrial energy efficiency. Energy 162:45–59

International Energy Agency (2009) Progress with implementing energy efficiency policies in the G8. International Energy Agency, Paris

Karathodorou N, Graham DJ, Noland RB (2010) Estimating the effect of urban density on fuel demand. Energy Econ 32(1):86–92

Liu J, Cheng ZH, Zhang HM (2017) Does industrial agglomeration promote the increase of energy efficiency in China? J Clean Prod 164:30–37

Metcalf GE (2008) An empirical analysis of energy intensity and its determinants at the state level. Energy J 29(3):1–26

Metcalf GE, Hassett KA (1999) Measuring the energy savings from home improvement investment: evidence from monthly billing data. Rev Econ Stat 81(3):516–528

Ministry of Economy, Trade and Industry (2020) Energy White Paper 2020. https://www.enecho.meti.go.jp/en/category/whitepaper/. Accessed January 2021

Morikawa M (2012) Population density and efficiency in energy consumption: an empirical analysis of service establishments. Energy Econ 34(5):1617–1622

Newman PWG, Kenworthy JR (1989) Gasoline consumption and cities: a comparison of US cities with a global survey. J Am Plan Assoc 55(1):24–37

Nordhaus WD (1979) The efficient use of energy resources. Yale University Press, New Haven and London

Otsuka A (2019) Natural disasters and electricity consumption behavior: a case study of the 2011 Great East Japan Earthquake. Asia-Pac J Reg Sci 3(3):887–910

Otsuka A (2020a) Determinants of energy demand efficiency: evidence from Japan's industrial sector. In: Tanar T (ed) Energy Policy. IntechOpen, London, pp 85–103. https://doi.org/10.5772/intechopen.81482

Otsuka A (2020b) Energy intensity and population density in Japan. In: Madden J, Shibusawa H, Higano Y (eds) Environmental economics and computable general equilibrium analysis. Springer, Singapore, pp 233–252. https://doi.org/10.1007/978-981-15-3970-1_11

Otsuka A, Goto M (2015) Estimation and determinants of energy efficiency in Japanese regional economies. Reg Sci Policy Pract 7(2):89–101

Otsuka A, Goto M (2018) Regional determinants of energy intensity in Japan: the impact of population density. Asia-Pac J Reg Sci 2(2):257–278

Otsuka A, Goto M, Sueyoshi T (2014) Energy efficiency and agglomeration economies: the case of Japanese manufacturing industries. Reg Sci Policy Pract 6(2):195–212

Porter ME, Van der Linde C (1995) Toward a new conception of the environment competitiveness relationship. J Econ Perspect 9:97–118

Reiss PC, White MW (2008) What changes energy consumption? Prices and public pressures. Rand J Econ 39(3):636–663

Rosenthal S, Strange W (2004) Evidence on the nature and sources of agglomeration economies. In: Henderson JV, Thisse JF (eds) Handbook of regional and urban economics, vol 4. Elsevier, Amsterdam, pp 2119–2171

Su Q (2011) The effect of population density, road network density, and congestion on household gasoline consumption in U.S. urban areas. Energy Econ 33(3):445–452

Thompson P, Taylor TG (1995) The capital-energy substitutability debate. Rev Econ Stat 77 (3):565–569

Wu Y (2012) Energy intensity and its determinants in China's regional economies. Energy Policy 41:703–711

Xu C, Bin Q, Shaoqin S (2021) Polycentric spatial structure and energy efficiency: evidence from China's provincial panel data. Energy Policy 149. https://doi.org/10.1016/j.enpol.2020.112012

Yao XL, Kou D, Shao S, Li XY, Wang WX, Zhang CT (2018) Can urbanization process and carbon emission abatement be harmonious? New evidence from China. Environ Impact Assess Rev 71:70–83

Zeng DZ, Zhao L (2009) Pollution havens and industrial agglomeration. J Environ Econ Manag 58 (2):141–153

Zheng QY, Lin BQ (2018) Impact of industrial agglomeration on energy efficiency in China's paper industry. J Clean Prod 184:1072–1080

Chapter 9
Regional Sustainability and Energy Efficiency

Abstract Energy intensity has not been deemed a suitable index of energy efficiency because it depends on various socioeconomic factors, such as energy prices and production size. Therefore, this chapter identifies desirable energy efficiency indices that overcome the concerns of energy intensity using the stochastic frontier analysis (SFA) approach. The SFA approach controls for prices and income, mechanization, vintage, and climate factors to derive accurate energy efficiency levels. By using this approach, this chapter clarifies the energy efficiency level for Japan's industrial and commercial sectors and evaluates the impact of regional agglomeration and inter-regional networks on energy efficiency. The results reveal that improved inter-regional networks have a positive impact on energy efficiency. Regions with well-developed transportation networks are highly energy efficient. This result suggests that policies aimed at strengthening inter-regional networks can significantly contribute to improving energy efficiency in Japan. Meanwhile, the results reveal that regional agglomeration has mixed effects on energy efficiency. That is, there are positive and negative impacts on energy efficiency. Initially, agglomeration economies inherently have a mixture of advantages and disadvantages, such as spatial externalities, congestion, and heat islands. By considering the nonlinear effects, this chapter identified that there is a threshold in the agglomeration effects, and both a positive and negative effect of agglomeration are at play. This result suggests that agglomeration sizes beyond the threshold level are necessary to enjoy agglomeration benefits.

Keywords Agglomeration · Energy efficiency · Energy intensity · Inter-regional networks · Stochastic frontier analysis (SFA)

This chapter is based on Otsuka (2020a).

A. Otsuka, *A New Driver of Regional Sustainability in Japan*, New Frontiers in Regional Science: Asian Perspectives 54,
https://doi.org/10.1007/978-981-16-3709-4_9

9.1 Introduction

Energy consumption is greatly affected by energy intensity, defined as the energy consumption per gross value added (GVA).[1] In Japan, energy intensity has been improving mainly in the manufacturing industry, but overall energy consumption has been rising due to economic growth that exceeded the improvement in sectoral energy intensity.[2] Therefore, determining whether it is possible to improve energy intensity to the extent that exceeds economic growth is vital for formulating policies to achieve regional sustainability. However, energy intensity is not deemed to be suitable as an index of energy efficiency because it depends on a variety of socioeconomic factors such as energy price and production size.[3] Furthermore, because energy intensity focuses on the relationship between energy input and output, it ignores factor substitution with other inputs in the production process. Therefore, many researchers have attempted to identify desirable energy efficiency index measurements (e.g., Murillo-Zamorano 2004; Shui et al. 2015). Energy efficiency indices have two approaches: stochastic frontier analysis (SFA) and data envelopment analysis (DEA). The SFA method is a parametric approach and is usually used to analyze productive efficiency and addresses statistical noise that DEA cannot handle well. Furthermore, utilizing SFA allowed us to identify the determinants of energy efficiency indices. Therefore, this chapter defines energy efficiency indices using SFA and analyzes its determinants.

Regarding the determinants of energy efficiency, we focus on the role of inter-regional networks in energy efficiency improvement as well as regional agglomeration. As discussed in Part II (Chaps. 5, 6, and 7), the upgrading of inter-regional networks expands the range of agglomeration economies and improves regional productivity. This is called the "borrowed size" effect and has been discussed in the context of urban network externalities (Camagni 1993; Capello 2000; Camagni and Capello 2004; Boix and Trullen 2007; Otsuka 2018a, 2020b). Reduced inter-regional travel time leads to an increase in regional productivity via this effect. Firms with increased productivity can turn their gains into energy conservation investments. Therefore, in an economy under environmental constraints, increased productivity is compatible with improved energy efficiency. Furthermore, when public transportation networks are designed well, people can avoid using private vehicles, thus saving energy consumption because the energy efficiency of passenger vehicles is worse than that of public transportation such as railways.[4] The

[1]See Chap. 8 for discussions on energy intensity.

[2]See Appendix 2 in Chap. 8 on the current trend of energy consumption in Japan's regions.

[3]Whether energy intensity is a suitable indicator for energy efficiency is debatable (e.g., Ang et al. 2010; Proskuryakova and Kovalev 2015).

[4]Passenger vehicles consume larger amounts of energy per unit than railways in Japan. In other words, the energy efficiency of railways is higher than that of passenger vehicles. To help solve global environmental problems, railways are therefore preferable to passenger vehicles as a means of travel. The modal shift possibility is considered in Chap. 10 in depth.

upgrading of inter-regional networks also affects commercial activities as time spent in the office can be reduced drastically by utilizing business trips and remote working. This is likely to make the energy consumption of commercial buildings more efficient. To the best of our knowledge, no empirical study has analyzed these effects. Therefore, this chapter aims to provide new insights into the effects of inter-regional networks on energy efficiency.

The remainder of this chapter proceeds as follows. Section 9.2 reviews studies on energy efficiency indices. Section 9.3 describes the framework of the analysis. Section 9.4 presents and discusses the results of the analysis. Finally, Sect. 9.5 presents the conclusions and policy suggestions.

9.2 Energy Efficiency Indices

Conceptually speaking, there are two categories of energy efficiency indicators: partial factor energy efficiency (PFEE) indicators and total factor energy efficiency (TFEE) indicators (Du and Lin 2017). The PFEE indicator is defined as the relationship between energy input and output. There are two well-known PFEE indicators: energy intensity (ratio of energy input to output) and energy productivity (ratio of energy output to input). The PFEE indicator is widely used because of its ease of use (Energy Information Administration 1995, 2013). However, the PFEE indicator does not consider the roles of other input factors. This has been criticized in recent studies because it is not consistent with actual production activities (Hu and Wang 2006; Boyd 2008; Stern 2012).

In contrast to the PFEE index, the TFEE index is defined as the ratio of the optimal to the actual energy input in a multifactor framework (Zhou and Ang 2008; Chang and Hu 2010). Conceptually, the TFEE indicator is based on neoclassical production theory. Filippini and Hunt (2011, 2012) defined TFEE indicators in terms of energy demand. There are two main approaches to estimating the TFEE indicator: DEA and SFA.

The DEA and SFA methods are nonparametric and parametric frontier approaches for estimating frontier functions, respectively (Murillo-Zamorano 2004; Shui et al. 2015).[5] Since Charnes et al. (1978), many researchers have used DEA in theoretical and applied research; it is known as one of the most effective tools for measuring the management efficiency of decision-makers such as firms. However, this method does not assess statistical errors and thus cannot address errors or outliers in frontier identification. It cannot handle the statistical noise that occurs in the data. As a result, the credibility of the DEA findings partially depends on data quality. With this limitation in mind, Filippini and Hunt (2011, 2012, 2015), Stern (2012), Zhou et al. (2012), Lin and Du (2013, 2014, 2015), and Filippini et al. (2014) favor the application of the parametric frontier approach.

[5]See Mardani et al. (2017) for detailed reviews of the DEA approach to energy efficiency.

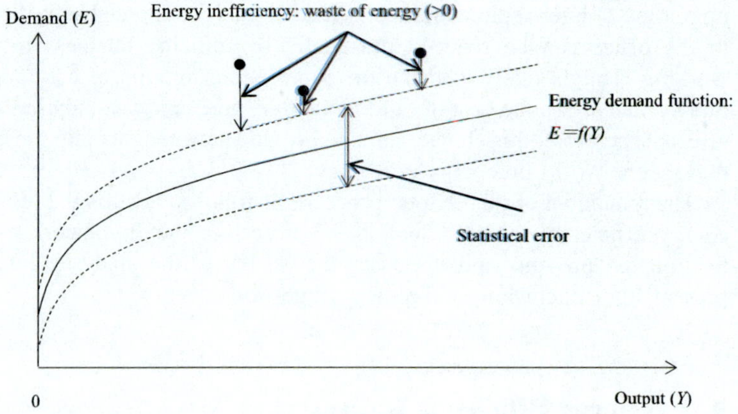

Fig. 9.1 Stochastic energy demand frontier function. Source: Otsuka and Goto (2015)

The parametric approach, SFA, assumes a particular functional type for the production frontier. Statistical noise and abnormal values can be considered error terms. Therefore, the SFA can separate the stochastic noise from inefficiency. Since SFA usually measures the economic performance of a production process, it is based on production theory applied to an econometric approach for efficiency measurement. This approach is generally based on the idea that the frontier function will provide the maximum output level or the minimum cost level feasible for the production entity. For example, in the case of the cost function, the frontier represents the minimum feasible cost to produce a given level of output. The same idea can be applied to the energy demand function (Otsuka and Goto 2015): When the output under a production activity is given, the difference between the observed energy demand and the minimized energy demand represents inefficiency (see Fig. 9.1). In the case of the aggregate energy demand function used here, the frontier provides the minimum level of energy usage that the economy requires for production activity to achieve a given level of output. In other words, estimating the frontier function for energy demand enables us to estimate the baseline energy demand, which reflects the managed energy usage in regional production processes achieved by such means as utilizing highly efficient equipment. This frontier approach enables us to assess whether a given region is located on the frontier. If a given region is not on the frontier, the distance from the frontier represents the energy consumption over the baseline demand and becomes an indicator of energy inefficiency.

In general, regional energy efficiency involves the influence of numerous factors that vary by region. They include local government regulations, differences in social environments, differences in industrial structures, and differences in cultures, lifestyles, and values. Since the energy efficiency linked to the upgrading of manufacturing equipment and production processes cannot be observed directly, we must estimate it by statistical methods. The SFA method is helpful for estimating the precise level of regional energy efficiency because it identifies the best practice in energy usage as a benchmark. Therefore, in many studies, SFA is applied to measure energy efficiency levels in various countries (see Appendix).

9.3 Methods

9.3.1 Empirical Model

This study assumes that an aggregate energy demand function f exists in a region:

$$E_{jt} = f\left(P_t, Y_{jt}, KL_{jt}, IK_{jt}, CDD_{jt}, HDD_{jt}, EF_{jt}\right), \tag{9.1}$$

where j is the region ($j = 1, \cdots, J$) and t is time ($t = 1, \cdots, T$). E is the final energy consumption, P is the energy price, and Y is corporate income. KL is the capital-labor ratio and indicates the degree of mechanization of factories and offices. IK is the investment-capital ratio and indicates the investment vintage. CDD and HDD are the cooling and heating degree days, respectively, and account for the temperature component. EF is the energy efficiency level in this region.

The level of energy efficiency is not directly observed in the economic system and therefore needs to be estimated using the SFA. The logic of the SFA is first to estimate the efficiency frontier and then measure efficiency by calculating the relative distance from the actual data point to the frontier as mentioned. The SFA employed in this study follows the assumptions of the stochastic frontier functional approach proposed by Aigner et al. (1977). We employ the one-step approach of Battese and Coelli (1995) and simultaneously estimate the determinants of the energy demand frontier function and the energy inefficiency term.[6]

The SFA model approximates the energy efficiency level of the economy to a one-sided non-negative error term. Thus, it is assumed that the logarithmic specifications of Eq. (9.1) can be described as follows[7]:

$$\begin{aligned} \ln E_{jt} = \alpha_0 + \alpha_P \ln P_t + \alpha_Y \ln Y_{jt} + \alpha_{KL} \ln KL_{jt} + \alpha_{IK} \ln IK_{jt} \\ + \alpha_{CDD} \ln CDD_{jt} + \alpha_{HDD} \ln HDD_{jt} + v_{jt} + u_{jt}, \end{aligned} \tag{9.2}$$

---

[6]Not only can SFA deal with statistical noise, but it is also very flexible in describing technological heterogeneity. In the traditional SFA, a fixed-effects SFA model is used. For this model, Battese and Coelli (1995) use the maximum likelihood estimation, but Greene (2004, 2005) uses true fixed-effects estimates. However, it has been pointed out that there are concerns with Greene's estimation approach, and Chen et al. (2014) and Du and Lin (2017) have suggested ways to improve it. For further detail, see Lin and Du (2013, 2014, 2015) and Du and Lin (2017).

[7]This energy demand function can be derived from the producer's profit maximization behavior. That is, it is assumed that Eq. (9.1) is the reduced form of the energy demand function. See Li et al. (2019) for details on the derivation method.

where α is an estimated parameter. The error term ($v_{jt} + u_{jt}$) consists of two parts: the random error term v_{jt} and the error term u_{jt} reflecting inefficiency. It is assumed that v_{jt} has a distribution $N(0, \sigma^2)$ and is independent of u_{jt} and all explanatory variables; u_{jt} is a non-negative random variable with a distribution $N(\mu, \sigma_u^2)$ and indicates that the energy efficiency level EF_{jt} in Eq. (9.1) can be interpreted as an indicator of energy inefficiency.

Given Eq. (9.2), the energy efficiency level EF_{jt} is estimated using the conditional expectation of the efficiency term, $E(u_{jt}| v_{jt} + u_{jt})$, as in Jondrow et al. (1982). The energy efficiency level EF_{jt} is measured as the ratio of the observed energy demand E_{jt} to the estimated energy demand frontier E_{jt}^F; thus, $EF_{jt} \equiv E_{jt}^F / E_{jt} = e^{-u_{jt}}, \ \ 0 < EF_{jt} \leq 1$.

Improved energy efficiency can be achieved through technological and organizational factors of energy demand, as well as social innovation in the production and consumption of energy services. In this study, the average energy inefficiency μ is formulated as follows:

$$\begin{aligned}\mu_{jt} = \beta_0 + \beta_{DENS} \ln DENS_{jt} + \beta_{DENS2} \ln DENS_{jt}^2 + \beta_{ACC} \ln ACC_{jt} \\ + \beta_{ACC2} \ln ACC_{jt}^2 + \beta_{MR} \ln MR_{jt},\end{aligned} \tag{9.3}$$

where β is the estimated parameter. The sign of β is negative if the determinants improve efficiency.

DENS is a proxy variable for regional agglomeration and represents the ratio of the population to the residential area (i.e., population density).[8] *The ACC* is a general index indicating the strength of inter-regional networks, and it is calculated based on Hansen (1959) as follows:

$$ACC_{jt} = \sum\nolimits_{k \neq j} \frac{GRP_{kt}}{d_{jkt}}, \tag{9.4}$$

where GRP_{kt} is the gross regional product in region k in period t and denotes the market size. d_{jkt} is the distance resistance (travel time) to travel from region j to region k over period t.[9] The degree of inter-regional networks depends not only on the size of the market but also on the travel time needed to access the market. In other words, *ACC* is more significant in regions with shorter time distances to other regions, while it is smaller in regions with less access and longer time distances.

The quadratic term in Eq. (9.3) represents the nonlinearity of the agglomeration economies and inter-regional network economies. Regional agglomeration is partially associated with external diseconomies such as increased congestion and the "heat island" phenomenon (e.g., Ihara et al. 2008; Hirano and Fujita 2012), wherein

[8]See Sect. 2.2 in Chap. 4 for discussions on the relationships between population density and agglomeration economies.

[9]See Chaps. 5 and 6 for the calculation procedure on travel time.

the concentration of population in urban areas increases the temperature of urban centers and reduces the performance of air-conditioning, thus deteriorating energy efficiency. Recent studies have verified that the impact of regional agglomeration on energy efficiency has an inverted U-shape (Wang et al. 2020; Zhao and Lin 2019). Additionally, some scholars have proved the nonlinear impact of regional agglomeration on the energy efficiency of carbon emissions and smog pollution in China (Xu and Lin 2015; Hao and Peng 2017; Zhang et al. 2017; Li et al. 2018; Xie et al. 2019). Therefore, the impact of regional agglomeration on energy efficiency has both positive and negative dimensions. This study controls for these nonlinear effects.

Finally, *MR*, the proportion of manufacturing industries in production activities, is a control variable for the effects of the industrial structure on energy efficiency. Japan's manufacturing industry has a higher energy intensity than other industries (see Appendix 2. in Chap. 8). Therefore, the sign of the coefficient for the *MR* is expected to be positive.

9.3.2 Data

This study uses panel data from 47 prefectures covering 1990 to 2013. Data on the final energy consumption of each prefecture are taken from the *Energy Consumption Statistics by Prefecture* (Ministry of Economy, Trade and Industry).[10] The data of this study are from the industrial and commercial sectors. Thus, this study covers the energy consumption of industrial activities in the industrial and commercial sectors (i.e., the total amount of energy consumed in factories and offices). The energy price is the real energy price index of the industrial and commercial sectors, published by the International Energy Agency. Corporate income data are obtained from the *Annual Report on Prefectural Accounts* (Cabinet Office) and converted to real figures based on the gross regional product deflator. The capital-labor ratio is the ratio of private capital stock to the number of employees. The investment-capital ratio is the ratio of private capital investment to private capital stock. The data on private capital investments and private capital stock are estimates from the Central Research Institute of Electric Power Industry. The number of employees was obtained from the *Annual Report on Prefectural Accounts* (Cabinet Office).

Data on the cooling degree day and heating degree day were obtained from meteorological observation points. The annual number of cooling degree days is the cumulative difference in temperature between 22 °C and the average temperature on each day in a year whose average temperature exceeds 24 °C. The annual number of heating degree days is the cumulative difference in temperature between 14 °C and the average temperature on each day in an annual period whose average temperature is below 14 °C. Population density is the ratio of the population to a

[10]See Sect. 2.4 in Chap. 8 for the definition of final energy consumption.

habitable land area. Data on population and habitable land area were extracted from the *Basic Resident Registers* and the *System of Social and Demographic Statistics*, respectively (Statistics Bureau, Ministry of Internal Affairs and Communiscations). Data on the gross regional product used to calculate the *ACC* index were obtained from the *Annual Report on Prefectural Accounts* (Cabinet Office). Data on travel time used to calculate the *ACC* index were obtained from the *National Integrated Transport Analysis System* (Ministry of Land, Infrastructure, Transport, and Tourism). The manufacturing industry ratio is based on data obtained from the *Annual Report on Prefectural Accounts* (Cabinet Office).

Descriptive statistics of the variables are presented in Table 9.1. The industrial and commercial sectors' final energy consumption rose from the 1990s to the 2000s as energy prices declined and corporate income increased. The capital-labor ratio increased, and mechanization continued to progress. However, between 2000 and 2013, the energy consumption of the industrial and commercial sectors declined. Population densities gradually increased throughout the observation period, and population agglomeration in urban areas was accelerated. The *ACC* index rose sharply between 1990 and 2000 and then began to decline in 2013. These results indicate a significant impact of shortening time distances due to the development of high-speed transportation systems in the 1990s.

9.4 Results and Discussion

9.4.1 Estimation Results

The maximum likelihood estimation results for the energy demand frontier function obtained using Eqs. (9.2) and (9.3) are listed in Table 9.2. The determinants of inefficiency are estimated simultaneously with the energy demand frontier function. Eight models are estimated from two perspectives: whether to introduce nonlinear effects for population density and the *ACC* index and whether to introduce time effects.

We look at the four models (A-D) on the left-hand side of Table 9.2. Concerning the energy demand frontier function, the estimated coefficients have the expected signs and are statistically significant for almost all variables. Since each variable is expressed in logarithmic form, the estimated parameters can be interpreted as elasticities. The estimated price elasticity ranges from 0.185 to 0.195, which is small and inelastic compared to income elasticity. This reflects the nature of energy goods as essential goods: Energy demand is more responsive to income changes than to prices. The sign on the capital-labor ratio is positive, indicating that capital and energy are complements rather than substitutes. In other words, the higher the mechanization, the more energy is consumed. The sign on the investment-capital ratio is positive. However, the values of the regression coefficients are minimal and are not statistically significant in the models that consider time effects. The coefficients on cooling degree day and heating degree day are significant but very small.

Table 9.1 Descriptive statistics for the industrial and commercial sector

		Final energy consumption (TJ)	Energy price index (2010 = 100)	Corporate income (JPY, millions)	Capital-labor ratio	Investment-capital ratio	Cooling degree day	Heating degree day	Population density (person/km^2)	ACC index (JPY, millions)	Manufacturing industry ratio (%)
		(*E*)	(*P*)	(*Y*)	(*KL*)	(*IK*)	(*CDD*)	(*HDD*)	(*DENS*)	(*ACC*)	(*MR*)
1990	Mean	224,845	80.7	1,506,889	10.72	0.099	412.5	971.2	1335.6	119,893,909	18.97
	Standard deviation	237,742	0.0	1,863,510	1.80	0.009	162.9	412.6	1573.9	36,481,908	7.28
	Maximum	1,089,664	80.7	11,090,526	14.80	0.117	863.5	2213.6	8455.8	225,478,388	38.29
	Minimum	24,922	80.7	280,522	7.29	0.072	45.6	3.7	259.3	66,087,556	4.39
2000	Mean	258,220	80.4	1,952,189	15.93	0.056	411.8	1117.6	1350.2	140,132,895	20.04
	Standard deviation	282,921	0.0	2,615,059	2.34	0.006	140.3	494.3	1585.0	36,190,932	7.39
	Maximum	1,410,306	80.4	17,450,509	21.25	0.078	836.3	2657.2	8412.9	248,414,172	37.38
	Minimum	36,771	80.4	416,615	11.21	0.045	65.8	3.9	259.5	92,980,292	5.32
2013	Mean	241,791	126.8	2,759,684	21.67	0.046	445.5	1152.6	1353.9	138,295,080	22.27
	Standard deviation	271,329	0.0	3,450,554	3.27	0.003	190.1	483.6	1692.1	34,067,397	8.92
	Maximum	1,314,587	126.8	22,242,515	29.81	0.053	993.9	2565.6	9163.9	239,525,670	39.97
	Minimum	29,844	126.8	436,306	13.91	0.034	51.0	0.6	245.2	88,778,384	4.85
1990–2013	Mean	245,922	90.5	2,012,368	16.11	0.059	373.7	1100.5	1354.8	135,176,002	20.41
	Standard deviation	267,563	13.7	2,739,355	3.84	0.016	174.9	469.4	1601.6	35,900,997	7.81
	Maximum	1,467,304	126.8	25,527,210	29.81	0.117	1190.3	2707.1	9163.9	253,542,836	41.66
	Minimum	24,922	77.7	256,171	7.29	0.034	0.0	0.3	245.2	66,087,556	4.28

Table 9.2 Estimation results

	Estimation for 1990–2010								Robustness estimation for 1990–2007							
	A		B		C		D		E		F		G		H	
Frontier function																
Constant (α_0)	−0.662	**	−0.621	**	−0.669	**	−0.615	**	−0.677	**	−0.605	**	−0.693	**	−0.602	**
	(0.028)		(0.036)		(0.032)		(0.041)		(0.041)		(0.053)		(0.052)		(0.063)	
α_P	−0.189	**	−0.185	**	−0.195	**	−0.190	**	−0.329	**	−0.317	**	−0.371	**	−0.342	**
	(0.021)		(0.021)		(0.029)		(0.029)		(0.044)		(0.047)		(0.064)		(0.061)	
α_Y	0.618	**	0.643	**	0.621	**	0.650	**	0.626	**	0.654	**	0.627	**	0.659	**
	(0.017)		(0.020)		(0.019)		(0.021)		(0.021)		(0.024)		(0.023)		(0.025)	
α_{KL}	0.158	**	0.137	**	0.174	**	0.151	**	0.239	**	0.224	**	0.268	**	0.246	**
	(0.036)		(0.036)		(0.045)		(0.040)		(0.042)		(0.048)		(0.049)		(0.050)	
α_{IK}	0.066	**	0.045	**	0.044		0.024		0.110	**	0.091	**	0.101	**	0.084	**
	(0.026)		(0.026)		(0.034)		(0.031)		(0.030)		(0.033)		(0.034)		(0.036)	
α_{CDD}	−0.090	**	−0.101	**	−0.090	**	−0.103	**	−0.087	**	−0.097	**	−0.088	**	−0.099	**
	(0.011)		(0.012)		(0.012)		(0.013)		(0.013)		(0.013)		(0.013)		(0.013)	
α_{HDD}	−0.053	**	−0.046	**	−0.059	**	−0.052	**	−0.069	**	−0.063	**	−0.077	**	−0.070	**
	(0.012)		(0.012)		(0.013)		(0.012)		(0.014)		(0.015)		(0.015)		(0.015)	
Inefficiency model																
Constant (β_0)	−0.453	*	−0.423	*	−0.167		−0.206		−0.484		−0.485		−0.206		−0.341	
	(0.265)		(0.247)		(0.284)		(0.286)		(0.330)		(0.334)		(0.375)		(0.370)	
β_{DENS}	0.763	**	1.221	**	0.662	**	1.102	**	0.727	**	1.251	**	0.595	**	1.114	**
	(0.124)		(0.211)		(0.127)		(0.205)		(0.159)		(0.239)		(0.152)		(0.236)	
β_{DENS2}			−0.240	**			−0.220	**			−0.292	**			−0.268	**
			(0.078)				(0.076)				(0.103)				(0.101)	
β_{ACC}	−0.708	**	−0.858	**	−0.624	**	−0.788	**	−0.767	**	−0.942	**	−0.655	**	−0.861	**
	(0.112)		(0.126)		(0.122)		(0.131)		(0.156)		(0.175)		(0.155)		(0.171)	
β_{ACC2}			0.075				0.066				0.086				0.074	

			(0.046)				(0.043)				(0.057)				(0.054)	
β_{MR}	0.947	**	0.926	**	0.868	**	0.884	**	0.957	**	0.957	**	0.815	**	0.876	**
	(0.144)		(0.134)		(0.145)		(0.131)		(0.183)		(0.172)		(0.187)		(0.172)	
Time effects	Excluded		Excluded		Included		Included		Excluded		Excluded		Included		Included	
σ^2	0.911	**	0.868	**	0.812	**	0.777	**	0.868	**	0.801	**	0.765	**	0.726	**
	(0.131)		(0.125)		(0.114)		(0.112)		(0.159)		(0.150)		(0.141)		(0.136)	
γ	0.937	**	0.914	**	0.929	**	0.899	**	0.911	**	0.870	**	0.899	**	0.851	**
	(0.013)		(0.023)		(0.015)		(0.029)		(0.022)		(0.039)		(0.026)		(0.049)	
Log-likelihood	−863.16		−856.68		−851.15		−845.47		−644.62		−638.95		−637.70		−632.64	
Observations	1128		1128		1128		1128		846		846		846		846	

Notes: (1) ** and * indicate 1% and 5% significance levels, respectively
(2) The values in parentheses indicate standard errors
(3) The software used for the estimation is Frontier 4.1 (Coelli 1996)

This indicates that the effects of temperature on the industrial and commercial sectors' energy demand are minor. The sign of the coefficient on temperature is negative, perhaps because the scale of the plant or office located in a climatically harsh area is small, and the energy consumption is also low.

To determine whether the deviations from the estimated frontier are due to the effects of inefficiency, the null hypothesis $\gamma = 0$ is tested against the alternative hypothesis $\gamma > 0$. The statistical test reveals that the null hypothesis is rejected at a significance level of 1%; thus, γ is statistically different from zero. This suggests that significant inefficiency is at play; hence, the estimates of the determinants of inefficiency are reliable.

Model A assesses the impact of regional agglomeration and inter-regional networks as determinants of inefficiency. The sign of the coefficient on population density is positive, which indicates that increased regional agglomeration has an adverse impact on energy efficiency. This result contrasts with the results of Chap. 8, which represents the total energy consumption. The results for the industrial and commercial sectors show that the disadvantages of regional agglomeration overshadow its advantages in this sector. However, the coefficient on inter-regional networks has a negative sign. This indicates that regions with well-developed transportation infrastructure are more energy efficient. At the same time, it also suggests that the development of high-quality transportation networks increases energy efficiency.

Model B considers the nonlinear effects of both variables. The results showed that all the terms of population density were statistically significant. The sign of the quadratic term is negative, which indicates the existence of an inverted U-shaped relationship. This suggests a threshold for the impact of regional agglomeration on energy efficiency: The negative phenomenon of agglomeration prevails until the population density reaches the threshold, and energy efficiency then deteriorates; when the population density of the region exceeds the threshold value, the positive effects of regional agglomeration increase and energy efficiency improves. The results of this model show that the relative magnitudes of the advantages and disadvantages of regional agglomeration depend on population density. However, the quadratic terms are not statistically significant for the *ACC* index; thus, the impact of inter-regional networks on energy efficiency can be considered linear for the industrial and commercial sectors.

The results of Models C and D, which introduce time effects, show no significant differences from Models A and B. The coefficients of the manufacturing industry ratio are positive and statistically significant in all models, indicating low levels of energy efficiency in the manufacturing-concentrated areas.

9.4.2 Efficiency Score

Table 9.3 reports the descriptive statistics of the energy efficiency scores for the industrial and commercial sector obtained from the estimation results of Model

Table 9.3 Descriptive statistics of energy efficiency score

Mean	0.588
Standard deviation	0.226
Minimum	0.105
Maximum	0.956
Median	0.657

Note: The energy efficiency score was calculated based on the results of Model D (Table 9.2)

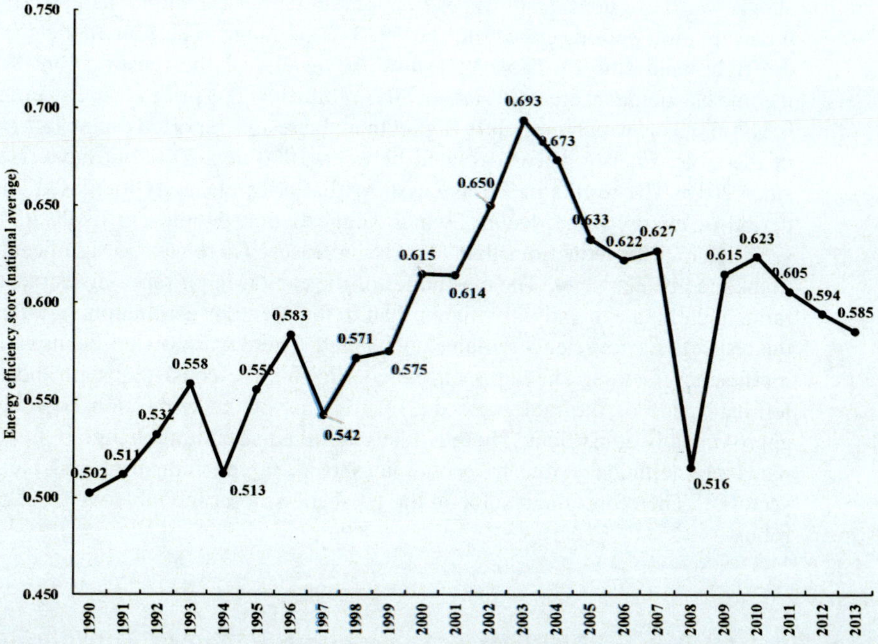

Fig. 9.2 The trend of the national average energy efficiency score. Note: The energy efficiency score was calculated based on the results of Model D (Table 9.2)

D. An efficiency score equal to 1 indicates the highest efficiency, and values smaller than one reflect lower levels of energy efficiency. The average energy efficiency is 0.588, and the median is 0.657. The maximum value is 0.956, while the minimum value is 0.105, which indicates significant regional differences in energy efficiency levels.

Figure 9.2 shows the national averages of the energy efficiency scores for the industrial and commercial sectors. Energy efficiency rose consistently from 1990 to 2003. It peaked in 2003, then exhibited a downward trend, and fell sharply in 2008. The Japanese economy experienced two economic shocks in the 2000s. The first was caused by the 2008 Lehman crisis (the financial crisis), which had a significant impact on production activity in large metropolitan areas. The second was the Great East Japan Earthquake in 2011. These two shocks have considerably changed the production structure of the industry. These shocks caused significant changes in industrial productivity and affected regional energy consumption patterns.

9.4.3 Robustness Analyses

To assess the robustness of the estimation results, periods that experienced economic shocks were excluded from the estimation, and a reestimation was performed with the estimation period reduced to the 1990–2007 range. The four models (E–H) on the right-hand side of Table 9.2 show the results of the reestimation. Price and income elasticities were both statistically significant. The price elasticity ranges from 0.317 to 0.371, which is slightly higher than the results reported on the left-hand side of the table. Energy prices declined between 1990 and 2007 but have risen again since 2010. The results in Table 9.2 show that price elasticity increased during the period of energy price decline, which suggests that people are likely to be more sensitive to price reductions than to price increases. There was no significant change in the income elasticity. The elasticities of the capital-labor ratio, investment-capital ratio, and climate are slightly higher than in the previous estimation, but the sign on the respective coefficients remains unchanged. There was no significant variation in inefficiency factors. The signs on the coefficients are consistent with those on the left-hand side of the table, and the magnitudes of the regression coefficients are approximately equivalent. There is likely to be no structural change in the determinants of inefficiency due to economic shocks in the industrial and commercial sectors.[11] Therefore, the results on the left-hand side of the table were judged to be robust.

9.4.4 Regional Efficiency Score and Efficiency Contributions

Table 9.4 reports the energy efficiency scores for regions derived from the estimation of Model D. Hokkaido, Tohoku, and Hokuriku exceed the national averages, with Okinawa at the top. On the contrary, the large metropolitan areas such as the Greater Tokyo Area, Kansai, and Chubu are below the national average, and their energy efficiency levels are low. Furthermore, the efficiency level of the Chugoku region, where the manufacturing industry is concentrated, is 0.39, which is only half the national average. However, energy efficiency has improved in most regions when the average efficiency score for the period before 2003 is compared with the period after 2003, which represents the peak of energy efficiency across the country. Since 2003, despite the downward trend in energy efficiency, the energy efficiency score

[11]For the residential sector in Japan, it is found that the Great East Japan Earthquake changed electricity consumption behavior. See Otsuka (2019) in detail.

Table 9.4 Energy efficiency scores and relative contribution (%) of determinants

	Panel A: Energy efficiency scores across regions			Panel B: Relative contribution (RC) of each determinant on energy efficiency (%)		
	Average score (1990–2013)	Average score (1990–2003)	Average score (2004–2013)	Population density	Inter-regional networks	Manufacturing industry ratio
Hokkaido	0.63	0.67	0.57	−0.17	−1.35	0.49
Tohoku	0.71	0.70	0.73	−1.50	−6.48	2.89
North Kanto	0.61	0.59	0.64	−0.01	−1.26	1.74
Greater Tokyo Area	0.52	0.51	0.53	0.17	−0.69	−1.49
Chubu	0.51	0.48	0.54	−0.09	−2.56	2.26
Hokuriku	0.73	0.71	0.75	−0.19	−0.78	1.06
Kansai	0.59	0.58	0.62	0.04	−1.89	0.63
Chugoku	0.39	0.38	0.41	−0.67	−2.96	1.18
Shikoku	0.55	0.53	0.58	−0.61	−3.57	1.71
Kyushu	0.60	0.58	0.63	−0.56	−6.19	4.83
Okinawa	0.83	0.81	0.86	0.15	−0.24	0.21
National average	0.61	0.60	0.62	−0.31	−2.54	1.41

Notes: (1) The energy efficiency score is calculated based on the results of Model D (Table 9.2)
(2) See Fig. 1.2 in Chap. 1 for the regional classification

has consistently exceeded the level achieved before 2003. The ratio of the 2013 energy efficiency to the 1990 energy efficiency exceeds 1 in all regions. This indicates that energy efficiency has improved throughout the observation period.

Table 9.4 also shows the relative contribution of determinants to energy inefficiency. Relative contribution (*RC*) calculations are based on the following formulation:

$$RC_{DENS} = \beta_{DENS} \cdot \ln \frac{DENS_{2013}}{DENS_{1990}} + \beta_{DENS2} \cdot \ln \frac{DENS^2_{2013}}{DENS^2_{1990}},$$

$$RC_{ACC} = \beta_{ACC} \cdot \ln \frac{ACC_{2013}}{ACC_{1990}} + \beta_{ACC2} \cdot \ln \frac{ACC^2_{2013}}{ACC^2_{1990}},$$

$$RC_{MR} = \beta_{MR} \cdot \ln \frac{MR_{2013}}{MR_{1990}}.$$

A negative sign indicates a reduction in inefficiency, and thus an increase in efficiency, whereas a positive sign indicates increased inefficiency.

The sign of regional agglomeration is positive only for the Greater Tokyo Area, Kansai, and Okinawa. This result suggests that the negative impact of agglomeration overrides its advantages. In other areas, the disadvantages of regional agglomeration are less evident. The sign of improved inter-regional networks is negative in all regions; thus, the effects of improved inter-regional networks are evident. In local areas, consolidating branch offices to core cities, along with improving transportation networks, significantly helps reduce the local office's energy consumption. The contribution of inter-regional networks is high in Tohoku and Kyushu, probably due to the opening of bullet trains (Akita Shinkansen, Yamagata Shinkansen, and Kyushu Shinkansen). The relative contributions of the manufacturing industry ratio are positive in all regions other than the Greater Tokyo Area. This reflects an increase in plant operating hours due to the increased value of shipments of manufactured goods in the observation periods.

9.5 Conclusions

This chapter focuses on energy efficiency in the industrial and commercial sectors and evaluates the impact of regional agglomeration and inter-regional networks on energy efficiency. Our SFA approach controls prices and income, mechanization, vintage, and climate factors to derive accurate energy efficiency levels. Energy intensity, used as a proxy for energy efficiency indicators, tends to depend on socioeconomic variables such as prices and income; our derivation of energy efficiency scores is accurate because we control for these variables.

The results reveal that improved inter-regional networks have a positive impact on energy efficiency. Regions with well-developed transportation networks are highly energy efficient. Meanwhile, the results reveal that regional agglomeration has mixed effects on energy efficiency. That is, there are positive and negative impacts on energy efficiency. Initially, agglomeration economies are inherently a mixture of advantages and disadvantages, such as spatial externalities, congestion, and heat islands. By considering the nonlinear effects, we identified that there is a threshold in the effects of regional agglomeration, and both positive and negative effects of regional agglomeration are at play. This result suggests that agglomeration size beyond the threshold level is necessary to enjoy the benefits of regional agglomeration for the industrial and commercial sectors.

Thus, strengthening inter-regional networks leads to increased energy efficiency by reducing travel time between regions. Improving inter-regional transportation networks is an effective policy for enhancing the energy efficiency of the industrial and commercial sectors. Therefore, it is essential to make cities more compact and connect core cities through transportation networks in order to increase environmental efficiency. The installation of high-quality transportation systems has the potential to be a driving force for energy efficiency and regional sustainability. To ensure the effectiveness of such a policy, Chap. 10 considers the impact of high-speed railways on energy conservation from a modal shift perspective.

Appendix: Brief Review of Studies on Energy Efficiency Using the SFA Approach

This appendix briefly reviews previous studies on energy efficiency measures using the SFA approach. The SFA approach is applicable to many countries by many scholars. Feijoo et al. (2002) and Buck and Young (2007) measured energy efficiency in Spanish industry and commercial buildings in Canada, respectively, using SFA. Boyd et al. (2008) used SFA to analyze the energy efficiency of wet corn milling plants, arguing that SFA is advantageous because it can avoid problems related to the definition of energy intensity. Boyd et al. (2008) applied SFA to estimate the energy efficiency in the US manufacturing industry. Aranda-Uson et al. (2012) measured energy efficiency in the Spanish manufacturing industry and evaluated its magnitude. Filippini and Hunt (2011) used SFA to measure energy efficiency in 29 OECD countries. Filippini and Hunt (2012) measured energy efficiency in the US household sector. Filippini and Hunt (2011, 2012) concluded that SFA-measured energy efficiency levels are uncorrelated with energy intensity and that energy intensity is not an appropriate proxy indicator for energy efficiency levels.

Among studies in Asia, Lin and Du (2013, 2014) measured energy efficiency in a region of China. Lin and Yang (2013) measured energy efficiency in China's thermal power industry, and Wei et al. (2007), Lin and Long (2015), and Lin and Wang (2014) measured the energy efficiency of the iron, steel, and chemical industries in China. Honma and Hu (2014) use SFA and DEA to measure the energy efficiency of Japan's regions and find high correlations in average efficiency using the two estimation methods. Otsuka and Goto (2015) identify that regional agglomeration has a significant impact on improving energy efficiency in Japan's regions based on SFA. Furthermore, Otsuka (2017, 2018b) applied the SFA to residential energy and electricity demand in Japan and identified the energy efficiency level of the residential sector.

As recent studies that consider the dynamic effect, Filippini and Hunt (2015) distinguish heterogeneity in energy efficiency and identify long-run and short-run efficiency. Filippini and Lin (2016) measured the levels of energy efficiency in China's states using various econometric models. Lin and Du (2015) and Du and Lin (2017) measure energy efficiency based on a parametric Malmquist index approach and perform international and regional comparisons that include regions in Asia. Yulan et al. (2020) disentangle the long-run and short-run efficiencies of energy use and demonstrate the effects of urbanization on energy efficiency in China using SFA models.

References

Aigner DJ, Lovell CAK, Schmidt P (1977) Formulation and estimation of stochastic frontier production function model. J Econ 6:21–37

Ang BW, Mu AR, Zhow P (2010) Accounting frameworks for tracking energy efficiency trends. Energ Econ 32(5):1209–1219

Aranda-Uson A, Ferreira G, Mainar-Toledo MD, Scarpellini S, Liera E (2012) Energy consumption analysis of Spanish food and drink, textile, chemical and non-metallic mineral products sectors. Energy 42:477–485

Battese GE, Coelli TJ (1995) A model for technical inefficiency effects in a stochastic frontier production function for panel data. Empir Econ 20(2):325–332

Boix R, Trullen J (2007) Knowledge, networks of cities and growth in regional urban systems. Pap Reg Sci 86(4):551–574

Boyd G, Dutrow E, Tunnessen W (2008) The evolution of the ENERGY STAR® energy performance indicator for benchmarking industrial plant manufacturing energy use. J Clean Prod 16:709–715

Boyd GA (2008) Estimating plant level energy efficiency with a stochastic frontier. Energ J 29:23–43

Buck J, Young D (2007) The potential for energy efficiency gains in the Canadian commercial building sector. Energy 32:1769–1780

Camagni R (1993) From city hierarchy to city networks: reflections about an emerging paradigm. In: Lakshmanan LTR, Nijkamp P (eds) Structure and change in the space economy: festschrift in honor of Martin Beckmann. Springer Verlag, Berlin, pp 66–90

Camagni R, Capello R (2004) The city network paradigm: theory and empirical evidence. In: Capello R, Nijkamp P (eds) Urban dynamics and growth. Elsevier, Amsterdam, pp 495–532

Capello R (2000) The city network paradigm: measuring urban network externalities. Urban Stud 37(11):1925–1945

Chang TP, Hu JL (2010) Total-factor energy productivity growth, technical progress, and efficiency change: an empirical study of China. Appl Energ 87(10):3262–3270

Charnes A, Cooper WW, Rhodes E (1978) Measuring the efficiency of decision making units. Eur J Oper Res 2(6):429–444

Chen YY, Schmidt P, Wang HJ (2014) Consistent estimation of the fixed effects stochastic frontier model. J Econ 181(2):65–76

Coelli TJ (1996) A guide to frontier version 4.1: a computer program for stochastic frontier production and cost function estimation (CEPA Working Papers No. 96/07). University of New England, London

Du K, Lin B (2017) International comparison of total-factor energy productivity growth: a parametric Malmquist index approach. Energy 118:481–488

Energy Information Administration (1995) Measuring energy efficiency in the United States' economy: A beginning. Energy Information Administration, DOE/EIA-0555(95)/2, Washington DC

Energy Information Administration (2013) International energy outlook 2013. U.S. Energy Information Administration, DOE/EIA-0484(2013), Washington DC

Feijoo ML, Franco JF, Hernández JM (2002) Global warming and the energy efficiency of Spanish industry. Energ Econ 24:405–423

Filippini M, Hunt LC (2011) Energy demand and energy efficiency in the OECD countries: a stochastic demand frontier approach. Energy J 32:59–79

Filippini M, Hunt LC (2012) U.S. residential energy demand and energy efficiency: a stochastic demand frontier approach. Energ Econ 34:1484–1491

Filippini M, Hunt LC (2015) Measurement of energy efficiency based on economic foundations. Energ Econ 52:S5–S16

Filippini M, Lin B (2016) Estimation of the energy efficiency in Chinese provinces. Energ Effic 9 (6):1315–1328

Filippini M, Hunt LC, Zoric J (2014) Impact of energy policy instruments on the estimated level of underlying energy efficiency in the EU residential sector. Energ Policy 69:73–81

Greene W (2004) Distinguishing between heterogeneity and inefficiency: stochastic frontier analysis of the World Health Organization's panel data on national health care systems. Health Econ 13(10):959–980

Greene W (2005) Reconsidering heterogeneity in panel data estimators of the stochastic frontier model. J Econ 126(2):269–303

Hansen WG (1959) How accessibility shapes land use. J Am Inst Plan 25:73–76

Hao Y, Peng H (2017) On the convergence in China's provincial per capita energy consumption: new evidence from a spatial econometric analysis. Energ Econ 68(9):31–43

Hirano Y, Fujita T (2012) Evaluation of the impact of the urban heat island on residential and commercial energy consumption in Tokyo. Energy 37:371–383

Honma S, Hu JL (2014) Industry-level total-factor energy efficiency in developed countries: a Japan-centered analysis. Appl Energ 119:67–78

Hu JL, Wang SC (2006) Total-factor energy efficiency of regions in China. Energ Policy 34 (17):3206–3217

Ihara T, Kikegawa Y, Asahi K, Genchi Y, Kondo H (2008) Changes in year-round air temperature and annual energy consumption in office building areas by urban heat-island countermeasures and energy-saving measures. Appl Energ 85:12–25

Jondrow J, Knox Lovell CA, Materov IS, Schmidt P (1982) On the estimation of technical inefficiency in the stochastic frontier production function model. J Econ 19(2):233–238

Li J, Huang X, Kwan MP, Yang H, Chuai X (2018) The effect of urbanization on carbon dioxide emissions efficiency in the Yangtze River Delta, China. J Clean Prod 188:38–48

Li J, Liu H, Du K (2019) Does market-oriented reform increase energy rebound effect? Evidence from China's regional development. China Econ Rev 56. Article 101304

Lin B, Du K (2013) Technology gap and China's regional energy efficiency: a parametric metafrontier approach. Energ Econ 40:529–536

Lin B, Du K (2014) Measuring energy efficiency under heterogeneous technologies using a latent class stochastic frontier approach: an application to Chinese energy economy. Energy 76 (1):884–890

Lin B, Du K (2015) Modeling the dynamics of carbon emission performance in China: a parametric Malmquist index approach. Energ Econ 49:550–557

Lin B, Long H (2015) A stochastic frontier analysis of energy efficiency of China's chemical industry. J Clean Prod 87:235–244

Lin B, Wang X (2014) Exploring energy efficiency in China's iron and steel industry: a stochastic frontier approach. Energ Pol 72:87–96

Lin B, Yang L (2013) The potential estimation and factor analysis of China's energy conservation on thermal power industry. Energ Pol 62:354–362

Mardani A, Zavadskas EK, Streimikiene D, Jusoh A, Khoshnoudi M (2017) A comprehensive review of data envelopment analysis (DEA) approach in energy efficiency. Renew Sust Energ Rev 70:1298–1322

Murillo-Zamorano LR (2004) Economic efficiency and frontier techniques. J Econ Surv 18 (1):33–77

Otsuka A (2017) Determinants of efficiency in residential electricity demand: stochastic frontier analysis on Japan. Energy Sustain Soc 7:31. https://doi.org/10.1186/s13705-017-0135-y

Otsuka A (2018a) Dynamics of agglomeration, accessibility, and total factor productivity: evidence from Japanese regions. Econ Innovat New Tech 27(7):611–627

Otsuka A (2018b) Regional determinants of energy efficiency: residential energy demand in Japan. Energies 11:1557. https://doi.org/10.3390/en11061557

Otsuka A (2019) Natural disasters and electricity consumption behavior: a case study of the 2011 great East Japan earthquake. Asia-Pac J Reg Sci 3(3):887–910

Otsuka A (2020a) How do population agglomeration and interregional networks improve energy efficiency? Asia-Pac J Reg Sci 4(1):1–25

Otsuka A (2020b) Inter-regional networks and productive efficiency in Japan. Pap Reg Sci 99 (1):115–133
Otsuka A, Goto M (2015) Estimation and determinants of energy efficiency in Japanese regional economies. Reg Sci Policy Pract 7(2):89–101
Proskuryakova L, Kovalev A (2015) Measuring energy efficiency: is energy intensity a good evidence base? Appl Energ 138:450–459
Shui H, Jin X, Ni J (2015) Manufacturing productivity and energy efficiency: a stochastic efficiency frontier analysis. Int J Energ Res 39(12):1649–1663
Stern DI (2012) Modeling international trends in energy efficiency. Energ Econ 34(6):2200–2208
Wang N, Zhu Y, Yang T (2020) The impact of transportation infrastructure and industrial agglomeration on energy efficiency: evidence from China's industrial sectors. J Clean Prod 244. Article Number 118708
Wei YM, Liao H, Fan Y (2007) An empirical analysis of energy efficiency in China's iron and steel sector. Energy 32(12):2262–2270
Xie R, Wei D, Han F, Lu Y, Fang J, Liu Y, Wang J (2019) The effect of traffic density on smog pollution: evidence from Chinese cities. Technol Forecast Soc Change 144:421–427
Xu B, Lin B (2015) How industrialization and urbanization process impacts on CO_2 emissions in China: evidence from nonparametric additive regression models. Energy Econ 48:188–202
Yulan L, Chen W, Cheng J (2020) Effects of urbanization on energy efficiency in China: new evidence from short run and long run efficiency models. Energ Policy 147. Article Number 111858
Zhang N, Yu KR, Chong ZF (2017) How does urbanization affect carbon dioxide emissions? A cross-country panel data analysis. Energy Policy 107:678–687
Zhao HL, Lin BQ (2019) Will agglomeration improve the energy efficiency in China's textile industry: evidence and policy implications. Appl Energy 237:326–337
Zhou P, Ang BW (2008) Linear programming models for measuring economy-wide energy efficiency performance. Energ Policy 36:2911–2916
Zhou P, Ang BW, Zhou DQ (2012) Measuring economy-wide energy efficiency performance: a parametric frontier approach. Appl Energ 90(1):196–200

Chapter 10
Inter-regional Network Formation and Modal Shift Potential

Abstract Energy conservation is a crucial policy agenda for solving global environmental problems and enhancing sustainability. This chapter quantifies the possibility of decreasing energy consumption in the passenger vehicle sector by improving inter-regional networks and provides a way to realize sustainable development goals (SDGs). The efficient design of high-speed transportation networks enables economic agents to avoid using private vehicles, which saves transportation energy. The results reveal a nonlinear relationship between improvements in inter-regional networks and reduced energy consumption in the passenger vehicle sector. There is an inverse U-shaped relationship between the two. That is, a modal shift from passenger vehicles to railways occurs if the improvement in the regional network reaches a threshold value. Furthermore, this chapter clarifies the changes in energy consumption patterns due to the installation of the *Linear-Chuo Shinkansen*, a high-speed magnetic levitation train. The *Linear-Chuo Shinkansen* has the potential to improve both firm productivity and energy efficiency because firms facing environmental constraints can invest in energy conservation by increasing their profits. Notably, the *Linear-Chuo Shinkansen* can drive a modal shift from passenger vehicles to railways, thereby improving the energy efficiency of the regions. Through a sensitivity analysis, this chapter shows that the *Linear-Chuo Shinkansen* installation has the potential to switch the mode of inter-regional travel from passenger vehicles to railways. These results suggest that the installation of the new high-speed railway leads to a reduction in greenhouse gas emissions and is a trump card to achieve SDGs.

Keywords Energy intensity · High-speed railway (HSR) · Inter-regional network · Modal shift · Panel data analysis

This chapter is based on Otsuka (2020a).

A. Otsuka, *A New Driver of Regional Sustainability in Japan*, New Frontiers in Regional Science: Asian Perspectives 54,
https://doi.org/10.1007/978-981-16-3709-4_10

10.1 Introduction

The formation of inter-regional networks contributes to increasing productivity in networked areas. Many studies have demonstrated the impact of inter-regional networks on economic activity (Burger and Meijers 2016; Camagni et al. 2016; Van Meeteren et al. 2016; Otsuka 2018, 2020b; Otsuka 2021). Inter-regional networks facilitate business travel between regions and expand the spatial range of agglomeration economies. As a result, the increased accessibility by improving inter-regional networks opens up new opportunities for revitalization for cities connected to networks, thereby offering sustainability to both short- and long-distance regions.[1]

This chapter considers the role of the high-speed railway (HSR) as an inter-regional transportation infrastructure. The HSR era began with Tokaido Shinkansen in Japan in 1964. It began in Europe in 1981 with France's TGV. HSR technology for passenger transportation has expanded worldwide. By the end of 2018, 42,978 km of HSR networks were operating worldwide. Given the planning and route networks under construction, 98,504 km of HSR networks are projected to be operational in 44 different countries by 2025 (International Union of Railways 2018). Among these countries, the development of HSRs in China has been remarkable in recent years. Since the early 2000s, the Chinese government has pursued a national strategy for developing railway infrastructure systems. This strategy calls for the development of HSR systems spanning over 16,000 km by 2020. China's HSR has evolved into the world's most extensive system over the last decade, with a total track length of more than 11,028 km, 425 newly constructed HSR stations, and more than 1000 HSR train sets covering over 28 rural areas and 28 cities, serving more than five million people (Chen and Haynes 2015a).

In light of the spread of HSRs in China, Chinese studies demonstrate that continuous investment in HSRs significantly impacts the overall Chinese economy from multiple aspects (Chen and Haynes 2015b, c, d). For example, studies in China provide empirical evidence that HSRs have a positive impact on tourism demand and housing value growth. In addition, it is argued that the new railway network systems serve as catalysts for accelerating urbanization, thus strengthening the productivity of the service and manufacturing sectors and promoting economic growth. Furthermore, studies have identified that railway investment has had a positive impact on social welfare through the asset effect on household income. Studies also provide evidence that railway infrastructure contributes to the improvement of fiscal balance by reducing transport costs.

However, studies in many countries, including China, do not provide a coherent conclusion about whether the continuous investment in HSRs increases greenhouse gas emissions and negatively impacts the environment (Westin and Kågeson 2012; Chen et al. 2016). HSR operations increase greenhouse gas emissions by stimulating economic activity but also have the potential to decrease the usage of passenger vehicles that have higher levels of greenhouse gas emissions. However, to the best of

---

[1]See Part II (Chaps. 5, 6, and 7) for detailed considerations on inter-regional network economies.

Table 10.1 Comparison of energy intensities of various passenger transport facilities

Passenger transport facilities	Energy consumption per unit (kcal/person km, 2015)
Private vehicle	516
Bus	199
Railway	46
Aviation	483
Total	356

our knowledge, few studies have robustly examined which effect is dominant. The growth of inter-regional transportation infrastructure, especially HSR, is expected to mitigate current transportation issues such as road traffic congestion and air pollution generated by the automobile and airline sectors. Thus, a comprehensive environmental impact assessment of high-quality inter-regional infrastructure investment is a fundamental and vital requirement. This assessment would help to better understand the effectiveness and benefits of transportation infrastructure investment policies and help the international community formulate sound strategies for HSR development. Therefore, this chapter quantitatively analyzes how inter-regional networks that include HSRs affect energy consumption patterns in Japan.

There are three perspectives on the impact of inter-regional networks on energy consumption patterns (Otsuka 2020c). First, the formation of inter-regional networks increases productivity and enables energy conservation investment, which improves energy intensity. Second, the installation of high-speed transportation networks contributes to the promotion of remote work and reduces the time spent by employees in office buildings, which improves energy intensity. Third, as the use of passenger vehicles in passenger travel decreases, the overall energy intensity improves. This chapter focuses on the third perspective: the possibility of modal shifts in passenger travel.

The efficient design of high-speed transportation networks enables economic agents to avoid using private vehicles, which saves transportation energy because the energy efficiency of passenger vehicles is lower than that of public transportation such as railways (see Table 10.1). HSRs are preferred to passenger vehicles as a means of travel to help solve global environmental problems.[2] In this chapter, we quantify the possibility of decreasing energy consumption in the passenger vehicle sector by improving inter-regional networks and provide a way to realize sustainable development goals (SDGs). Thus, the first novel aspect of this chapter is that it discusses the potential for improving energy intensity in the passenger vehicle sector.

The second novel aspect is that this chapter clarifies the changes in energy consumption patterns due to the installation of the *Linear-Chuo Shinkansen*, a high-speed magnetic levitation train. The *Linear-Chuo Shinkansen* has the potential to improve both firm productivity and energy efficiency because firms facing

[2]This argument is based on the use of gasoline cars as passenger vehicles. It should be noted that the premise of the argument changes when electric vehicles become prevalent in the future.

environmental constraints can invest in energy conservation by increasing their profits. These investments promote research and development on energy conservation and encourage the renewal of manufacturing facilities, thereby balancing the increase in productivity with improvements in energy efficiency. Furthermore, the *Linear-Chuo Shinkansen* can drive a modal shift from passenger vehicles to railways and thereby improve the energy efficiency of regions. Through a sensitivity analysis, this chapter simulates the changes in the energy consumption pattern of the passenger vehicle sector due to the installation of the *Linear-Chuo Shinkansen*. Based on the empirical evidence of this chapter, we define the role of high-speed transportation infrastructure in improving regional energy efficiency and achieving SDGs.

The remainder of this chapter proceeds as follows. Section 10.2 explains the methods used in the empirical analysis. Section 10.3 presents the estimation results for the energy demand function and simulates the extent of the reduction in energy consumption in the passenger vehicle sector triggered by the installation of the *Linear-Chuo Shinkansen*. Finally, Sect. 10.4 concludes the chapter and discusses future research agendas.

10.2 Methods

10.2.1 Framework of Analysis

To analyze the energy consumption patterns, we must estimate the relevant energy demand functions. Energy demand functions have often been identified through static models and partially adjusted models (e.g., Cuddington and Dagher 2015). The static model calculates the price and income elasticities for energy demand under the assumption of long-run equilibrium. Therefore, the elasticity cannot be calculated separately for short and long runs. In contrast, the partial adjustment model enables the calculation of both short- and long-run elasticities by relaxing the long-run equilibrium assumption in the static model. However, because the time lag of the dependent variable is included in the independent variable in the partial adjustment model, the independent variable and error term correlate with each other and are therefore inconsistent in the ordinary least squares estimation (Cameron and Trivedi 2009). Hence, dynamic models are required to precisely identify the energy demand function (Alberini and Filippini 2011; Blázquez et al. 2013; Otsuka and Goto 2018).

There are two types of dynamic models: the autoregressive distributed lag (ARDL) model and the dynamic generalized method of moments (dynamic GMM). The ARDL model deals with the relationships of cointegration among the variables. This model requires a long time series for estimation. However, there is no consensus on the required length of the time series, and Pesaran et al. (2001) note that the ARDL framework works well for observation periods of at least 30 years or more. Further, Pedroni (2001) and Costantini and Martini (2010) contend that the ARDL framework does not work well if the length of the time series is less than 20 years. The second dynamic model, the dynamic GMM, works efficiently if a broad cross section is obtained for even a short observation period (Arellano and Bond 1991). The dynamic GMM is suitable for the current study because our dataset covers a short observation period (24 years) and a broad cross section (47 units).

This study uses the following model to perform dynamic panel estimation:

$$\Delta EI_{jt} = \alpha\Delta EP_t + \beta\Delta IC_{jt} + \gamma\Delta ACC_{jt} + \delta\Delta ACC_{jt}^2 + \lambda\Delta EI_{jt-1} + \Delta\varepsilon_{jt}, \qquad (10.1)$$

where all the variables are logarithmic values, j is the region ($j = 1, \cdots, J$), and t is the time ($t = 1, \cdots, T$). Δ represents the differences in values. EI is the energy intensity of the passenger vehicle sector, which represents energy consumption per capita, EP is the energy price, and IC is household income. Furthermore, ACC is an index representing the strength of inter-regional networks. The Greek letter of the regression coefficient in Eq. (10.1) is the estimated parameter, and ε represents the error term.

The sign of α is expected to be negative because an increase in the energy price (EP) reduces energy consumption. The sign of β can be both positive and negative. An increase in household income (IC) increases energy consumption because passenger vehicles represent a nominal good. However, it is possible to select alternative transportation modes and replace the passenger vehicle with a fuel-efficient mode if household income is high. In this case, an increase in income reduces energy consumption. In other words, increases in household income have positive and negative effects on energy consumption.

ACC is a general index indicating the strength of inter-regional networks and is the same index adopted in Chap. 9:

$$ACC_{jt} = \sum\nolimits_{k \neq j} \frac{GRP_{kt}}{d_{jkt}}, \qquad (10.2)$$

where GRP_{kt} is the gross regional product in region k in period t and denotes the market size. d_{jkt} is the distance resistance (travel time) to travel from region j to region k over period t.[3] The degree of inter-regional networks depends not only on the size of the market but also on the travel time required to access the market. In other words, ACC is more significant in regions with shorter time distances to other regions, while it is smaller in regions with less access and longer time distances.

The quadratic term in Eq. (10.1) represents the nonlinearity of energy consumption patterns in inter-regional network economies. Nonlinearity means that there are two sides to the energy consumption pattern of the passenger vehicle sector. On the one hand, the travel range of a passenger vehicle expands along with networking, which increases its energy consumption. On the other hand, an increase in the convenience provided by HSR leads to modal shifts from passenger vehicles to railways. Thus, the energy consumption of the passenger vehicle sector decreased. Both possibilities imply a threshold value for the impact of inter-regional networks

[3]See Chaps. 5 and 6 for the calculation procedure on travel time.

on energy consumption patterns: The degree of improvement of inter-regional networks increases the energy consumption of the passenger vehicle sector until it reaches the threshold value. However, the modal shift advances when the degree of improvement exceeds the threshold value, and the energy consumption of the passenger vehicle decreases. Thus, we assume that the sign of γ is positive or negative while that of δ is negative to account for the nonlinear effects of the inter-regional network.

Relevant short- and long-run elasticities were obtained from Eq. (10.1). We expect the short-run energy demand to be less responsive to price than long-run demand because it is not possible to change the behavioral habits of energy demand abruptly. Some habits, such as the frequency of the use of automobiles and mileage, can readily accommodate rising fuel prices, but others, such as passenger vehicle replacement, cannot occur immediately. Thus, we cannot expect a quick replacement of passenger vehicles in response to changes in energy prices. Therefore, short-run energy demand deviates from long-run optimal consumption, and energy demand is not immediately adjusted for long-run equilibrium but gradually converges to an optimal level if consumers have rational behaviors.

Partial adjustment models were derived based on these behavioral habits.[4] Because a partial adjustment model accounts for the adjustment process of energy demand, a slow adjustment process is allowed between the long-run (optimal) and short-run consumption levels. In the model, the estimated parameter λ captures the impact of the historical energy intensity on the current energy intensity. If this parameter is positive and significant, this indicates behavioral habits related to energy consumption.

10.2.2 Data

This study uses panel data for 47 prefectures from 1990 to 2014 to estimate the energy demand functions. Hence, the dataset is characterized by a relatively brief period ($T = 24$) and a relatively large unit ($J = 47$).

Our data on energy consumption in the passenger vehicle sector in each prefecture are derived from the *Energy Consumption by Prefecture* (Ministry of Economy, Trade, and Industry). Energy intensity was defined as energy consumption per person, and relevant population data were obtained from the *Basic Resident Registers* (Ministry of Internal Affairs and Communications). The energy price represents the regular gasoline prices specified in the *Petroleum Products Price Survey* (Ministry of Economy, Trade, and Industry), and it is deflated by the *Consumer Price Index* (Ministry of Internal Affairs and Communications). Household income is the taxable income per household published by the Ministry of Internal Affairs and

[4]See Filippini et al. (2018) and Otsuka (2019) for detailed discussions on the behavioral habits of energy demand.

Table 10.2 Descriptive statistics for the passenger vehicle sector

		Energy intensity (GJ/person)	Energy price (JPY/ ℓ)	Household income (JPY, ten thousand)	ACC index
		(*EI*)	(*EP*)	(*IC*)	(*ACC*)
1990	Mean	5.49	145.76	375.03	119,893,909
	Standard deviation	1.32	0.84	84.91	36,481,908
	Maximum	8.47	147.36	527.52	225,478,388
	Minimum	2.27	144.31	212.69	66,087,556
2000	Mean	8.41	102.33	380.61	140,132,895
	Standard deviation	2.25	1.36	64.04	36,190,932
	Maximum	12.77	104.49	481.55	248,414,172
	Minimum	2.67	100.97	250.32	92,980,292
2010	Mean	9.22	137.99	313.23	132,916,869
	Standard deviation	2.53	2.49	55.88	34,032,865
	Maximum	15.04	146.14	426.59	236,725,583
	Minimum	2.59	133.13	215.57	78,895,675
2014	Mean	8.28	164.62	303.88	140,484,593
	Standard deviation	2.45	2.47	55.06	34,369,271
	Maximum	12.85	172.05	440.49	242,287,154
	Minimum	2.10	159.89	210.53	90,675,783

Communications; like the energy price, it is deflated by the *Consumer Price Index* (Ministry of Internal Affairs and Communications). The data on gross regional products used to calculate the *ACC* index were obtained from the *Annual Report on Prefectural Accounts* (Cabinet Office). Data on the travel time used to calculate the *ACC* index were obtained from the *National Integrated Transport Analysis System* (Ministry of Land, Infrastructure, Transport, and Tourism).

Table 10.2 depicts the descriptive statistics for the specific year data. Time-series changes in the energy intensity of the passenger vehicle sector increased significantly from 1990 to 2010, whereas the average declined from 2010 to 2014. The energy price significantly declined from 1990 to 2000 and then increased from 2000 to 2014. Household income slightly increased from 1990 to 2000 but declined significantly from 2000 to 2014. In other words, during the 1990s, energy prices declined and household income increased, which probably increased the passenger vehicle sector's energy consumption. Further, a significant increase in energy prices and a decline in household income are likely to have reduced the sector's energy consumption after the 2000s. Finally, the *ACC* index increased from 1990 to 2000, declined once in 2010, and then increased again.

Figure 10.1 shows the trend of energy intensity in the passenger vehicle sector by regions when the level in 1990 is set to 100. In the 1990s, energy intensity increased in all regions, but especially in Hokkaido and Hokuriku. In the 2000s, the growth of

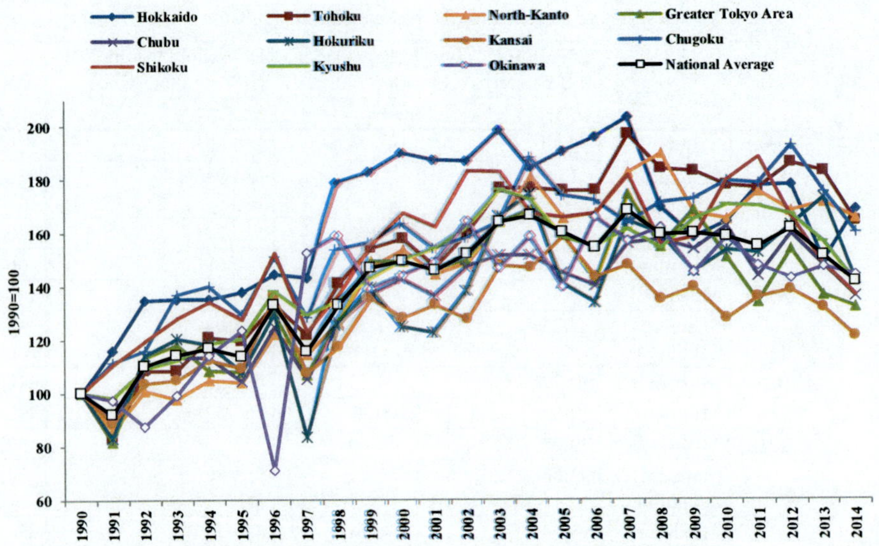

Fig. 10.1 Regional trend of energy intensity in the passenger vehicle sector. Source: Calculations based on the *Energy Consumption Statistics by Prefecture* (Ministry of Economy, Trade and Industry). Note: See Fig. 1.2 in Chap. 1 for the regional classification

energy intensity has been declining in the Greater Tokyo Area and Kansai, while no clear downward trend is observed in other regions.

Figures 10.2 and 10.3 show the corresponding static and dynamic relationships between the passenger vehicle sector's energy intensity and the *ACC* index. Figure 10.2 shows the static relationship between the two variables. The figure depicts an inverse relationship: The higher the *ACC* index, the smaller the energy intensity of the passenger vehicle sector. This relationship suggests that passenger vehicles are less frequently used in regions that have well-formed inter-regional networks. Figure 10.3 depicts the dynamic relationship between the two variables for the 1990–2014 period. It shows a concave nonlinear relationship between the change in energy intensity and that in the *ACC* index. This relationship suggests that energy consumption in the passenger vehicle sector increases until the degree of improvement in inter-regional networks reaches the threshold; once it exceeds the threshold, the consumption decreases. Section 10.3 examines in detail how these improvements in inter-regional networks affect the energy intensity of the passenger vehicle sector.

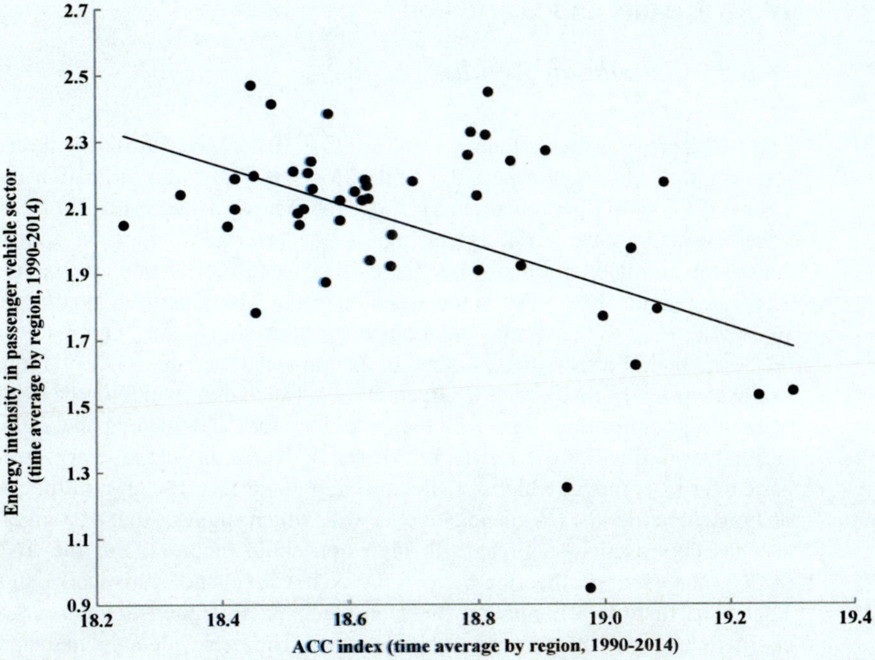

Fig. 10.2 Static relationship between energy intensity and the *ACC* index

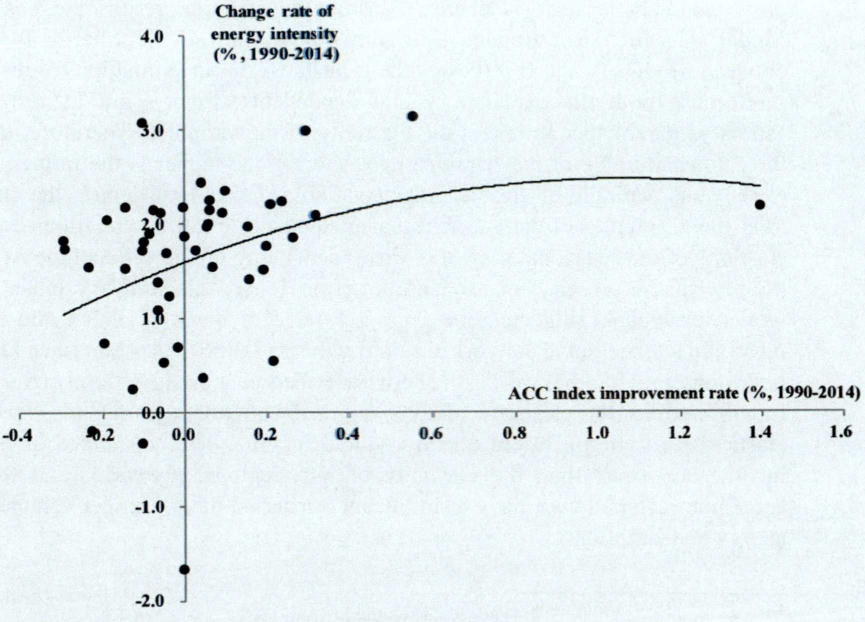

Fig. 10.3 Dynamic relationship between energy intensity and *ACC* index

10.3 Results and Discussion

10.3.1 Estimation Results

Table 10.3 presents the estimation results of Eq. (10.1). Model A shows the estimation results for all observation periods, while Model B shows the estimation results for limited observation periods to confirm the robustness of the results. In the dynamic panel estimation, the serial correlation in the error term must be confirmed. A consistent estimator is obtained if there is no serial correlation in the error term. Accordingly, the first-order autocorrelation should be significant in the Arellano-Bond test, whereas the second-order autocorrelation should not.[5] Our results satisfied this condition. Further, the number of instrumental variables is not found to be excessive from the results of the Sargan-Hansen test of exogeneity for the instrumental variables. Therefore, we satisfy all the conditions for the dynamic panel estimation.

First, we consider the results of Model A. The sign of the energy price (*EP*) parameter is negative, which satisfies the sign condition. The sign of the parameter on household income (*IC*) is negative as well, which suggests that passenger vehicle use has decreased in regions with high household incomes. For the *ACC* index (*ACC*), the sign of the quadratic term is negative and statistically significant. Therefore, there is a nonlinear effect on the impact of inter-regional networks on energy intensity in the passenger vehicle sector. The energy demand in the passenger vehicle sector decreases if the degree of improvement in inter-regional networks exceeds a certain threshold level. This result suggests that modal shifts occur depending on the degree of improvement in inter-regional networks, reducing the passenger vehicle sector's energy consumption. Similar results are observed in Model B, which is estimated with limited samples; this similarity in findings between Models A and B indicates the robustness of our estimation results.

Because both the explanatory and dependent variables are logarithmic, the estimated parameters represent the elasticity of the variables. Therefore, the larger the estimated value of the parameter (elasticity), the higher is the influence of the explanatory variable on the dependent variable. Table 10.4 depicts the short- and long-run elasticities of the variables calculated based on the estimation results. The elasticity of inter-regional networks varies depending on the value of the *ACC* index because of the presence of a quadratic term. Hence, this study evaluates the networks' elasticity using the time-averaged value of the *ACC* index and finds the measured inter-regional network elasticities to be −0.986 in the short run and − 1.512 in the long run. In other words, the network effects change significantly over the long run. Moreover, the elasticity of inter-regional networks significantly exceeds the elasticities of energy prices and household income. The elasticities of price and income are lower than the elasticity of inter-regional networks, and these two economic factors do not have a significant impact on the passenger vehicle sector's energy consumption.

[5]See footnote 6 in Chap. 5 for details on Arellano-Bond tests.

Table 10.3 Estimation results for energy intensity regression in the passenger vehicle sector

	Model A		Model B	
Regressors	1990–2014		1990–2010	
$\Delta lnEI(t-1)$	0.348	**	0.261	**
	(0.016)		(0.015)	
$\Delta lnEP$	−0.123	**	−0.088	**
	(0.006)		(0.006)	
$\Delta lnIC$	−0.522	**	−0.636	**
	(0.043)		(0.035)	
$\Delta lnACC$	0.535	**	0.637	**
	(0.054)		(0.057)	
$\Delta\ ln\ ACC^2$	−0.081	*	−0.137	**
	(0.036)		(0.044)	
Number of observations	1081		893	
J-statistic	46.070		46.462	
Probability (J-statistic)	0.308		0.294	
m-statistic (AR(1))	−5.782	**	−4.607	**
m-statistic (AR(2))	1.445		1.914	
Instrumental variable	EI(t-2)		EI(t-2)	

Notes: (1) Estimates are a two-step dynamic generalized method of moments estimates
(2) ** and * indicate significance at the 1% and 5% levels, respectively
(3) The values in parentheses indicate standard errors
(4) The J-statistic is the Sargan-Hansen test (a test of exogeneity) for the instrumental variable
(5) The m-statistics are the Arellano-Bond test for first- and second-order serial correlation

Table 10.4 Short- and long-run elasticities

	Short run	Long run
Price	−0.123	−0.188
Income	−0.522	−0.800
Inter-regional networks (ACC)	−0.986	−1.512

Note: The elasticity of inter-regional networks changes according to the ACC value for the quadratic term. In this table, elasticity is evaluated using the period average value of the ACC

10.3.2 Sensitivity Analysis

Finally, we examine the marginal energy consumption reduction effect of the *ACC* index using the estimation results. The *Linear-Chuo Shinkansen*, a new HSR using magnetic levitation trains, is being constructed in Japan. It currently starts at Shinagawa in Tokyo, and projects are underway to expand the line to Nagoya by 2027 and Shin-Osaka by 2045. The MLIT (2017) estimates the extent of time-distance reductions by installing a new HSR. Based on this estimation procedure, this study calculates the future *ACC* index values $\widehat{ACC}_{jt}$ that should be achieved following the installation of the new HSR. The magnitude of the marginal variation in the energy intensity is evaluated using the following equation:

$$\widehat{\Delta EI_{jt}} = 0.535 \times \widehat{\Delta ACC_{jt}} - 0.081 \times \widehat{\Delta ACC_{jt}^2}, \quad (10.3)$$

where $\widehat{\Delta EI_{jt}}$ represents the marginal variation in the energy intensity in the passenger vehicle sector according to the variation in the *ACC* index. The parameters (0.535 – 0.081) of the *ACC* variables in Eq. (10.3) are the estimates of Model A as listed in Table 10.3.

Table 10.5 shows the calculation results for the magnitude of the marginal effects. Case (1) represents the connection up to Nagoya station from Shinagawa station, and case (2) represents the connection up to Shin-Osaka station from Shinagawa station. As Table 10.5 shows, the evaluation of the marginal effects of the new HSR on energy intensity reveals that Yamanashi has the highest effect, and the effects are

Table 10.5 Marginal effects of *Linear-Chuo Shinkansen* installation on energy intensity improvements

Prefecture	Marginal effects for case (1)	Marginal effects for case (2)	Prefecture	Marginal effects for case (1)	Marginal effects for case (2)
Hokkaido	−0.34	−0.49	Kyoto	−19.93	−19.93
Aomori	−2.76	−3.87	Osaka	−13.18	−28.43
Iwate	−5.04	−6.72	Hyogo	−13.69	−26.06
Miyagi	−5.71	−7.02	Nara	−11.64	−11.65
Akita	−2.50	−2.80	Wakayama	−7.30	−16.61
Yamagata	−4.58	−5.96	Tottori	−3.70	−6.95
Fukushima	−8.04	−9.93	Shimane	−3.92	−7.97
Ibaraki	−7.12	−9.36	Okayama	−13.72	−25.85
Tochigi	−12.43	−14.91	Hiroshima	−11.86	−22.98
Gunma	−5.61	−7.92	Yamaguchi	−7.13	−14.93
Saitama	−7.44	−8.92	Tokushima	−1.86	−5.23
Chiba	−7.29	−9.71	Kagawa	−8.20	−15.97
Tokyo	−16.61	−21.34	Ehime	−4.87	−9.49
Kanagawa	−10.71	−14.56	Kochi	−2.07	−4.42
Niigata	−5.35	−6.74	Fukuoka	−4.70	−9.80
Toyama	0.00	0.00	Saga	−2.35	−5.20
Ishikawa	−0.01	−0.01	Nagasaki	−1.45	−3.29
Fukui	−10.81	−10.81	Kumamoto	−1.61	−3.52
Yamanashi	−37.35	−40.21	Oita	−1.66	−3.71
Nagano	0.00	−2.22	Miyazaki	−1.85	−3.25
Gifu	−20.84	−25.09	Kagoshima	−1.06	−2.27
Shizuoka	−0.01	−3.99	Okinawa	0.00	0.00
Aichi	−29.20	−36.98			
Mie	−20.75	−21.67			
Shiga	−15.81	−15.81			

Notes: (1) Case (1) is the simulation result when expanding the line up to Nagoya station
(2) Case (2) is the simulation result when expanding the line up to Shin-Osaka station

high along Aichi and Gifu in case (1). These three prefectures were located along the HSR line. Moreover, Mie and Kyoto, which are not located along this HSR line, show a similar trend because the time distance to Tokyo can be shortened if the line passes through Nagoya. Case (2) shows significant effects along several lines, such as Yamanashi, Aichi, and Gifu, because the distance traveled per hour is expanded via the expansion of the network to Osaka. The effect in Hyogo is high because it lies adjacent to Osaka. Furthermore, in Okayama and Hiroshima, the time distance to Tokyo via Osaka was reduced, and the marginal effect increased. These results suggest that the widening of the travel range by the new HSR could cause modal shifts from passenger vehicles to railways and significantly reduce the passenger vehicle sector's energy consumption.

10.4 Conclusions

Improving energy intensity is a crucial policy agenda designed to solve global environmental problems. This chapter focuses on the passenger vehicle sector and analyzes how improving inter-regional networks affects energy consumption patterns from a dynamic perspective.

This chapter presents two significant findings. First, improving the inter-regional network reduces the energy consumption of the passenger vehicle sector. We reveal a nonlinear relationship between improvements in inter-regional networks and reduced energy consumption in the passenger vehicle sector. There is an inverse U-shaped relationship between the two. That is, a modal shift from passenger vehicles to railways occurs if the improvement in the inter-regional networks reaches a threshold value. Second, the *Linear-Chuo Shinkansen* installation has the potential to switch the mode of inter-regional travel from passenger vehicles to railways. In other words, the installation of the new HSR realizes a modal shift and improves the regional energy intensity. This result suggests that the installation of the new HSR leads to a reduction in greenhouse gas emissions and is a trump card to achieve SDGs. This finding provides significant policy evidence for researchers and policymakers.

However, two notes are included in the analysis in this chapter. First, we should note that the results in this chapter are produced from an analysis using aggregate data. As we well know, there are various types of vehicles, such as gasoline vehicles, electric vehicles, and hybrid vehicles (e.g., electric and gasoline). Therefore, it is necessary to verify the validity of the findings of these vehicle types. In particular, as mentioned in footnote 2, the consideration in this chapter is based on the use of gasoline vehicles. However, there is a high possibility that EVs will replace gasoline vehicles in the future. Therefore, there is a need for a deeper consideration of the relationship between the spread of EVs, public transportation, and inter-regional networks.

Second, we used a partial adjustment model for the energy demand in this study. The model was built on adaptive expectations regarding the behavior of energy consumption. However, economic agents generally act based on a forward-looking expectation of variation in energy prices or incomes. Therefore, we should consider an energy demand model that reflects decision-making based on rational expectations as a more desirable model.

References

Alberini A, Filippini M (2011) Response of residential electricity demand to price: The effect of measurement error. Energ Econ 33:889–895

Arellano M, Bond SR (1991) Some tests of specification for panel data: Monte Carlo evidence and an application to employment equations. Rev Econ Stud 58(2):277–297

Blázquez L, Boogen N, Filippini M (2013) Residential electricity demand in Spain: New empirical evidence using aggregate data. Energ Econ 36:648–657

Burger MJ, Meijers EJ (2016) Agglomerations and the rise of urban network externalities. Pap Reg Sci 95(1):5–15

Camagni R, Capello R, Caragliu A (2016) Static vs. dynamic agglomeration economies. Spatial context and structural evolution behind urban growth. Pap Reg Sci 95(1):133–158

Cameron CA, Trivedi PK (2009) Microeconometrics using Stata. Stata Press, College Station

Chen Z, Haynes KE (2015a) Chinese railway in the era of high-speed. Emerald Group Publishing Limited, Bingley

Chen Z, Haynes KE (2015b) Impact of high speed rail on housing values: An observation from the Beijing-Shanghai line. J Transp Geogr 43:91–100

Chen Z, Haynes KE (2015c) Multilevel assessment of public transportation infrastructure: A spatial econometric computable general equilibrium approach. Ann Reg Sci 54(3):663–685

Chen Z, Haynes KE (2015d) Impact of high-speed rail on international tourism demand in China. Appl Econ Lett 22(1):57–60

Chen Z, Xue J, Rose AZ, Haynes KE (2016) The impact of high-speed rail investment on economic and environmental change in China: A dynamic CGE analysis. Transport Res A 92:232–245

Costantini V, Martini C (2010) The causality between energy consumption and economic growth: A multi-sectoral analysis using non-stationary cointegrated panel data. Energ Econ 32 (3):591–603

Cuddington JT, Dagher L (2015) Estimating short and long-run demand elasticities: a primer with energy-sector applications. Energy J 36:185–209

Filippini M, Hirl B, Masiero G (2018) Habits and rational behavior in residential electricity demand. Resour Energy Econ 52:137–152

Otsuka A (2018) Dynamics of agglomeration, accessibility, and total factor productivity: Evidence from Japanese regions. Econ Innovat New Tech 27(7):611–627

Otsuka A (2019) Natural disasters and electricity consumption behavior: A case study of the 2011 Great East Japan Earthquake. Asia-Pac J Reg Sci 3(3):887–910

Otsuka A (2020a) Assessment of the improvement in energy intensity by the new high-speed railway in Japan. Asia-Pac J Reg Sci. https://doi.org/10.1007/s41685-020-00165-5

Otsuka A (2020b) Inter-regional networks and productive efficiency in Japan. Pap Reg Sci 99 (1):115–133

Otsuka A (2020c) How do population agglomeration and interregional networks improve energy efficiency? Asia-Pac J Reg Sci 4(1):1–25

Otsuka A (2021) A new approach to inter-regional network economies in Japan. Reg Sci Policy Pract 13(3):1051–1067

Otsuka A, Goto M (2018) Regional determinants of energy intensity in Japan: The impact of population density. Asia-Pac J Reg Sci 2(2):257–278

Pedroni P (2001) Purchasing power parity tests in cointegrated panels. Rev Econ Stat 83 (4):727–731

Pesaran MH, Shin Y, Smith RP (2001) Bounds testing approaches to the analysis of level relationships. J Appl Econ 16(3):289–326

International Union of Railways (2018) High Speed lines in the world, UIC High Speed Department. https://uic.org/IMG/pdf/20181001-high-speed-lines-in-the-world.pdf. Accessed January 2021

Van Meeteren M, Neal Z, Derudder B (2016) Disentangling agglomeration and network externalities: A conceptual typology. Pap Reg Sci 95(1):61–81

Westin J, Kågeson P (2012) Can high speed rail offset its embedded emissions? Transport Res D-Tr E 17(1):1–7